# HOWARD

## THE ART OF PERSUASION

Selected Speeches of
John Howard

# HOWARD
## THE ART OF
## PERSUASION
### Selected Speeches of
### John Howard

**David Furse-Roberts**
**Editor**

**Jeparit Press**

Published by Jeparit Press, 2018

Jeparit Press was established in 2017 as an imprint of Connor Court Publishing Pty Ltd, in association with the Menzies Research Centre, dedicated to publishing enduring works of Australian political philosophy and history. The imprint is edited by Nick Cater.

Connor Court Publishing Pty Ltd

PO Box 7257

Redland Bay QLD 4165

sales@connorcourt.com

www.connorcourt.com

ISBN: 9781925826173

Cover design by Branded Graphics

Front cover photograph: John Howard (1996)

(AUSPIC COPYRIGHT: Commonwealth of Australia, Photographer: David Foote)

# CONTENTS

CONTENTS

# Foreword

*Nick Cater*

Executive Director, Menzies Research Centre

The Australian people were not looking for razzmatazz when they elected John Howard as the 25th Prime Minister of Australia on 2 March 1996.

As that fateful election day approached, the five-term Labor administration, tired and out of touch, battled to thwart Howard's advance towards office. His informal but business-like style was mercilessly mocked by his opponents and adversaries, but it was exactly what the voters wanted.

John Howard spoke plain, unadorned English, the sort of English which Australians themselves used daily, at home and at the workplace, with family and friends.

The power of Howard's language came from the convictions lying behind it, never from rhetorical flourish.

More than a decade after leaving office, Howard remains the major advocate of liberalism in Australia and, indeed, the English-speaking world.

His words and wisdom thus display an unchallengeable relevance for our times. He has much of value to say about the continuing tasks of government in Australia, whether guiding its economy, meeting the social, educational and health requirements of the people, or steering the nation through the complexities of international affairs.

With this diverse, wide-ranging collection of speeches, David Furse-Roberts has provided Australians and all people committed to liberalism with ready access to Howard's thinking on many key matters of public policy in a form of which he was a master – the public address.

It is a most worthy successor to David's earlier book, *Menzies: the Forgotten Speeches*. And it is a very welcome addition to the publications of the Menzies Research Centre, celebrating the Liberal legacy and demonstrating how much that legacy has to offer Australia as it grapples with government, and politics and public policy in the 21st century.

# Foreword
## (paperback edition)

### *The Hon John Howard OM AC*

That great political philosopher Edmund Burke bequeathed to us many memorable phrases. One of them was society's "little platoons". It described the myriad of small clusters of individuals in our society who came together for a common purpose. That purpose was always to improve society.

As an individual, I belonged to many little platoons. There was the local soccer club, my daughter's ballet group, the local church, and the school parents' associations.

Another numerically small, but in every other way not little, was the Federal Parliamentary Liberal Party, which I had the honour to lead for more than 16 years. It was the most significant of all the little platoons in which I was involved.

The speeches in this book comprise some of the many that I made in the almost 12 years that I was Prime Minister. The atypical turnover of Prime Ministers in recent years has attracted attention to the roles and responsibilities of a Prime Minister in the Australian version of the Westminster system. I use the expression "Australian version" quite deliberately. There are some special home-grown features, which we should recognise, but without question ours is a Westminster system.

The sole determinant in Australia of whether or not a person is commissioned as Prime Minister is the Governor General being satisfied that he or she commands a majority on the floor of the House of Representatives. This is fundamental to the Westminster system. It also underscores the special character of the relationship between the leader and his or her parliamentary party. It is leadership of that group, and that group alone, which delivers the Prime Ministership. That is why, in my opinion, election of a leader should always be the sole preserve of the parliamentary party.

In those countries which embrace Westminster, the Prime Minister is but the first amongst equals. For the system to work the members of the parliamentary party must accept the primacy of their leader, as Prime Minister. In return he or she must recognise and respect their equality. Their relationship is unique. Of all the relationships which a serving Prime Minister has, none is more sensitive or important as the relationship between the Prime Minister and the men and women who from time to time comprise the parliamentary party.

In our system a Prime Minister is both a private counsellor and a public advocate. Members of Parliament are overwhelmingly ambitious, opinionated and energetic. Most believe they are capable of doing the jobs of their more senior colleagues better than those who hold the positions at any given time. This includes the party leader. Much of the time of a party leader must be spent talking to his colleagues, either in the formality of cabinet or party room meetings or, informally, in one-on-one meetings. Failure to do this can prove fatal.

Politics in its best sense is a contest of ideas and values. It is not a public relations tournament. Effective presentation is crucial to political success, but unless the source of the presentation is sound and compelling the presentation will ultimately fail. The most important quality a political leader can bring to his or her public presentation is a core set of beliefs, firmly and clearly held. To know and understand what an individual believes in is the most important measure of his or her success as a public figure.

As is well known I have always seen the Liberal Party of Australia as the custodian of two great political traditions: the conservative and classical liberal traditions. Our Party, which I frequently describe as a broad church, best succeeds when both elements operate together. It stumbles when one or other strand stakes a greater claim to the Party's soul. I am confident that Scott Morrison holds strongly to this belief.

In the speech delivered on 8 September 2005 (p. 28) I cited the Party's commitment to labour market reform as an example of our commitment to the classical liberal tradition. I said, "labour market reform is about transferring power from institutions to individuals… the essence of our drive for labour market reform is to create flexibility at the individual workplace level, to empower the individual, with appropriate protection, to make the bargain that he or she thinks is best for that person's individual circumstances and that person's family."

I frequently instanced my support for the constitutional monarchy as an example of the Liberal Party's conservative tradition. Conservatism does not reject all change. Edmund Burke himself said "a state without the means of some change is without the means of conservation". In 1999 Australia demonstrated that it had the means to remove the constitutional monarchy but decided to keep it. The people rightly concluded that the case for change had not been made.

Preserving the broad church character of the Liberal Party is all the more important given the frayed political environment so evident in liberal democracies around the world.

The past decade has shaken the political orthodoxy of many countries. Donald Trump's victory over his opponents within the Republican Party and, ultimately, his Democratic Party rival confounded most of the pundits. The vote of the British to leave the European Union, something I welcomed, surprised most commentators. The list goes on. Emanuel Macron, a virtual newcomer, overwhelmed the traditional parties of both the right and the left. Even Angela Merkel appears to have lost her magical touch, through mishandling the immigration issue.

There are reasons for this. The decade since the global financial crisis has produced an irritable middle class, for the pure and simple reason that in many of the comparable societies with which most of us are familiar, such as Britain, the United States and New Zealand, real wages have remained stagnant. Unemployment has not risen as feared in 2009. In a number of countries it has fallen. For many years before 2009, political leaders and policy makers craved a trade-off, namely minimal real wage growth in exchange for lower unemployment. The late Frank Crean, Labor's first Treasurer after the election of the Whitlam government in 1972, often said "one man's wage rise can be another man's job" when appealing for wage restraint. It was a sentiment echoed by senior figures on both sides of politics in the decades that followed. But the apparent arrival of this trade-off has not produced a contented society.

Our communities have taken greater employment stability for granted. The old adage that one only worries about unemployment when it is thought that your job is at risk has been validated.

The middle class – which in Australia is most of us – is increasingly conscious of real wage stagnation and, understandably, is unhappy. In the United States this unhappiness has been aggravated by the realisation that quantitative easing (or money printing) by the Federal Reserve, which puts more money into the system, has further enriched the very well off. Their already substantial assets have grown.

The really good news is that there has been a dramatic reduction in poverty in the developing world. The past twenty years have seen more people lifted from poverty than at any time since the industrial revolution. In the process real wages have increased markedly for many millions in the developing world. But the juxtaposition of flatlining real wages in the developed world, with such wages surging in the developing world, has presented huge challenges for policy makers in mature capitalist societies.

A further characteristic of the changed political environment has been that the dividing line between the parties of the left and the right is less clear than was once the case. In many ways the Cold War shaped the old political divide. In earlier years parties of the left were strongly attracted to much greater government involvement in and ownership of the economy, whereas the parties of the right pointed in the opposite direction, with a greater stress on the individual's ownership of property. Those differences remain, but they are less emphatic.

One consequence of this has been the rise of identity politics. Increasingly political parties, particularly of the left, seek to build support by tailoring policies to suit defined groups in the community. This was a fatal flaw in Hillary Clinton's 2016 Presidential campaign. For example, she targeted particular groups of women, black Americans and gays. But there was no philosophical coherence in her appeal. In the process she alienated others, even calling them "deplorables".

Such an approach breaks a fundamental tenet of political persuasion. A party's manifesto should be broad enough to appeal to individuals in all sections of the community irrespective of gender, race or other identity. Political parties should welcome the support of any defined group of citizens, but it is problematic to imply that the goal is to build majority support within a group irrespective of the impact on others. It will inevitably result in parties becoming beholden to special interest groups.

All of the post 2016 analysis of the Trump victory suggests that the Clinton campaign alienated the very people who felt they had been left behind by the economic impact of the Global Financial Crisis. Hillary's emphasis on particular groups facilitated Donald Trump's appeal to those very Americans who were not numbered amongst her target groups.

Modern politics is much less tribal. More than fifty years ago, when I first became active in politics it was broadly true to say that forty percent of the community normally voted Labor, with another forty percent supporting the Coalition. The rest moved around. Those rough figures no longer hold true. In recent times both of the two major parties have seen their primary voting intentions in opinion polls regularly below forty percent.

The decline in political party memberships, which reflects a lesser disposition on the part of citizens in general to join organisations, means that active members of political parties now are probably less representative of the generality of those who might vote for those parties.

Thus the Liberal Party needs the broad church more than ever before. The party I hold dear must have a widely based appeal, which rejects special interest groups and always projects a sense of balance. This, and an emphasis on the central role of the family, as well as the place of small business in the life of the nation, is most likely to deliver political success.

# Preface

## *John O'Sullivan, CBE*

A Prime Minister – and, to some extent, a Leader of the Opposition – is a generalist. By the very nature of the job, he must comment, decide, and act on a large range of matters on which he is not expert but of which he knows enough to question those who are. Initially he will acquire that knowledge by study; eventually, if he survives long enough, he will acquire it more intimately and securely by the experience of dealing with the same or similar challenges along the way. One can see this process working itself out over a period of more than twenty years in speeches delivered by Australia's elder statesman, John Howard, who stands with Robert Menzies as one of Australia's greatest prime ministers.

Howard's speeches are all well-argued, lucid, and simply interesting (on the page, readable). They link his government's immediate policies to enduring principles of Australian Liberalism. More than once we come across a list of such principles: opportunity and choice; a fair go for all; increasing self-reliance; working in partnership; and mutual obligation. When he reflects on their relative importance, however, he orders them in a very significant hierarchy: "I have never seen economic liberalism as an end in itself or a stand-alone political credo. Sound money, responsible budgets and efficient markets are nothing more than the mechanisms to support resilient families, cohesive communities and a stronger Australia."

Howard's well-known blending of the conservative and liberal traditions in Australian politics shows itself especially in his insistence that "the principle of mutual obligation" should shape not only economic and social policy but a much wider range of government actions, including immigration, first Australians, and reconciliation. [Thus, he writes, "we who live in Australia have an obligation of welcome, of acceptance, of decency . . . those who come have an obligation to embrace . . . the values that bind us together as Australians . . ."] Able to draw on the two traditions, each correcting the excesses of the other, Howard's speeches have a flexibility, a pragmatism, and a humanity that monist and more rigid ideologies lack.

An impressive consistency of thought and sense mark these speeches. They would appeal – as, indeed, they did – to a broad spectrum of Australians. One can sense a change in them, too. Earlier speeches are more formal in tone, more carefully structured; more guarded against attack – the product of study and the midnight oil. Later ones are just as carefully argued, but have a relaxed colloquialism, a sense of easy command of topics, and more jokes – in short, the result of having mastered the constant stream of problems that life throws at a prime minister.

Speeches are composed not for the ages, but for particular occasions. That shapes them. And since Howard is addressing a variety of audiences, he employs a variety of styles. Talking to old friends – a Rotary function or a *Quadrant* anniversary dinner – he does so as a congenial neighbour celebrating fellowship as well as the common cause. But dealing with tough political topics on which he has had to fight and think hard, he is a sharp polemicist – his analysis of the "soft Left" national history curriculum in 2012 is a model of logical demolition. When he defends the late Bill Leak against vicious persecution by the Human Rights Commission over a "racist" cartoon that was plainly no such thing, he is angry, direct, and to the point – which is that bureaucratic political correctness is incompatible with free speech. When he examines "the insidious rise of identity politics" before an international audience, he both defines and refutes it as seeking "to gather the support of a group based on what that group has in common, not the support of that group for a common principle which might gain acceptance throughout the entire community." And if there should be another referendum on the monarchy, his prime minister's advice to the nation at the close of the campaign in 1999 could be re-issued by constitutional monarchists without amending a single word.

All are essays in persuasion which is indispensable to the successful practice of democratic politics.

What we have in this collection, therefore, is a rich education in almost all aspects of politics in Australia and abroad. If you happen to have the self-sacrificial desire to be a prime minister or, more ambitiously, to govern a free people successfully for four terms, here's how.

Budapest, February 2018

# John Howard and the Advocacy of Australian Liberalism

## *David Furse-Roberts*

Throughout the history of liberalism in Australia, public addresses and speeches have been a major means for the advocacy and exposition of its philosophies and principles. As the 20th century drew to a close, and in the opening decades of the 21st century, John Howard, Prime Minister of Australia from 1996 to 2007, has been liberalism's pre-eminent advocate.

It is the purpose of this volume to ensure that Howard's advocacy is readily accessible to the Australian community. The aim is not only to lay significant addresses on great national issues before the public but also to furnish others on particular topics. For Howard's contribution to be understood properly, it needs to be seen in a broad context, embracing local and community themes as well as those which are national and international.

As a major advocate of Australian Liberalism, John Howard stands in a distinguished line. Among the most prominent in this line have been predecessors in the office of Prime Minister, Alfred Deakin in the formative years of the Federation, and Sir Robert Menzies, whose oratory, mid-century, was such a compelling force in the founding and development of the Liberal Party of Australia, and in the years of government, 1949-1966, a key influence in the shaping of modern Australia.

*Howard: the Art of Persuasion* seeks to showcase the speeches of John Winston Howard, Australia's second-longest serving prime minister. Howard held the highest political office in Australia for nearly twelve years from March 1996 to late 2007. Longevity alone does not ensure impact but, as one observer has noted, "the prime ministers whose words have been subject to the most sustained scrutiny and who had the most practice and influence in this respect are those who served the longest".[1]

---

[1] Sally Young, "Political and Parliamentary Speech in Australia", *Parliamentary Affairs*, Vol 60, No.2, 2007, 236.

Yet in an age where the public's perception of prime ministers and political leaders is all too frequently based on sound-bites and second-hand media reporting, commentary and analysis, the purpose of this volume is to take readers directly to the primary source materials where they can appraise the ideas and thoughts of John Howard for themselves. Whilst the media can undoubtedly perform a great service for the public in bringing their expertise and insight to bear on the pronouncements and speeches of leaders, the original message is often selectively filtered or even misconstrued. The public is left with a less than full understanding of what a prime minister or party leader was intending to convey to the people or achieve for the country.

It is critically important, given the significance of John Howard's prime ministership in recent Australian history, that speeches concerning watershed decisions and policies of his Government are easily available.

From this volume, readers will be better able to understand, for example, the rationale behind the Howard Government's controversial reforms to workplace relations, especially the Australian waterfront, in the late 1990s and the reasons why Howard took the "practical reconciliation" approach that he did to Indigenous affairs. From his speeches on international relations, readers will be able to appreciate the subtlety and nuance of Howard's direction of foreign policy, and appreciate how he linked Australia's traditional associations with the United Kingdom and, later, the United States, with a sustained endeavour to cultivate closer and deeper ties with Australia's Asian neighbours.

Howard's speeches on ethnic and cultural diversity, whether about Aboriginal and Torres Strait Islanders or the migrants from more than 140 countries around the globe, provide a rounded picture of his policies and more so of his thinking about the increasingly diverse character of modern Australian society. They thereby furnish a more holistic perspective on which to appraise his contribution and his legacy.

In substance, style and delivery, Howard's speeches "often drew on simple, family-orientated messages and imagery". This was evident in his "Tough on Drugs" address to Anglicare in March 1999, where he told the heartfelt story of a distraught mother unable to get her drug-dependent daughter into a treatment programme because there were no available places. Indeed, much of the key to Howard's electoral success lay in his capacity to empathise with the concerns of ordinary voters in Australia's towns and cities.

Howard has prided himself on his "ordinariness" and directness. He delivered his speeches with an educated yet "general Australian accent" that resonated readily with middle Australia. Howard focussed on "modest objectives which were deliverable".[2] His distinctive talent was for extempore, "off the cuff" speeches, in marked contrast to tightly controlled, pre-scripted delivery. One observer perceived that, "by not having a speech-writer, Howard endeavoured to position himself as the authentic voice of 'middle' Australia – practical, no-nonsense and suspicious of grand visions".[3] No one ever asked who was John Howard's speech-writer – it was the man himself.

----------------------------------

Howard led the Liberal Party to victory in four elections. Only Sir Robert Menzies surpasses him in length of service at the apex of politics. In the past half-century, the record and achievements of Howard remain unmatched by any other centre-right leader in Australia. To be sure, the next longest-serving Liberal prime minister, Malcolm Fraser, did win three elections and his government deserved credit for not only reining in the fiscal extravagance of the Whitlam era but for its policy initiatives in foreign affairs, immigration and social security. While the Fraser Government achieved some success in restoring a responsible approach to government, its record of serious economic reform did, however, remain fairly modest owing to its attachment to the older Keynesian economic paradigm. The Howard Government, on the other hand, seized the opportunity after winning office in 1996 to lead a proactive reform government committed to modernising the Australian economy. The decidedly bold approach of the Howard Government paid dividends. The

---

[2] Young, "Political and Parliamentary Speeches in Australia", 237
[3] James Curran, *The Power of Speech: Australian Prime Ministers Defining the National Image* (Melbourne: Melbourne University Press, 2004), 21.

economy markedly improved on most indicators from unemployment to inflation during his term in office. The economic record of Howard and his Government, alone, earns him a secure place in the top league of Australian prime ministers

As well as enabling Australia to flourish economically and socially, Howard's other great contribution to public life was that he gave both his own Liberal Party, and Australia at-large, a surer sense of itself and the values for which it stood. Howard emerged as the authoritative voice of Australian Liberalism in the late twentieth century, tirelessly communicating its philosophies, principles, values and aspirations to the public. It was his special contribution to interpret and apply the Liberal creed fashioned by Menzies in the middle of the 20th century to Australian society, politics, economy and culture in its turn of the century context.

Howard frequently explained that the Liberal Party, a "broad church", united both classical liberal and conservative thought; it was thus the heir of both John Stuart Mill (1806-1873) and Edmund Burke (1729-1797). For Howard, Australian Liberalism was at its best when it accommodated both these strands, bringing classical liberalism to bear more on economic policy and the conservative tradition more on matters of cultural identity and the social fabric.

As Prime Minister, Howard was not only committed to this synthesis in a philosophical sense but also, at a practical level, with his decision to engage both "small-l liberals" and "conservatives" in the Cabinet and the party room. In articulating the vision of Australian Liberalism to a new generation and finding space for both its philosophical limbs, Howard brought a renewed unity, cohesion and purpose to the Liberal Party as Australia entered the second century of its life as a nation.

Howard's resolve to reassert the identity of his own Party extended to that of Australia at large. An unabashed patriot, he was determined to see a united Australia proud of its past achievements and assured about its own national identity and place in the world. He maintained that Australia had spent far too long navel-gazing about national identity instead of being inspired by the best of its past to celebrate the demonstrated virtues of liberal democracy, egalitarianism, a "practical mateship", and the notion of a "fair go". Never afraid to acknowledge the injustices of the past, he desired Australia's first people to be reconciled to the nation at large. He believed this was best done not by visiting blame for past wrongs on the present generation but by introducing forward-looking, practical measures to advance Indigenous welfare.

For Howard, the influx of millions of new arrivals from around the world since 1945 did not suggest Australia was simply a land of disparate tribes, but a family of culturally diverse members bound together by shared Australian values. Far from viewing Australia's British heritage as a handicap to the nation's engagement with Asia, Australia, as a Western nation in the Asia-Pacific, was able to cherish historic affinity with the United Kingdom and the United States at the same time as enjoying increasingly closer ties with its Asia-Pacific neighbours. Howard repeatedly displayed a definitive sense of what Australia and its people represented and what they could aspire to be.

Together with Margaret Thatcher, Ronald Reagan and Chancellor Helmut Kohl of Germany, Howard numbers among the great centre-right leaders of the Western world in recent decades. His election as Prime Minister of Australia in 1996 brought this grand renaissance of the centre-right to the South Pacific; he became one of its chief standard-bearers in the 1990s and 2000s. In the same vein as Thatcher, Reagan and Kohl, Howard worked to advance the ideals of liberal democracy, the freedom of the individual, and the need for economic growth based on individual initiative and competitive free enterprise economies. His Government succeeded in calibrating this agenda in the Australian setting by restructuring industrial relations on the Australian waterfront and in the workplace, by reforming the Australian taxation system to provide a more competitive environment for businesses and industries, by privatising assets such as Telstra and by brokering free-trade agreements with Australia's major trading partners. Like the experience of his North Atlantic counterparts, his programme of economic liberalisation and reform made his country stronger, freer and more prosperous in the longer term. Howard's stature as a modern centre-right reformer was such that he became a model and mentor to emerging centre-right leaders Stephen Harper, of Canada and John Key in New Zealand, both of whom frequently consulted the Australian statesman for guidance.

Howard looms large in the popular memory for the steady hand he brought to government and for the long period of economic growth and prosperity his government oversaw. Howard's objective to modernise the Australian economy was evident very early in his political career when he served as the Treasurer in the Fraser Government from 1977 to 1983. As Treasurer, Howard had been responsible for establishing the Campbell Committee in 1979 to report on the efficacy of Australia's existing financial system. Released late in 1981, the Campbell Report recommended a move from a fixed to a market-based exchange rate for the Australian dollar, permitted the entry of foreign banks and a general deregulation of the banking sector. Despite some dissent within the Fraser Government, Howard endorsed the recommendations of the Report and sought to modernise the Australian economy in his remaining years as Treasurer. As Prime Minister from 1996 to 2007, Howard lost none of his reforming zeal to strengthen the Australian economy and this would ultimately define much of the success behind his prime ministership. Professor Geoffrey Blainey spoke for many when he observed that "[in] the end, John Howard will be seen by vast numbers of Australians as one of the great prime ministers".[4]

Blainey's judgment was soon vindicated by polling in which Howard has enjoyed a clear lead as Australia's greatest prime minister of the modern era. In an Essential Research poll published by *The Australian* in March 2016, 34 per cent of voters judged Howard to be the best prime minister since 1972. This was well ahead of his old adversary, Bob Hawke, whom 13 per cent of voters considered to be the best.

-------------------------------------

From his 1995 Headland speech in the lead up to the 1996 election which brought him to power, to his victory speech on 2 March 1996 and his speech accepting of the Edmund Burke Award on 1 November 2016, the sixty speeches in this volume cover a full range of Howard's prime ministerial tenure and life after politics. They are a mixture of

---

[4] Geoffrey Blainey, "From Triumph to a Tragic", *Herald Sun*, Tuesday, 27 November 2007.

addresses, statements, lectures, orations and contributions to parliamentary debates. They vary markedly in both style and substance, from the poetic quality of the poignant tribute he delivered to the fallen heroes of the Thai-Burma Railway on Anzac Day 1998 to the studied analysis he gave of Federal-State relations in a 2006 lecture to the Menzies Research Centre. Drawn from a vast catalogue of prime ministerial transcripts, the speeches for this volume were selected on the basis of both the insight they provide into the Liberal philosophy of John Howard and the extent to which they each expressed the salient policy themes and achievements of the Howard years. The featured speeches, however, reveal not only his ideals and philosophies, together with his agenda for governing the nation, but also something of his own personal interests, not least his abiding affection for the game of cricket.

They were delivered in a range of locations from the floor of the House of Representatives, the chamber of the United States House of Representatives and the Guildhall in London, to town halls, lecture theatres, clubs, open air assemblies, party conferences and conventions throughout Australia. In terms of audiences and speaking venues, he frequently spoke to community organisations such as church groups, charities, RSL and Rotary clubs, retirement villages, surf lifesaving clubs, sporting organisations, the Australian Women's National League, Arthritis Australia and universities as well as Liberal Party functions.[5] He esteemed these associations and institutions as the backbone of civil society as well as in their purpose of serving as vital intermediaries between the government and the individual. They reveal a conviction that governing in a democracy was not simply something done on high, in the Parliament or the Cabinet room, but was also something done locally, among communities themselves.

In contrast to the large rallies or public meetings characteristic of the 1950s and 1960s, Howard typically spoke to smaller and sometimes exclusive audiences which included business organisations and centre-right think tanks. Such changes are also attributable, no doubt, to the heightened security procedures and protocols that now attend the office

---

[5] Young, "Political and Parliamentary Speech", 238.

of prime minister which frequently determine which, and how many, members of the public can freely hear the prime minister speak in person.

Like Sir Robert Menzies, Howard maintained that there was a world of difference between *speech-reading* and *speech-making*. Taking Menzies' aphorism to heart that "People are not roused and stimulated by the reading of an essay but by the passion and persuasion of a human being", Howard had a singular distaste for simply reading a text at the podium. The delivery of such a speech was not only wooden and artificial, but also disengaged from the audience as the speaker constantly looked at notes instead of the people being addressed. Howard preferred his words to flow directly from his own lips and to fashion his speeches spontaneously from the podium.

All this, however, did not mean that Howard was simply able to pluck a desired speech magically from "thin-air" to deliver on-the-spot. On the contrary, Howard would read and think critically and creatively about the topic on which he was to speak, write out dot-points of the message he wanted to convey, mull over the words and phrases he intended to use and, finally, deliver his speech without notes. Howard recalled that he employed this method for most of his speeches, the remainder being essentially formal statements to the House of Representatives that he would deliver from the despatch box.

On one occasion where the journalist and author, Margaret Simons, enquired about Howard's speechwriter(s), his staffers responded that "nobody wrote for him: He talks to his advisers to gather facts, but he either speaks without a script or writes his speeches himself." [6] If Howard, for example, needed to speak on a topic requiring specialist input, he would consult an economics and industry policy adviser for the necessary facts and figures and then prepare the speech himself. Even his contributions to parliamentary debate were largely "off-the-cuff" performances in a manner reminiscent of an earlier time.

What was the inspiration and explanation behind Howard's penchant for "off-the-cuff" speeches, a style increasingly unusual in the late 20th century? One well-placed student of Australian politics believes it was

---

[6] Young, "Political and Parliamentary Speech", 240.

most likely a pattern of speaking that Howard imbibed from his Methodist upbringing. Stretching back to its founder, John Wesley (1703-1791), the Methodist movement had a long and proud tradition of extempore preaching where ministers would dispense with written notes to speak directly to their congregants from the pulpit. The object of the classic Methodist preacher was always to inspire the congregation with the gospel message through frequent eye-contact, animated hand gestures and an expressive extempore delivery. Howard remembers this style of preaching from his Methodist youth and learnt the lesson that, like the best of preachers, the best of politicians are those who could engage and persuade an audience through the power of speech.

To speak thus was no doubt aided by a good memory. As a former practitioner of law and a keen student of history, Howard was adept at recalling the chronological sequence of events. He had also excelled as a debater at school and this gave him the experience of being able both to think on his feet whilst delivering a speech and to engage with opponents. With this combination of experiences and natural faculties, Howard emerged as the pre-eminent extemporaneous orator of modern Australian politics. As Geoffrey Blainey concluded, "He was one of the outstanding debaters in the nation's history. On any topic, almost without notice, he could speak energetically and persuasively".[7]

..............................

The speeches in this collection are assembled thematically, thus allowing readers to appreciate the various elements of Howard's political outlook. The first chapter takes Howard's famed "broad church" characterisation of the Liberal Party. These speeches address Howard's conception of the modern Liberal Party as custodian of both the classical liberal philosophy deriving from John Stuart Mill and the conservative tradition stemming from Edmund Burke. Throughout its long period in the political wilderness during the Hawke and Keating years, the Liberal Party had struggled to define its philosophical identity as "wets" battled "dries" and "conservatives" clashed with "moderates" over both economic and social policy. Howard sought to resolve this internal debate

---

[7] Blainey, "From Triumph to a Tragic".

and finally led a party that "knew what it stood for". In these speeches the Prime Minister both affirmed the Party's deep philosophical roots and explained their continuing relevance and applicability to contemporary public policy.

The second theme, "Governing for all Australians", was founded upon the view that governments are elected by the people to serve the interests of all Australians. As such, governments could not afford to be beholden to powerful sectional interest groups at the expense of governing in the broad public interest. Howard affirmed the need for governments to serve not only the people who voted for them but also those who did not. This approach was reinforced by what could be described as the "Australian middle-way", whereby governments afforded individuals maximum freedom to flourish whilst providing a necessary safety-net for those in need. In so doing, Australian governments could avoid the pitfalls of either a *laissez-faire* approach to public policy or the paternalism characteristic of many governments in Europe. In his own phrase, Howard believed not in getting government "out of people's lives but getting it off people's backs".

Howard's views about Australia in all its complexities and diversities, at once wide-ranging and deeply felt, were especially evident when addressing the nation in times of both celebration and tragedy. Chapter III features speeches on watershed events of his prime ministership, ranging from the celebration of the 2000 Olympics in Sydney to the killings at Port Arthur in 1996 and the tragedy of the Bali bombings in 2002. On each occasion, the Prime Minister gave voice to the joys and sorrows of the nation. The Howard Government is as much remembered for its key reforms on gun control as it is for social welfare and drug policy.

For governments to advance the welfare of the people, Howard believed that they had a critical responsibility for the project of necessary economic reform to maximise the growth, productivity, competitiveness and prosperity of the nation. He acknowledged that Australia had enjoyed a lengthy phase of economic growth, but maintained that continuous modernisation of the economy was needed for such growth to be sustained over the longer term. To shed light on this reforming vision of Howard in office, chapter IV brings together speeches in which the

Prime Minister outlined his bold plans to strengthen Australia's economy. Chief amongst these were reforms to the Australian waterfront to boost the nation's export performance; introduction of a new taxation system to stimulate individual initiative and enterprise; and modernisation of Australia's industrial relations system both as part of the streamlining of the national economy and to create a climate even more favourable to free enterprise and productivity.

For Howard, however, economic growth and prosperity also had a vital human dividend whereby wealth creation never represented an end in itself but a means by which Australia could better help those experiencing hard times. After five years in office, the Prime Minister remarked in 2001 that a strong economy had enabled Australia to strengthen the social safety net for people in need. In speeches on this theme, Howard articulated his guiding philosophy and objectives of contemporary social welfare policy. These were based principally on the ethic of "mutual obligation" that embraced society's obligation to help its less fortunate members and a corresponding obligation from those receiving assistance to contribute back to the community. In the formulation and implementation of welfare programmes, Howard favoured forging what he called a "social coalition" of government agencies, churches, charities and businesses to help the disadvantaged. Vital as the role and responsibility of government was, it alone had neither all the knowledge nor expertise required, nor the skills and competence for successful delivery.

A sixth theme focusses on the growing diversity of Australian society and culture. As a nation built by immigrants, Howard valued the immense contribution successive waves of new arrivals had made to enriching Australia's cultural tapestry but, at the same time, affirmed their membership of one Australian family with an ethos and identity of its own. Howard took pride in describing modern Australia as a nation "drawn from the four corners of the Earth, but united behind a common set of Australian values". In speeches on these features of modern Australia, the Prime Minister affirmed the importance of cultural diversity together with the need to foster a common Australian citizenship. Integral to Howard's vision of a culturally rich and cohesive Australian community was one in which Australia's first people could feel an acute sense of pride and belonging. To this end, he frequently spoke of including Aboriginal and Torres Strait Islander people in the social, cultural and economic development of mainstream Australian society in forms sensitive to their cultural heritage and customs.

Chapter VII encompasses Howard's vision for Australia, and his desire not only for a cohesive and harmonious national community but one with a sense of national pride about its character and accomplishments. A self-confessed "passionate Australian nationalist", he believed it was high time for Australia to move beyond the "seemingly endless seminar" about its national identity to assert instead its traditional values and take pride in its history. Fully recognising the blemishes of Australia's past, Howard believed that Australia's history was a narrative of survival, progress and achievement from which grew its national traits of mateship, egalitarianism and "a fair go".

His speeches on Australia's national identity range from those delivered in the rugged settings of Gallipoli, where he spoke poignantly of the Anzac legend and its manifestation of Australian mateship, to the gentle slopes of Sydney's lower Blue Mountains where he lauded the accomplishments of Australian democracy since the days of Sir Henry Parkes in the nineteenth century.

Howard's thinking about Australia's fate and fortune was as much international as domestic. Viewing Australia as a "projection of Western civilisation" in the Asia-Pacific region, Howard's oft-repeated refrain was that Australia did not need to choose between its history and geography. At the same time as deepening Australia's engagement with Asia through closer economic, trade, and often defence ties with Singapore, Thailand, Malaysia, Indonesia, China, Japan and South Korea, Howard and his government was resolved to reaffirm Australia's cultural affinity with its traditional allies in the North Atlantic. In addition to his project of rebalancing Australia's foreign policy orientation, Howard emerged as a lead advocate of free trade and globalisation. He saw trade liberalisation and open markets as not only advantageous to Australia's national interest but as eminently conducive to a more free, prosperous and peaceful world. In what he described as a "humanising globalisation", the internationalisation of the world economy had been the greatest force for lifting millions of people out of poverty in developing countries.

A concluding group (chapter IX) of speeches on "Anniversaries and Australian Achievements" show Howard reflecting publicly on historic milestones, movements and achievements that could be a source of inspiration and pride for all Australians. These included introduction of Australian citizenship, in legal terms, in 1949; celebration of Australia's historic political and cultural ties with Great Britain at the centenary of the Federation; the welcome advancement of women in professional and public life; and the enduring spiritual and moral capital to be derived from Australia's Judeo-Christian inheritance. For Howard, the role of Prime Minister was never simply about giving leadership and direction to his government. It was also about giving voice to the inspirations and aspirations of the Australian people he was so privileged to represent.

This diverse collection of John Howard's speeches seeks to provide readers with a first-hand insight into the ideas and thinking of the man who led one of the most enduring and reformist governments in the modern Western world. This collection serves to acquaint readers with Howard's distinctive style of extempore speech-making on an extraordinary range of subjects, from deeply serious matters of policy to the pleasures of national life, especially, in his case, cricket. Along with his own best-selling autobiography, *Lazarus Rising*, *Howard: the Art of Persuasion* will furnish readers with a comprehensive portrait of the philosophies and thinking a major Australian statesman brought to the prime ministership and which marked a distinguished tenure in which he guided the nation into its second century.

# Chronological Order of Speeches

# I

# "A Broad Church"

## Australia's Liberal-Conservative Tradition

# The Liberal Tradition

## The Beliefs and Values which Guide the Federal Government

## 1996 Sir Robert Menzies Lecture

### Melbourne – 18 November 1996

Eight months into his prime ministership, John Howard was invited by the Sir Robert Menzies Lecture Trust to deliver their annual lecture in Melbourne. His 1996 Lecture was his second appearance at the Trust. As Treasurer in the Fraser Government he had delivered the lecture in 1980. As Prime Minister in a relatively new Liberal Government, the third such government since the Second World War, Howard saw this lecture as a timely opportunity to restate the philosophical foundations of Australian Liberalism to a new generation.

Recognising Menzies as the great founder of modern liberalism, Howard used this lecture to address both the political convictions and pragmatic approach of his distinguished predecessor. The Prime Minister argued that liberalism was not a fixed ideology but a directional touchstone with principles that could be applied to the circumstances of today. Taking both a historical and a contemporary focus, the Prime Minister lauded the past achievements of Australian Liberalism whilst making the case that it remained the best philosophy with which to approach the contemporary challenges facing Australia.

We honour tonight the memory of Sir Robert Menzies as a great Australian leader and as the founder of modern Australian Liberalism. We recall the achievements of the national governments that he led, as well as the values that were the driving force behind them. But our purpose tonight is also a much broader one: one that is focussed squarely on the challenges of Australia's future, and on the central role of Liberal values and ideals in ensuring that they are met successfully. Menzies himself always had such a focus. He forged modern Australian Liberalism not as a fixed ideology but as a political philosophy with values that need to be related to the great issues of the day, and of the future.

Australian Liberalism has always been evolving and developing. It always will be. We are constantly relating liberalism's enduring values to the circumstances of our own time. Enduring values such as the commitment to enhance freedom, choice and competition, to encourage personal achievement, and to promote fairness and a genuine sense of community in Australian society … The achievements of the Menzies era laid the groundwork for the achievements of the Liberal political tradition more generally. And we need to ensure that those achievements are properly recognised as our political history is re-interpreted by a new generation of Australians.

The Liberal political tradition has made a decisive contribution to nation-building in Australia. It has been the Liberal political tradition which has overseen the periods of greatest sustained economic growth in our history and which, through policies in support of free enterprise, laid the foundations for Australia's modern manufacturing, agricultural and industrial development.

It is our political tradition which facilitated the establishment of a modern national economic infrastructure. It is our tradition which has championed not only the rights of small business but opportunities in general for individuals to work hard and to achieve for themselves and their families.

It is our tradition which dramatically expanded educational opportunities for all Australians and which, through the decision over 30 years ago to provide direct government assistance to independent schools, ended many of the deep sectarian divisions and bitterness which had afflicted Australian society for more than a century.

It is our tradition which opened up regional co-operation through economic initiatives beginning with the 1957 Australia-Japan Commerce

Treaty, through educational initiatives beginning with the Colombo Plan and through immigration reforms such as the ending of the White Australia Policy. It is our tradition which provided one of the world's most generous and compassionate responses to the Indo-Chinese refugee crisis of the late 1970s and 1980s. It is our tradition which expanded Australia's own defence capabilities and underpinned them with the negotiation of the ANZUS alliance. It is our tradition which oversaw the great surge of post-war migration to Australia and laid the foundations of our modern Australian society drawn from the four corners of the Earth and united together by a common set of Australian values.

It is our tradition which has had a "fair go" for all as one of its driving forces and which has strengthened the social security safety-net through such advancements in social policy as the extension of child endowment, pensioner medical services, health services, pharmaceutical benefits, housing, invalid and other pensions, mental health care, family allowances, and many other initiatives. It is our tradition which has led, and won, the great debate of ideas over issues such as greater choice and security for Australian families, industrial relations reform, financial deregulation and privatisation.

It is our tradition which oversaw the extension of the full rights of citizenship to Aboriginal Australians. It is our tradition which has made an historic contribution in so many other policy areas such as regional development, technology, environmental protection, child-care and the growth of new industries such as tourism.

And it is our tradition with our emphases on incentives for achievement, deregulation and competition which is best suited to the demands of our economic future: a future in which economic enterprise will become more decentralised, in which small businesses will be even more important as generators of jobs and national wealth, and in which technology will change patterns of work and diversify the options for achieving growth. ...

The personality of Sir Robert Menzies, and the achievements of his governments, lay at the centre of many of the historical achievements of the Liberal tradition to which I have referred.

Tonight, however, is not the occasion for a detailed recitation of all of them. But I would like to take the opportunity to reflect in a personal way on what I see as the enduring legacy of Menzies' contribution to public life in Australia.

Menzies, above all, was a great Australian nation-builder in the true sense of the word. He understood better than any political leader of his generation the nation-building capacities of private enterprise and a strategic but limited role for government. That is clearly evident in the record of his achievements in government in areas as diverse as national development, economic growth, trade and foreign policy, science and education, and the arts. It was his essential Australianness that underpinned his unequalled period of dominance in Australian political life.

One of the most perverse myths about Menzies was his alleged subservience to Britain and, subsequently, America. Like most Australians of his time, Menzies did have a special admiration for the English inheritance of the rule of law, democratic constitutionalism and personal liberty. But that did not make him any lesser Australian. In fact, it made him a more robust one as he applied that unique inheritance to Australia's own national circumstances. Menzies fiercely attacked British indifference to Australian interests whether it was in strategic policy (as in the Second World War), in trade policy or in any other aspect. For example, in the 1930s Menzies was a consistent opponent of British governments over their application of the 1932 Ottawa Agreement. He argued that the need for Australia to develop its own manufacturing base demanded greater understanding than Britain was prepared to extend. Furthermore, immediately after the Australian declaration of war in 1939, Menzies resisted British pressure to commit Australian forces immediately to Europe. He argued that the situation in 1939 was not the same as 1914. He agreed to send Australian forces to Europe only after he had an assessment of Japan's likely intentions and after he had insisted on, and received, a reassurance from Britain on its commitment to send a fleet to Singapore if Japan did move south.

Menzies' intense Australianness was highlighted in the political re-

5

lationship he had with the Australian people. He articulated the hopes and concerns of the Australians of his time more effectively, more representatively and for a longer period than any other national leader. Menzies' political genius lay in that basic affinity with the aspirations of the Australian people. He understood the priority they placed on jobs, on rising living standards, on home ownership, on high economic growth, on a sense of national unity, and on opportunities for their children that were greater than they themselves had experienced. And he developed priorities in national policy-making and a role for national government that enabled those aspirations to be achieved.

Menzies had his finger on the pulse of the Australian nation in a way that few other leaders have matched and none has surpassed. But the quality of his political leadership did not lie in perceiving or anticipating every shift in public opinion. He responded to public opinion, but he also shaped it. He respected it, but he also guided it. He knew the difference between short-term public opinion and long-term public interest.

Another aspect which I see as central in Menzies' enduring legacy is, of course, his role as the Founding Father of modern Australian Liberalism. Menzies knew the importance for Australian Liberalism to draw on both the classical liberal as well as the conservative political traditions. He knew the importance for liberalism of upholding people's rights and freedoms as individuals. He also knew the importance of values and priorities that had both a proven record of past achievement and a relevance to advancing Australia's national interests into the future. He opposed change for the sake of change, just as he opposed blind adherence to outmoded and ineffective practices that no longer served the national interest. He was a traditionalist in that he respected the wisdom that is shaped by experience. But where he was convinced of the need for change, he became its powerful advocate. This was clearly evident in the changing emphases of Menzies' foreign policy with his awareness of the importance of the Asia-Pacific region in Australia's future and his creation of the framework for greater interaction with it.

It was also evident in a range of his social and economic policies, and none more so than the new directions he charted for secondary and tertiary education. Menzies' practical approach to policy issues reflected the dualism in liberalism's political philosophy. He believed in a liberal political tradition that encompassed both Edmund Burke and John Stuart Mill, a tradition which I have described in contemporary terms as the broad church of Australian Liberalism. Part of Menzies' legacy, therefore, is that liberalism has developed political values that are neither ideological, on the one hand, nor mere bellwethers of every changing circumstance, on the other.

Menzies valued a broad-based political philosophy because he knew that it was from such a philosophy that liberalism derived its enduring values, values such as individual freedom, choice, diversity, opportunity, and the importance of strong families and communities as bulwarks against the intrusive power of the state. That is why the modern Liberal Party has never been a party of privilege or sectional interests or narrow prejudice. Menzies always championed individual freedom and spirit over collective action based on a corporate state, and he did so not to promote narrow and selfish outcomes but for the purposes of enabling every Australian to fulfil their hopes and aspirations. liberalism has always pursued those purposes, and it will continue to do so.

Another aspect of Menzies' legacy is that liberalism has focussed on national interests rather than sectional interests. Menzies knew that a broad-based political philosophy is a necessary filter for the narrow aspirations of individual lobby groups. He understood that the weaker a political party's philosophical base, the more likely it is to be hijacked by single-issue groups which have a focus that is sectional and not national. These aspects of liberalism lay at the heart of Menzies' political views. They have an enduring relevance and value, and modern liberalism remains strongly committed to them.

Any assessment of Menzies' influence on Australian public life would be incomplete without reference to the great strengthening influence he exerted in support of democratic constitutionalism in Australia.

Throughout his long career in State and Federal politics, Menzies demonstrated consummate and, in my view, unrivalled skill as a political practitioner. But even more than that, he demonstrated his great commitment to parliamentary democracy. He never forgot that the responsibilities of democratic government are not some preordained right bestowed on a privileged few, but are a gift from the people. He understood that the strength of our national political institutions directly affect the value of the democratic rights exercised by individual Australians.

That is why Menzies placed the authority, standards and traditions of Parliament squarely at the centre of the national governments that he led. It is why he always insisted on adherence to the proper processes of Cabinet decision-making. It is why he championed the doctrine of the separation of powers. It is why he refused to compromise on the need for honest and competent administration and the accountability of government. It is why he turned his back on the attractions of a legal career in private practice in favour of fulfilling his deeply-felt sense of public duty. …

Menzies' political success lay in building an enduring and broadly-based constituency that supported liberalism's values and priorities. At the heart of that constituency were "the forgotten people" of that era, the men and women of the great Australian mainstream who felt excluded from the special interest elitism of the Liberal Party's immediate predecessors and from the trade union dominance of the Labor Party. They included small business people, farmers, employees in enterprises both large and small, women, families concerned for their security, older Australians, young people in search of jobs and opportunity, and many others.

Australia faces fundamentally different challenges to those of the Australia of the Menzies era. But liberalism faces the ongoing challenge of building an enduring and broadly-based constituency across the great mainstream of our rapidly changing society.

Over recent times, a new constituency has galvanised around new issues and in support of Liberal priorities. It includes many of the "battlers" and families struggling hard to get ahead. It includes Australians, young and old, who want Australia to break free of the legacy of debt and deficits. It includes small business people who want to expand, invest and employ more Australians. It includes all those who want the talents of Australians to be liberated so that Australia can achieve its full potential. It includes all those who do not want their national government to respond to the loudest clamour of the noisiest minority.

This new constituency does not represent a permanent realignment in Australian politics. Its continued support for Liberal priorities cannot be taken for granted. It must be earned through keeping faith, through staying in touch, and through continuing to be humbled by the privilege of governing a great country like Australia in the interests of all Australians.

Liberalism now has an opportunity, unparalleled for almost fifty years, to consolidate a new coalition of support among the broad cross-section of the Australian people. It will only prove enduring if liberalism continues to relate its fundamental values and principles to the concerns and aspirations of the Australian mainstream, rather than the narrower agendas of elites and special interests.

That means building a genuinely shared sense of national purpose rather than an amalgamation of special interests. It means not stepping back from implementing the reforms that will make our economy competitive with others into the future, that will generate jobs and investment for Australia, and that will raise Australian living standards. It means communicating clearly the rationale for change where change is necessary, and ensuring that consequent reforms and burdens impact fairly on different sections of the community.

It means not being a Government of economic dogma, but a Government of economic common sense. It means being concerned not only with economic efficiency, but also with equity and fairness as well. It means seeking a more productive economy, a more responsible fiscal policy and more effective markets not as ends in themselves or as articles of some rigid ideological faith but as the practical means for achieving rising living standards, expanding employment opportunities and an effective social safety-net.

It means achieving a practical balance between the limits of government and the limits of markets, between *laissez-faire* economics on the one side and a suffocating centralism by government and bureaucracy on the other.

It means understanding accurately in which direction the forces of change are taking the Australian economy towards smaller workplaces, towards more decentralised work patterns, towards more independent sources of employment in a dynamic and rapidly changing regional economy. It means enhancing job-creating investment in the Australian economy as we are doing through our Budget strategy of fiscal consolidation and enhanced competitiveness which is providing the climate for lower interest rates, as well as through our initiatives to make it easier to do business in Australia.

It means putting the interests of Australian families at the centre of national policy-making, as we are, through our family tax initiative, through our private health insurance rebates, through our maintenance of the social security safety net, through addressing the causes of family breakdown, and through many other measures.

It means giving Australians more choice in the way they live and work, more choice in industrial relations, more choice to join or not to join a trade union, more choice in education, more choice in child care and more choice in telecommunications. It means liberating and re-energising small businesses all around Australia, as we are through our industrial relations, taxation, paperwork and other initiatives that will give them more incentives to expand, invest and create more jobs.

It means strengthening the decentralised networks of families, workplaces and communities as far more effective guarantors of choice, freedom and opportunity than centralised political and bureaucratic controls. It means significantly expanding measures to protect Australia's unique environment as we will through our historic one billion dollar Natural Heritage Trust of Australia just as soon as the Senate passes the legislation on the one-third privatisation of Telstra which will provide the necessary funding. It means achieving the full potential of our rapidly developing partnerships with the countries of the Asia-Pacific region at the same time as we continue to build on our important and long-standing relationships with our traditional friends.

In meeting these challenges, liberalism draws on a rich store of ideas and values. But our clearest guiding principle will be to stay true to what we have always been, a political movement owned by no special interests, defending no special privileges and accountable only to the Australian people in meeting the responsibility to build a better and fairer future for all of them.

# A Great History

## National Convention of the Liberal Party
## Brisbane – 15 March 1998

At the 1998 National Convention of the Liberal Party in Brisbane, John Howard reminded the Party of who they represented and what it stood for. With the widely-held public perception that the previous Keating Labor Government had become beholden to vocal special-interest groups, the Prime Minister asserted that the Party he now led would belong to all Australians. Like Menzies, who believed that the Labor Party of his day, and even his own United Australia Party, had become dominated by sectional interests such as the trade union movement or the corporate sector, Howard was resolved to lead a party that would govern in the broad national interest. As well as endeavouring to represent all Australians, Howard's Liberal Party would remain firmly grounded in principles such as the dignity and freedom of the individual, the fundamental role of the family, the value of enterprise and hard work, the ethic of mutual obligation, the critical importance of small businesses to the community and a national vision for a tolerant and racially harmonious society.

The Liberal Party is a party that belongs to all Australians. When I accepted the mandate of the Australian people on that exhilarating night of 2 March 1996, that none in this room will ever forget, I said the proudest thing about being the Prime Minister-elect of Australia was that I led a party that was owned by no one section of the Australian community, that it was a party for all Australians. It was not owned by the business community. It was not owned by the noisy elites. It was not owned by political correctness. It certainly was not owned by the trade union movement. It was owned by the ordinary men and women of Australia and I remain immensely proud that we have demonstrated that in Government.

We are a party with a great history but an even greater future. We remember the great inheritance of Sir Robert Menzies, our founder, remember those long, uninterrupted years of social and economic stability after 1949 when we had an unemployment rate that was the envy of the rest of the world, when we welcomed in their millions the peoples of Europe and the Middle East, whether they came like Alex Somlyay's[8] parents from Budapest or whether they came from Italy or from Greece or from the Baltic States or from Poland or Czechoslovakia.

We welcomed them in their millions and they have all become, every last one of them, wonderful Australians and we thank them and we respect them for the contribution they have made to our great nation.

We also remember the inheritance from Menzies of great social reform. We remember the trail-blazing reforms of the Fraser Government. We remember the fact that it was the Holt Government and not the Whitlam Government that ended the inequity of the White Australia Policy. We remember the family allowance changes brought in by Malcolm Fraser, and of course, we also remember the 13 barren years under Hawke and Keating.

Our Party has always been rooted very firmly in principles. We believe, above all, in the supremacy and the sovereignty of the individual. We believe that the family unit is the bedrock of our society. We believe in the work ethic. We believe in rewarding hard work and achievement. We believe in the principle of mutual obligation. Those in the community who are down on their luck are entitled to our assistance and our compassion but we, as a community, are entitled to ask in return, where it is reasonable, that people who receive government help give something back to the community. That is the principle of mutual obligation and that is the principle that is enshrined in our Work for the Dole policy which has the overwhelming support of the Australian community.

We are a party that believes passionately in the place and the role of

---

[8] Alex Somlyay (born 1946) was a Liberal member of the House of Representatives representing the Queensland Division of Fairfax from 1990 to 2013.

small business in our society. I have often spoken very feelingly and proudly about my own background as the son of a garage proprietor in the inner suburbs of Sydney. I have never forgotten the upbringing I received. I have never forgotten what I was taught about the value of starting with nothing and building something by the dint of your own effort and your own achievement and I long for an Australia where every man and woman who wants to do that can do it without hindrance or without interruption.

We are also, above all, a party that believes in tolerance and racial equality. We have welcomed people from the four corners of the Earth. We have welcomed people of different religions and of different colour and of different ethnic backgrounds. We admire and we respect them all and they are all equal and entitled members of the great Australian family. …

# Nurturing the Natural Party of Middle Australia

## The Centenary of the Australian Women's National League
## Melbourne – 16 July 2004

In the history of Australian conservatism and liberalism, the Australian Women's National League (AWNL) looms large. As one of the peak political bodies for women on the centre-right, the League had a long history of promoting free enterprise and volunteerism, resisting socialism and championing the interests of women and the family. After reaching its zenith during the First World War, the League coalesced with other like-minded groups to form the Liberal Party of Australia in the 1940s. Long before affirmative action became fashionable, the AWNL's Elizabeth Couchman successfully brokered an agreement with Menzies to ensure women had equal representation in the structures of the Liberal Party.

At this dinner to celebrate the centenary of the foundation of the League, Prime Minister Howard paid tribute to the lasting contribution of the AWNL to the conservative-liberal movement in Australia. While the League had ceased to exist as a formal entity since its absorption into the Liberal Party, Howard observed that its enduring influence was certainly apparent in the modern party's advancement of women's interests. From being the first party to introduce child endowment in the 1940s to the party that helped present-day women balance work and family life, the ideals of the League continued to inform Liberal policies to assisting women and

> their families. Without dwelling too much on the past,
> the Prime Minister concluded that centenaries such as
> this were cause for Australian Liberals to take due pride
> in the rich legacy wrought by their pioneers.

It is a great pleasure to join you this evening and to commemorate the 100th anniversary of the Australian Women's National League (AWNL).

This gathering is particularly appropriate in a week when Liberal women have achieved yet another milestone. For the first time in Australia's history, there are now three women in the Federal Cabinet, a milestone that has been achieved without the use of patronising quotas.

The women in this room, especially from the Women's Section of the Victorian Division, are heirs to a tradition that has produced some great political warriors for the Liberal cause.

Established in 1904, the Australian Women's National League grew to become the largest and most effective women's political organisation in Australian history. It pursued a tough-minded, liberal agenda aimed at economic prosperity and freedom of thought and action. It participated in pre-selections on the non-Labor side of politics and, at its peak during the First World War, the League registered some 500 branches with more than 50 000 members.

And it played an important role in the formation of the Liberal Party. This year we also mark the 60th anniversary of the founding of our great party by Sir Robert Menzies. So it is doubly appropriate that tonight we celebrate the contribution of generations of Liberal women to our party and to the making of modern Australia.

Menzies was very conscious of the political power of the Australian Women's National League at the time he formed the Liberal Party in 1944. He was forever indebted to the League's president, Elizabeth ("May") Couchman, for helping to convince her colleagues to merge their organisation into the new party. And, in turn, women gained a strong voice in the Liberal Party.

## *A tradition of Liberal achievement*

In later life, Menzies would often reflect on the unique spirit of those who helped him form the Liberal Party, not least the members of the Australian Women's National League. It is worth reminding ourselves what led so many women to throw their support behind the Liberal Party in the 1940s and in later decades.

The Liberal Party was created at a time when the political winds could hardly have been more unfavourable. The momentum behind bigger, more intrusive government seemed almost unstoppable. The Great Depression and World War left many people, including much of the intelligentsia, convinced that socialism offered the only path to prosperity and happiness.

Into these headwinds came a remarkable group of Australians determined to resist Labor's collectivist social planning. And women like Elizabeth Couchman, Ivy Wedgwood and Edith Haynes were in the front rank of the new Liberal Party based on their organisational and political skills.

The founding fathers and mothers of the Liberal Party did not oppose Labor's big government agenda simply on economic grounds. They knew socialism was inefficient. But, more importantly, they were determined to resist what they saw as a dull and sterile world-view that negated the dignity and worth of the individual.

The men and women who formed the Liberal Party embodied a particular ideal of Australian society based on virtues of individual freedom, personal responsibility and social obligation. These are virtues with a timeless place in the Australian Liberal inheritance.

Menzies' great strength was his capacity to connect Liberal philosophy with the experiences, concerns and ideals of people in their daily lives. In broadcasts such as "The Forgotten People", his classic 1942 statement of Australian Liberalism, he articulated superbly the aspirations of men and women in Middle Australia for themselves, their families and their country.

Menzies also had a very clear idea of good government when he led the Liberal Party out of the political wilderness in 1949. The Menzies era is synonymous with rising living standards and expanded opportunities for the Australian people, years of full employment, low inflation, surging home ownership, increased education opportunities and large-scale immigration.

For Australians who had endured years of depression and war, it was a time of new and bigger horizons; a time when they could plan with confidence and aspire to give their children an even brighter future. In many ways, Menzies was ahead of his time in recognising the changing role of women in Australian society and in developing policies that appealed to women.

Of course, our political opponents have made it their mission to tear down the great and enduring Menzies legacy. We owe it to our past, our present and our future to reaffirm this tradition of Liberal achievement.

The growth rates achieved between 1949 and 1966 were the highest in Australia's history. Unemployment was consistently between one and one-and-a-half per cent. I well recall casting my first vote at the December 1961 Federal Election when the Menzies Government was almost thrown out of office because unemployment reached what was then the unthinkable level of 2.6 per cent.

Australia also became one of the world's great home-owning democracies in the Menzies years. In Melbourne, for example, between 1947 and 1961 home ownership rates rose from 50 per cent to 76 per cent. For the first time, thousands of Australian workers whose traditional allegiance was to the Labor Party could afford to buy their own home.

The expansion of education was another significant part of Menzies era nation-building. The Menzies Government's decision to grant state aid to religious schools in 1963 ended 100 years of discrimination against Australian Catholics. In the process, the Liberal Party became, emphatically, a more inclusive movement.

Menzies was also the driving force behind the great post-war expansion of higher education in Australia. Based on his clear vision of the role of universities in Australian society, his government paved the way for a massive transition from elite to mass higher education. In later life Menzies continued to rate the development of Australia's university system as one of his proudest achievements, notwithstanding the counter-cultural backlash on campuses against much of his legacy.

The Menzies era was a time of economic prosperity and social stability, two things that symbolise the Liberal inheritance to Australia. But, as Menzies well understood, Australian Liberalism is not a fixed ideology.

It is a broad-based political philosophy that relates a core set of enduring values to the changing realities and challenges of Australian society. And we face a continuing challenge to relate our Liberal inheritance to the hopes and aspirations of the Australian people.

## *The social dividend of economic strength*

My Government has pursued its own distinctively Australian synthesis of economic liberalism and modern conservatism. We have never lost sight of the fact that good economic management and sustained economic growth are not ends in themselves. Economic prosperity is valued for its contribution to building a stable, fair and cohesive Australian society.

Our economic prosperity and social advancement rest on many of the same requirements. Robust communities, cohesive families and responsible individuals are fundamental for building a strong economy. And without a strong economy, a caring community is much harder to achieve.

There is never a disconnect between economic policy and social policy. Good economic policy, generating growth, investment and jobs, is essential to sustaining a fair and decent society.

Let me illustrate by highlighting, in turn, just some of the Government's economic and social policy achievements over the last eight and a half years.

- More than 1.3 million new jobs have been created since March 1996.
- We are spending 60 per cent more on employment servic-

19

es for disabled Australians than was the case when Labor left office.

- Real wages have risen by 14 per cent, while inflation has remained low and stable.

- We have indexed the old-age pension to the strong growth in average male wages rather than to the lower rate of the consumer price index.

- Labor's $96 billion debt has been cut by $70 billion with interest savings averaging $5.5 billion a year.

- We have doubled annual spending on health, from $17 billion to $35 billion over our time in office.

- The number of strikes in Australia has fallen to a record low.

- We have created more than 256 000 extra child-care places since 1996.

- The profit share in Australia is at a record high.

- We are providing record support to carers in Australia, including through a five-fold increase in carer respite services.

Again, the point is a simple one. A strong economy and a fair and decent society are bound up together. Economic prosperity is the essential prerequisite for reaching all our other goals. ...

Today, our economy is stronger and more competitive than ever. The last eight and a half years have seen rising living standards, rising employment, low interest rates and low inflation. This prosperity has in turn translated into rising expenditure on health, aged care, education and all the other things that are important to improving the lives of Australians.

If we want to build a better Australia, we simply do not have the lazy option of taking this prosperity for granted.

### *More choice and opportunities for Australian women*

The Liberal Party and our political forebears have a very proud record, both in the area of women's representation and, more broadly, in the advancement of women in Australian society.

Women from the Liberal Party's forebears were the first elected to the House of Representatives, and almost all the State parliaments. The Liberal Party was the first political party in the country to make provision for equal numbers of men and women in some of its senior party positions, particularly in the Victorian Division.

It was a Liberal Government that introduced child endowment. It was a Liberal Government that established the first national childcare office. It was a Liberal Government that first recognised the rights of married pensioners in the tax system. It was a Liberal Government that introduced many of the provisions for private health insurance that are so important for women.

We are a party that values choice and individuality among women. We do not believe in advancing certain categories of women or, indeed, certain categories of men. We want to mobilise the talents of all women in Australian society with policies that promote wider opportunity and wider choice.

Our work and family package in this year's budget, 2004-2005, was based on the view that the government's role is to help facilitate choice for Australian women and that there is no single solution for managing demands of work and family.

With this package, total assistance to families will have increased by over $6 billion a year since 1996. The base rate of family assistance has increased from less than $600 per child in January 1996 to almost $1,700 per child in July 2004, a real increase of over 100 per cent.

Our workplace relations policies also reflect our commitment to expanding choice and opportunities for women. Increased labour force participation by women continues to be a major influence on our labour market. For example, female part-time employment is increasing at an annual average rate of 3.5 per cent, more than twice the rate for the labour force as a whole.

We have made it easier for women to negotiate working arrangements that provide a better balance between work and family. Women are now more likely than the average to be covered by a federal certified agreement that includes carer's leave or provisions for access to regular part-time work. At the same time, the workplace relations safety net has been strengthened to encourage the full participation of women in the workforce on a full-time, part-time, casual or job-sharing basis.

In a speech in Adelaide last week, I spoke about my Government's commitment to building an enterprise culture in Australia. Women are at the leading edge of new work arrangements and options, leveraging off information technology and the shift towards smaller, decentralised business models.

About one-third of Australia's 1.6 million small business operators are women. Our existing Small Business Enterprise Culture programme supports skills development projects and mentoring services tailored to the needs of women.

Many Australian women are looking for new options to work from home with the extra scope this gives them to achieve the right balance between work and family. I used the example in my speech last week of a woman with accounting skills setting up a home-based business to do tax returns and the Government aims to take additional steps to assist Australians wanting to establish home-based businesses.

I also spoke in Adelaide about helping mature-age Australians stay in touch with the labour market in a world of rapid economic change. The Coalition's Job Network is currently providing more than 100 000 mature age workers with targeted assistance to maximise their employ-ment opportunities. As a Government, we are committed to meeting the challenge of an ageing society in a way that expands opportunities and choices for older Australians.

The 2004-05 budget also included initiatives to deliver a more flex-ible and adaptable retirement system with significant benefits to Austra-lian women. As well as increasing the Government's superannuation co-contribution to assist low and middle income earners, we are providing people with more flexibility in using superannuation savings to purchase an income stream while continuing to do some work.

This is all part of what I have termed "getting the big things right" for Australians. Keeping our eye on the ball with responsible economic management, but also looking over the horizon at our nation's long-term social challenges.

## *Challenges for our Party's future*

None of us, least of all political parties, can afford to be overly nostalgic about the past or too self-congratulatory about the present. As Liberals, we need to face the challenges of the future.

First, the immediate one, we need to mobilise for the coming political battle with Labor at the Federal Election when it is called. As I have said to my colleagues in Canberra, the Government is in the fight of its life and only eight seats separate us from political oblivion.

It will be difficult but we have a very good story to tell. And all of us need to be out there telling it, in our communities, over the back fence and in our workplaces. So I appeal to you all to turn your minds and your energies (and perhaps even your wallets) to what is required for victory.

The second challenge is equally great, if less immediate. All political parties, the Liberal Party, the National Party, and the Labor Party, need to confront the fact that they are becoming too narrow. Their base of membership has narrowed and they need to find ways of relating more comprehensively to community concerns.

By and large, people are not joining institutions anymore in the way they used to when I was growing up and entering adult life. This is a challenge as much for churches, community and other voluntary groups as it is for political parties.

Political parties have to do a better job of attracting members and harnessing community support. This is very important to our body politic because, if you end up with political parties being dominated and run by people whose whole life has revolved around politics, then you are going to get a narrow set of perspectives and a shallow reservoir of experience.

The Liberal Party is the natural party of Middle Australia and we need to nurture that. That does not mean that we do not also attract high-profile candidates. Unlike the Labor Party, we actually make our high-profile candidates go through local pre-selection processes. But we do need to stay very much in tune with community sentiment and draw on wide community experience.

Finally, as Liberals, we need to be conscious of our history and our intellectual inheritance as a tool in the battle of ideas. Ultimately you need the courage of convictions in politics and, on our side, we have a rich intellectual tradition from both the classical liberal and conservative traditions. As I have said many times, the Liberal Party is a broad church that draws on both these traditions.

Australian Liberalism also has a great history going back to colonial politics, to the Federation years and on through Menzies and the great political battles of the twentieth century. And, without being overly sentimental, we should be proud of our history and draw on it to fight the political battles of today and tomorrow.

### Conclusion

The inheritance of Australian Liberalism is an important part of the broader history of Australia. A prosperous economy and a fair and decent society are central to this inheritance. And they have been central to what my Government has sought to deliver to the Australian people.

A century ago, at the time the Australian Women's National League was formed, a new nation's yearning for prosperity and fairness was expressed in policies that largely set Australia apart from the world. High industry protection, centralised industrial relations and the White Australia Policy betrayed a certain lack of ease about who we were and what we could be.

Today, a very different Australia faces the challenges of the twenty-first century. We are a strong, competitive economy no longer reliant on protection. We are a tolerant, diverse society, confident about our place in the world.

While we have made our mistakes as a country, this story of change and achievement is one all Australians can be proud of. And the Liberal Party can be proud of its role in that story.

Historically, the Liberal Party has never been a party of individualistic libertarians. With roots deep in the aspirations of Middle Australia, we have sought to strike a common sense balance between a healthy scepticism about what governments can achieve, and the Australian tradition of believing that there is a role for government beyond being simply a keeper of the ring.

A balance that understands the need for both a strong economy and a caring community. A balance that supports a decent safety net, but also aims to build greater self-reliance and personal responsibility.

A balance that, despite changing times, still embodies the values of those who founded the Liberal Party, including the members of the Australian Women's National League.

# Custodian of Two Great Traditions
## The Launch of *The Conservative*
### Parliament House, Canberra – 8 September 2005

In the fourth term of his prime ministership, John Howard was invited by his parliamentary colleague, Senator Nick Minchin, to launch a new journal, *The Conservative*. As a conservative journal of ideas, the publication would feature contributions by Liberal parliamentarians across a range of policy areas. At a time when the Prime Minister's own NSW Division of the Liberal Party was racked with factional in-fighting over ideology, the nation's most senior Liberal reminded the Party that it was, and must remain, a "broad church" with two complementary philosophical streams. According to Howard, the Liberal Party was always at its best and strongest when it could deftly blend and balance the conservative tradition of Edmund Burke (1729-1797) with the classical liberal tradition of John Stuart Mill (1806-1873). In short, the liberal emphasis on the personal liberty of the individual served to complement the conservative imperative for social order in society. The Prime Minister argued that the Liberal Party required both for it to be able to represent the present needs and aspirations of Australian society. On the one hand, the Party needed to accept the realities of change, modernisation and globalisation whilst, at the same time, deriving security and continuity from the institutions and values that had served Australia so well.

To all of my colleagues, ladies and gentlemen, I am truly delighted to have been asked to launch this publication. And the most important reason why I am delighted to be involved in this launch is that this is the latest piece of field evidence that when it comes to debating the great issues and the ideas that will shape Australia for decades into the future, there is only one party in town, this town, that is involved in the debate of ideas. And that is the most important thing, the most important thing of all about this publication and the other two publications, one that I launched and one that my colleague, the Deputy Leader of the Liberal Party, Peter Costello, launched. Both of those publications, along with this one, address serious issues. We are not afraid to debate ideas, we are not afraid to welcome a public contribution to a sensible debate. It is the mark of a mature, successful, cohesive political party that it can welcome debate on ideas. And if it is done in a respectful fashion, if it is done on the basis of merit and intellectual exchange, it can only be to the good of our Party and to the good of our society.

Appropriately enough, just before I came here, I took part in a very private and a very touching ceremony. The Ambassador from Poland came to see me and awarded me the Medal of Gdansk – the medal that has been struck to mark the 25th anniversary of the Solidarity movement. Solidarity is not a word that I normally allow to roll off my tongue with conservative alacrity. Solidarity is a word that is more normally employed by those who march to a different political drumbeat than I do. But Solidarity was the name that Lech Walesa gave to that great movement that did more than any other individual activity to bring about the collapse of communism in Poland and that played a major role in the collapse of communism around the world. As I look back on the events of my political lifetime none has been more transforming and none more important than the fall of communism, something which changed the world and represented the greatest single triumph for liberty in my lifetime and in the lifetime I am sure of everybody in this room.

The Liberal Party is a broad church. You sometimes have to get the builders in to put in the extra pew on both sides of the aisle to make sure that everybody is accommodated. But it is a broad church and we should never, as members of the Liberal Party of Australia, lose sight of the fact that we are the trustees of two great political traditions.

We are the custodian of the classical liberal tradition within our society. Australian Liberals should revere the contribution of John Stuart Mill to political thought.

We are also the custodians of the conservative tradition in our community. And if you look at the history of the Liberal Party, it is at its best when it balances and blends those two traditions. Mill and Burke are interwoven into the history and the practice and the experience of our political party.

Nick [Minchin][9] has quite rightly said that we are a party that is committed to the role of the individual. Our classic liberal tradition is manifest in our attitude to economic policy. ...It is important to take a moment to identify some of the things that we have done and we have stood for over the last few years to make my point. If you look for evidence of the classic liberal tradition within our embrace and within our activity, we think, I think instinctively, of our commitment to labour market reform. Labour market reform is not about transferring power from the States to the Commonwealth. Labour market reform is about transferring power from institutions to individuals. Because the essence of our drive for labour market reform is to create flexibility at the individual workplace level, to empower the individual with appropriate protection to make the bargain that he or she thinks is best for that person's individual circumstances and that person's family.

I have often described myself, and I do so again this morning, as somebody who is an economic liberal and a social conservative. I see no incompatibility between the two. And some of the oddest pieces of political philosophy that I have listened to or read is that philosophy or attitude that says, if you are an economic liberal, you have to be a social libertarian. Or, if you are somebody who is conservative in social policy, you have to have a conservative approach to economic policy.

My view is there is nothing incompatible with the blend of those two. And from my own personal point of view I have always thought that that mix best suits both the needs and the temper of contemporary Australian society. Contemporary Australian society understands that we do live

---

[9] Nick Minchin served as a Liberal member of the Australian Senate representing South Australia from 1993 to 2011.

in a world of change, they understand that globalism is with us forever, they may not like some aspects of it but they know they cannot change it and they therefore want a government that delivers the benefits of globalisation and not one that foolishly pretends, Canute-like, it can hold back the tide. They accept and they understand that. But they also want, within that change, sometimes that maelstrom of economic change, they want reassurance and they want to protect and defend those institutions that have given them a sense of security and a sense of purpose over the years.

And that is where our conservative tradition comes in. We carry the Burkean tradition of conservatism within our ranks. We believe that if institutions have demonstrably failed they ought to be changed or reformed. But we do not believe in getting rid of institutions just for the sake of change. We need to be persuaded that they are failed institutions. We should not rise to the clarion call of radical change just for its own sake.

It was Edmund Burke who famously said that "a state without the means of some change is without the means of its conservation". That is an interesting way of expressing the blend and the mix that we must, in contemporary Australian society, try and achieve. I am sceptical of radical reform of our society. In fact, I have been a profound opponent of radically changing the social context in which we live.

As Liberals we support and respect and promote the greatest institution in our society, and that is the family. There is no institution that provides more emotional support and reassurance to the individual than the family. There is no institution, incidentally, which is a more efficient deliverer of social welfare than a united, affectionate, functioning family. It is the best social welfare policy that mankind has ever devised.

But we also see liberty in our community as bound up with a sense of order. And we also, as Liberals, believe very much in a sense of individual and personal responsibility. And that is both a concomitant of personal liberty, and it is also an acknowledgement of the need that if we are to enjoy personal liberty we must have an ordered society. And we believe very strongly in the concept of mutual obligation. It is a concept that we have championed over the last 10 years and it is a concept that has won widespread support within the Australian community.

It is a concept that expresses the essential balance we must achieve, the compassion of looking after people who need help but the reasonable expectation of a society built on individual achievement that, having given people a fair go, they will return the compliment by themselves having a go. And that is really the philosophical basis of our ideal. And our strong belief in personal responsibility leads to, in fact flows from, our deep commitment to the obligation we have to each other.

Another thing that has united all Liberals and, in that collective unity, has separated ourselves from our political opponents, is our profound respect for and pride in the history of this country. We may have a debate about the appropriate balance between the central government and the States, we may talk about centralism and federalism. But there is one thing that Australians should never tire of talking about, and should never tire of identifying themselves with, and that is the cause of Australian nationalism.

Some people say I am a centralist – I have even heard one or two of my colleagues say that. I am certainly not a States' rightist, and I am not a centralist but I am an Australian nationalist. And my national sentiment transcends any regional parochial or State sentiment that I might in the dim distant past have had. I not only refuse to barrack for New South Wales in State of Origin rugby league matches out of respect for the marvellous generosity of the Queensland people at the Federal Election – that is one of the reasons why I refuse to barrack against my good friends from Queensland – but another reason is, much and all as I love the city in which I grew up, I have never felt any personal identification with the State. Perhaps that varies according to where you grew up. But a sense of commitment to the unity and wholeness of the Australian nation is something I think is very important to Australian Liberals.

Unlike occasionally our political opponents, we do not share the Manning Clark view of history that the history of this country started in 1972. We believe that this country has had a proud record of achievement. And, indeed, it is interestingly expressed in the equivocation that governments sometimes have about how they mark great political events. I can remember in the 1980s, as a member of the Fraser Government, we were starting the preparations to mark the Bicentenary. And the label, the description we wanted to give to it, was "The Australian Achievement". And when we were replaced by our political opponents in 1983 they got rid of that and I think they had the description, "Australians Living Together". Now, I mean that is nice and you know I am all in favour of that. But it said something to me, an equivocal view within that party about the history of this country. Now this country has blemishes in its history and I have said before, and I would say it again today, that the greatest blemish of all has been the treatment of Indigenous people. But if you look at the balance sheet of this country's history of achievement, it is not unimpressive, it is heroic and it is something that every individual Australian should be immensely proud of.

This publication will make a huge contribution to debate on ideas. I welcome it as I do the other two publications. I congratulate Santo [Santoro][10] for his indefatigable work in bringing this together and all others who have contributed to it.

Can I again say to you that we do occupy as the Liberal Party of Australia a special position amongst centre-right parties around the world. We are a party that must care for both of those traditions. We should never see it as our role as Australian Liberals to see the triumph of one of those traditions to the unfair detriment and certainly not the obliteration of the other. Our success has been to recognise that each has a rich contribution to make and, when we blend them in the right way, we are not only at our most compassionate and also most effective, but we are also at our most politically acceptable.

The average Australian, that overworked expression for which there is really no proper or valid alternative, the average Australian is a mixture of many things – he or she believes very much in the traditions of this country; he or she believes this country has been very successful; he or she does not think this country has much to be ashamed of; he or she believes that this country is well regarded around the world. But he or

---

[10] Reference to Senator Santo Santoro, Liberal Senator for Queensland, 2002 to 2007.

she also believes that individuals should be given a fair go, that if they are down on their luck, as he would describe it, they should be helped, but, having been helped, they should then get on with their lives and not expect the rest of the community to keep on assisting them.

The average Australian believes in traditional institutions, like the family and the traditional view of the family, but he or she does not want to persecute people who might have an alternative view. He or she is a very tolerant individual, but also a person who believes that when we face a common threat we need to be a united, cohesive people. Finally, and very importantly, the average Australian believes in a classless society. The average Australian believes that a person's worth should be determined by a person's character and hard work and not their religion, their race, their social background or their class.

Now that is not the most perfect definition of what an Australian believes in and what an Australian stands for but, after some, collectively at various stages and with the odd interruption here or there of some 14 years of leading the Liberal Party of Australia which is the custodian of this unique blend, that is my assessment humbly and respectfully of what I think the average Australian cares for and what matters to that person. And they want a government that responds to and expresses those values. They are in some respects universal values but they also contain a number of unique Australian values and I think they are very good values and it is our job to understand those values, constantly to keep them in mind and respond and I think, in the great debate of ideas, *The Conservative* will make a huge contribution as will the other two.

I thank the authors and I congratulate all of my colleagues for the willingness to engage in a debate of ideas. And I finish on this note, it is not a mark of fragmentation, it is a mark of cohesion and strength and maturity and success that we can engage in this debate of ideas and thus be an example to other political parties in Australia.

# All that is Worth Preserving in the Western Cultural Tradition

## *Quadrant* – the 50th Anniversary
## Sydney – 3 October 2006

Founded in 1956 by anti-communist intellectuals, James McAuley and Richard Krygier, the Sydney-based literary and cultural journal celebrated its fiftieth anniversary in 2006. Since its inception, *Quadrant* prided itself on providing a free platform for conservative-minded intellectuals, authors and poets to deliver a cogent counterpoint to the left-leaning ideologies prevailing in some quarters of academia and the media. As such, John Howard esteemed the journal as an intellectual standard-bearer for the Western cultural tradition of which Australia was a legatee.

In this address, Howard praised *Quadrant* for its historical contribution to the struggle against Soviet communism in the Cold War years and for its present-day role as a beacon for freedom against resurgent Islamist terrorism. In a world where traditional Western values were challenged by the ascendency of cultural relativism and political correctness, *Quadrant* represented the intellectual guardian of objective moral truths, individual liberty, liberal democracy and the rule of law. Whilst the magazine did not have any formal affiliation with a political party, Howard valued its essays, short stories and poetry for providing the cultural and intellectual ballast to the political cause of conservatism and liberalism.

I am finally succumbing to Peter Garrett's advice and it is great to embrace an evening of culture and poetry and all of that after overdosing on my Philistine sporting pursuits over the weekend in almost the four corners of the Earth, from one side of the country to the other.

It really is an enormous pleasure for Janette and me to celebrate this great event of a great literary journal. It has fought the good fight in the best sense of that expression for over half a century because it is true that over the last 50 years *Quadrant* has upheld, often as a lonely counterpoint to stultifying orthodoxies and dangerous utopias, the best of the Western cultural tradition.

It has helped many of us to navigate the battle of ideas, while staying true to its calling as an outlet for essays and poetry of the highest quality. Indeed, it is no exaggeration to say that *Quadrant* has been Australia's home to all that is worth preserving in that Western cultural tradition.

We recognise the debt that intellectual life in Australia owes to *Quadrant*, and to the people importantly who have sustained *Quadrant*'s free spirit over that 50 years.

As has already been remarked by both Paddy McGuinness[11] and Peter Coleman,[12] *Quadrant* has always attracted a very diverse group of people to its circle. People of different backgrounds, different faiths as well as those of no faith, people with different party political sympathies, but all united by a commitment to intellectual freedom and liberal democracy.

This diversity was nowhere more apparent than among the people who launched *Quadrant* in 1956, and this has already been alluded to, in the shadow of the Soviet suppression of the Hungarian uprising.

And I join others in paying tribute to three individuals: *Quadrant*'s founder and long-time publisher, Richard Krygier; its first editor James McAuley; and the first Chairman of the Australian Association for Cultural Freedom, Sir John Latham. Each in their own way was critical to *Quadrant*'s birth and its subsequent development.

Richard Krygier, the Jewish immigrant from Poland whose experiences of both Nazism and communism bred a passionate grasp of what was at stake in the great ideological contest of our time.

---

[11] Padraic "Paddy" McGuinness (1938-2008) was a former editor of *Quadrant* and a journalist, activist and commentator.

[12] Peter Coleman (born 1928) was a former editor of *Quadrant* and a Liberal member of the Legislative Assembly of New South Wales, 1965 to1978, and Leader of the Opposition, 1977-78; and held the House of Representatives seat of Wentworth for the Liberal Party from 1981 to 1987.

James McAuley, the poet and Catholic convert who edited *Quadrant* in its early years and who saw with great clarity the need for a cultural journal in Australia that stood apart from the canons of conformity of the left.

John Latham, the former Chief Justice and politician; the avowed humanist and rationalist whose involvement added prestige and stature to the *Quadrant* project.

I want also to recognise all of those who worked, often for very little money or no money, to produce some 430 issues of *Quadrant* down the years. Like most small magazines, *Quadrant* has invariably led a hand-to-mouth existence and been very much a labour of love for many committed people.

It is important on an occasion like this that we remember not just the big ideological struggles but also the individuals who took up the cause of cultural freedom and the defence of liberal democracy against its enemies.

With the fall of the Berlin Wall and the collapse of Soviet communism, it became all too easy to pretend that the outcome of the Cold War was an inevitable result of large-scale, impersonal forces that ultimately left totalitarianism exhausted and democratic capitalism triumphant. Nothing could be further from the truth. This was a struggle fought by individuals on behalf of the individual spirit.

And *Quadrant* holds an honoured place in Australian history for the stance it took for democratic freedom and a pluralist society and in opposition to collectivist ideologies that so many saw as the inevitable wave of the future.

It is worth recalling just a few incidences of the philo-communism that was once quite common in Australia in the 1950s and 1960s. For example, Manning Clark's book, *Meeting Soviet Man* (1960), where he likened the ideals of Vladimir Lenin to those of Jesus Christ. John Burton, the former head of the External Affairs Department, arguing that Mao's China provided a model for the "transformation" of Australia. All those who did not simply oppose Australia's commitment in Vietnam, but who actively supported the other side and fed the delusion that Ho Chi Minh was some sort of Jeffersonian Democrat intent on spreading liberty in Asia.

To quote George Orwell: "One has to belong to the intelligentsia to believe things like that: no ordinary man could be such a fool". There is a view that the pro-communist left in Australia in decades past was no more than a bunch of naive idealists, rather than what they were – ideological barrackers for regimes of oppression opposed to Australia and its interests.

In taking on the communist left and their fellow-travellers, people like Richard Krygier, James McAuley, Peter Coleman, Bob Santamaria, Heinz Arndt and Frank Knopfelmacher were not only right in practice, they were right in principle and part of a noble and moral cause.

The influence of the pro-communist left in Australian cultural circles did wane over time, after Hungary and Khruschev's secret speech in 1956 and further still after the brutal suppression of the Prague Spring in 1968. In the 1960s and 1970s, it largely gave way to a New Left counter culture, where once again *Quadrant* served as a beacon of free and sceptical thought against fashionable leftist views on social, foreign policy and economic issues.

In the eyes of the New Left, the Cold War became a struggle defined by "moral equivalence", where the Soviet bloc and the American-led West were equally to blame, each possessing their own dominating ideologies. It became the height of intellectual sophistication to believe that people in the West were no less oppressed than people under the yoke of communist dictatorship.

In time, the world would luckily see the emergence of three remarkable individuals whose moral clarity punctured such nonsense: Ronald Reagan, Margaret Thatcher and Pope John Paul II.

Reagan, the man who gave America back her confidence and optimism in the wake of a decade of setbacks and who began to talk openly and candidly about an "evil empire" – the sort of talk that sends diplomats the world over into panicked meltdown.

Thatcher, the Iron Lady who as well as anyone grasped and articulated the essential connection of personal, political and economic freedom.

Pope John Paul II – a man of enormous courage and dignity whose

36

words of faith and hope inspired millions behind the Iron Curtain to dream again of a Europe whole and free.

All of us here owe a particular debt of gratitude to these three towering figures of the late 20th century.

Beyond this defining ideological struggle, *Quadrant* has also been at the centre of various controversies and causes in Australia, often prepared to publish things that others would not touch, often taking stands which others shied away from taking. According to Peter Coleman, it was the Whitlam Government that inspired *Quadrant* to go from a bi-monthly to 10 issues a year and, based on some of the policies around at the time, I am not surprised. I do want to pay a special tribute to Peter as *Quadrant*'s longest serving editor.

Current editor Paddy McGuinness also deserves our special praise for the way he has carried on the *Quadrant* tradition of fine scholarship with a sceptical, questioning eye for cant, hypocrisy and moral vanity.

Of the causes that *Quadrant* has taken up that are close to my heart, none is more important than the role it has played as a counterforce to the black armband view of Australian history. Until recent times, it had become almost *de rigueur* in intellectual circles to regard Australian history as little more than a litany of sexism, racism and class warfare.

Again, it would take the brave voices of a few individuals to take a stand against the orthodoxies of the day. And, again, *Quadrant* has been an outpost of lively non-conformity in its willingness to defend both Geoffrey Blainey and Keith Windschuttle against the posse of political correctness.

Nowhere, I suggest, have the fangs of the left so visibly been on display as they were in a campaign based on character assassination and intellectual dishonesty through their efforts to trash the name and reputation of that great Australian historian, Geoffrey Blainey.

Despite a more diverse and lively intellectual environment in Australia compared with past decades, we should not underestimate the degree to which the soft-left still holds sway, even dominance, especially in Australia's universities, by virtue of its long march through the institutions.

*Quadrant* has always been a principled defender of what I might call a "traditionalist" view of a good education, and in opposition to the more fashionable, progressive views that have held sway in schools and universities. Earlier this year I called for a root and branch renewal of Australian history in our schools, with a restoration of narrative instead of what I labelled the "fragmented stew of themes and issues".

Armed with clear evidence of the decline of Australian history in our schools, the Government has made a start in our quest to ensure that the nation's history is an essential component of every Australian child's education, no longer an afterthought or an optional extra.

This is about ensuring children are actually taught their national inheritance, a nation like all others with its share of failures and mistakes, but one that has emerged at the start of this millennium as one of the most successful societies on Earth.

Few debates are as vital as those over education, whether it be in upholding basic standards on literacy and numeracy, promoting diversity and choice or challenging the incomprehensible sludge that can find its way into some curriculum material. That is why the Government will continue to be very tough on States and territories that fail to live up to their obligations for high standards in our schools.

Having spoken earlier about *Quadrant*'s role in the defining global struggle of the second half of the 20th century, let me say just a few words about the global struggle we now face at the start of the 21st century.

Today, free and open societies face a new tyranny, the tyranny of Islamist terrorism, one with at least a family resemblance to the great struggles against the forces of totalitarianism in the past. A Czech writer once wrote with great prescience that: "You can't build utopia without terror, and before long terror is all that's left".

And just as past struggles called for clear and unambiguous statements of belief and purpose, so we must again make very clear what is at stake. Let me say what I have said many times before. This is not a struggle against Islam. It is a struggle against a perverted interpretation of Islam. As we see on a daily basis, it is the terrorists and suicide bombers who eagerly set out to spread terror and to kill innocent Muslim civilians. Countries with their sons and daughters serving in Iraq and

Afghanistan today would like nothing more than to see them complete their job and return home.

To those who want to portray the West as anti-Muslim, I would say that it was not the Arab League who went to war in the 1990s on behalf of Muslim minorities in the Balkans. It was the governments of the United States, the United Kingdom and their NATO allies. Let me also remind people who now talk as if Iraq was some kind of pro-Islamic tranquillity before 2003 that the person who has probably killed more Muslims in history than anyone else is Saddam Hussein.

There are, as Owen Harries, an honoured guest tonight properly reminds us, people who legitimately opposed the original action to oust Saddam Hussein. However, it remains, to borrow a phrase, an inconvenient truth that if some countries such as the United States, the United Kingdom and Australia simply abandon the people of Iraq, this would be an enormous victory for the forces of terror and extremism around the world.

The fact is that we are part of a global campaign for the very ideals that some people wistfully dreamed were unchallengeable after the Cold War. No less than in that long, twilight struggle, this too will be a generational struggle for ideals of democratic freedom and liberty under the law.

I want to thank you for giving me the opportunity and paying me the honour of joining this celebration of this remarkable magazine. Its free and sceptical spirit has contributed enormously to intellectual and political debate in this country. It has displayed in relation to each of the great philosophical challenges that have come along through their domestic manifestations here in Australia, in my lifetime, tenacity towards principle, a consistency in advocating basic values and beliefs, and a broad-mindedness. By attracting an eclectic gathering of people from different backgrounds, this magazine has done itself and the values that unite it great credit indeed.

I wish *Quadrant* well. I thank it for its contribution to Australia. But even more importantly than that, I thank it for its contribution to the universal values of liberal democracy, and truth, and the spirit of the individual that is so important to all of us.

# The Liberal Party – a Broad Church

## The Inaugural John Howard Lecture
## Menzies Research Centre
## Melbourne – 19 February 2009

In 2009, the Menzies Research Centre instituted the "John Howard Lecture Series" to honour the former Prime Minister's contribution to Australian public life over three decades. While the lecture series would invite prominent Australian and international leaders from the centre-right of politics to discuss issues of importance to Australia's future, it was fitting that the inaugural 2009 lecture featured the eponymous former Prime Minister himself. After little more than a year since leaving the prime ministership, John Howard reflected on the essence of the Liberal Party and the social and economic policy aspirations it should continue to champion, be it in opposition or in government. By remaining true to its core beliefs, Howard argued that the Party during his years in office had accomplished several significant outcomes, not least delivery of critical reforms to the labour market and taxation system, reduction of tariff protection, creation of a balanced social security system, and a foreign policy that strengthened ties with both the Asia-Pacific and North Atlantic regions.

I am greatly honoured that the Menzies Research Centre has inaugurated an annual lecture in my name and I am touched that the Centre has asked me to deliver the first of these lectures. ...

The legacy of the former Liberal Government is one that we should all want to own. Australia was a stronger, prouder and more prosperous nation in November 2007 than it had been in March 1996. ...

When I resumed the leadership of the Liberal Party on 30 January

1995, I laid out five objectives. It is with some pride that I now reflect on the extent to which the Government I led acted in different ways to achieve the goals I enunciated so many years ago.

The Liberal Party of Australia is not a party of the hard right, nor does it occupy the soft centre of Australian politics. It is a party of the centre right. It is the custodian of two great traditions in Australia's political experience. It represents both the classical liberal tradition and the conservative tradition. Put another way, it is the party of both John Stuart Mill and Edmund Burke.

This is a view that I have held for a very long time, not only through the years when I was Prime Minister but well before that. The colloquial description of our Party, which I have frequently employed, as being a broad church is one that we should not only treasure but always give effect to as we reach our decisions. Ours is a party which rejects extremes. We should not, however, be a party which constantly seeks the mid-point between opposing arguments. I deliberately employed the expression, "mainstream", rather than "middle ground" or "consensus", to describe my position on particular issues.

This was because I believed that both the desirable outcome and community feeling were often anything but at the mid-point of opposing views on particular issues. I am by instinct an economic liberal and a social conservative. It will come as no surprise for me to state this tonight. To some this is a contradiction.

To the more thoughtful, it is a complementarity. Economic change of the type experienced by Australia over the past thirty years has been extensive and, to many, quite unsettling, but it has been accepted as necessary. In accepting the inevitability of economic change Australians, sometimes unconsciously, have sought reassurance in the continuation of the status quo in other areas. It is against the human condition to be comfortable with change in every aspect of life. We all seek balance.

We are a party of the individual rather than of the collective. We do not neglect our obligations as individuals to society, but we see the maximum good for the nation being achieved when each individual is encouraged to do his or her best. This was the philosophy which underpinned our successive reforms of the industrial relations system. The success of this policy was best illustrated by the extraordinary fall in unemployment during our twelve years in government.

We are a party that should always see the family as the most important unit in our society, not only as a source of love and emotional security, but also, quite pragmatically, as the most efficient social welfare system that mankind has ever devised. A properly functioning family is a greater antidote to poverty and low self-esteem than a plethora of labour market programmes and an army of counsellors.

The Liberal Party should always be a party of national pride and cultural self-belief. Many Western nations show signs of losing faith in their own cultural identity. They have developed the mistaken belief that if there is progressive accommodation with some of the more radical critics of their societies, then those critics will in time be absorbed into the mainstream of the nation. This is a mistaken belief. This nation is a magnet to millions from around the world because of who we are and not because of what others would want us to become.

Liberals should always retain their strong belief in the fundamental force of the market. That does not mean that the market always functions smoothly or that it is not open to abuse. The notion, gaining traction because of the world's financial turmoil, that in some way markets need extensive reregulation is based on a false reading of what has happened to the world economy in the past year and also ignores the reasons for the remarkable growth of the middle class in the Asia-Pacific region and the consequent reduction in levels of poverty, which have occurred during the past thirty years.

Our Party should always be the champion of small business. We should not only give rhetorical effect to this but should ensure that we support policies which explicitly help small business. That is why my Government frequently sought to reform the absurd unfair dismissal laws introduced by the Keating Government. Complaint about those laws was a constant theme of the years of dialogue I had with small business as Prime Minister.

We should always be a party which maintains what I choose to call the Australian safety net for the less fortunate. Economic issues inevitably dominated the policy analysis of the former government. This meant that the scale of the reforms within the area of social security was often overlooked. I have deliberately employed the expression, "the Australian safety net". One of the great achievements, often unremarked, is that in the area of social security it has struck the right balance between the hard edges, sometimes verging on indifference, of the American approach to social security and the overly paternalistic approach of many European countries.

It is never defensible to say to people, who, through no fault of their own, cannot find work, that after a certain period of time society will provide them with no financial support. Equally, however, a system which contains no incentives to move from welfare to work and thus perpetuates high levels of unemployment and welfare dependency should be repudiated.

In Australia we have got the balance right. The introduction, early in our term, of Work for the Dole was greeted with shrieks of horror from many commentators and the Labor Party. Yet, after a short period, it became fully accepted as part of our nation's approach. To most it struck the right balance. It provided support for people and, in return, if they were able-bodied, the people receiving the support were required to do some work or provide some other community service. Likewise, the Welfare to Work policy has lasting social benefits.

Internationally, Australia should never move far from the doctrine of enlightened self-interest. In the twelve years of the previous government, and against many predictions to the contrary, Australia not only deepened and strengthened her relations with the United States but simultaneously brought a new dimension to our association with the nations of Asia, particularly those of North Asia. To be able to say, at the end of 2007, that Australia enjoyed an even better relationship with both China and the United States than had been the case a decade or more earlier encapsulated the Coalition's success in this policy area.

As a counterpoise to the deepening relationship with China, Australia, in partnership with the United States, placed great emphasis on the democratic traditions we held in common with other Asian nations such as Japan and India. Not only did this send a clear message to China about the importance we attached to our common democratic values, it provided balance and reassurance to some other nations nervous about China's increasing muscle.

We should always remember that, for all the value of certain international organisations, friends are more enduring than forums, and that common values bind nations together more effectively and in a more enduring way than undue faith in the efficacy of process and international structures.

Finally, and very importantly, we should be a political party which always actively pursues desirable reform. As is well known, I have always brought an essentially "Burkean" approach to Australia's institutions. I support change and reform where that will clearly produce a better outcome. If it does not, then there is no point in disturbing the status quo.

If one had stood at the vantage point of Australian economic history in 1980 it would have been possible to say very clearly that our nation needed five great reforms. We needed to deregulate our financial system, fundamentally change our taxation system, make our labour markets freer, reduce excessively high levels of tariff protection and rid the government of ownership of commercial enterprises which would not only be better run by private enterprise but, by dissolving government ownership, conflicts of interest would be eliminated. By 2007 these five great reforms had been achieved....

If one can be philosophical, it is fair to say that those five reforms were an essential Australian contribution to what one might properly describe as the neo-liberal experiment of the past thirty years....

The highlights of the Coalition's economic achievements are well-known; the elimination of $96 billion of government debt, the introduction of major reforms to our taxation system, the lowest unemployment level for more than thirty years, a freer and more open labour market which capitalised on the natural trading advantages of Australia, and a level of fiscal rectitude which meant that Australia entered the current economic plunge in a stronger state than any other Western nation....

In the past thirty years the freer functioning of markets inherently involved in the globalisation process has lifted hundreds of millions of people out of poverty. Competitive capitalism has been integral to this historic development. So far from failing, it has succeeded....

# Politics – Battle of Ideas

## Speech Accepting Edmund Burke Award
## Alliance of Conservative Reformists in Europe
## London – 1 November 2016

In November 2016, the Alliance of Conservative Reformists in Europe conferred the Edmund Burke Award on John Howard. Founded in October 2009, the Alliance described itself as a "political family united by the centre-right values expressed in our Reykjavik Declaration". The values affirmed included individual liberty, national sovereignty, parliamentary democracy, private property, limited government, sound money, free trade, family values and the devolution of power.

In its desire to recognise world leaders credited with advancing conservative principles globally, the Alliance instituted the Edmund Burke Award. Named in honour of the eighteenth-century British Whig statesman and opponent of the French Revolution, Edmund Burke (1729-1797), the award recognised politicians who followed Burke's lead of campaigning against arbitrary power and injustice, whilst championing human freedom and the British common law constitutional tradition.

The recipient of the 2016 Award, John Howard, reflected on the relevance of Burke's conservative principles to the present state of politics in Australia and the world. In view of the recent referendum on Britain's membership of the European Union, the former Prime Minister affirmed the importance of the nation-state concept in the freedom of a nation to determine its own destiny. Emphasising Burke's vision for human freedom, Howard also stressed the primacy of free speech in a democratic society, citing recent incursions on the freedom of expression in Australia. Howard concluded by noting that Burke's legacy had informed the philosophy of his own Liberal Party with its synthesis of classical liberalism and conservatism.

We live in a time when there is – to use a biblical expression – a lot of wailing and gnashing of teeth about the state of politics. It is occurring in all of our countries. It is occurring in Great Britain, it is occurring in Australia and it is occurring particularly in the United States as we face an extraordinary presidential election where the level of disenchantment with the two major candidates is quite unparalleled.

And in the shadow of this great man, Edmund Burke, and conscious of the Award that I have been given, I could perhaps briefly reflect on the relevance of some of the things that Burke said through his career on the state of politics. It is true that the new swear word of the political commentariat is populism: if you are not happy with something, then it is a result of populism having won the day, and I can understand that. It is easy to run a populist campaign. But it is also easy to lose sight of the fact that we have always had populism. There have always been people unhappy with the impact of particular political decisions on their lives or on their community. And it is always more likely that that will be the case in the wake of more difficult world economic circumstances. And I think as we wail and gnash our teeth about what we see as populism around the world at the present time, we should not lose sight of the fact that it has come on the heels of a period of time when, between, I suppose, the early 2000s or even earlier than that through to the global financial crisis, many of the governments and many of the communities of the Western world were pushing against an open door when it came to economic expansion and economic activity. And it is also easy to lose sight of the tremendous gains that globalisation and competitive capitalism have brought to the world, not least the poor of the world.

I often hear those on the Left saying the great moral challenge of our age is climate change. I think that is nonsense. It is not the great moral challenge of our age. The great moral challenge of our age remains as it has been for many ages, and that is the removal, through fair means of free market-based growth, of the gap between the rich and poor. That is the great moral challenge and that is the methodology by which that gap should be closed: not by state ownership and redistribution, but rather by the fruits of competitive capitalism and globalisation.

We should never cease to remind the world and remind our electorates of what globalisation and what competitive capitalism have done for hundreds of millions of people lifted from absolute poverty in many parts of Asia and South America and now, increasingly, is beginning to occur in the continent of Africa. That is the great success story of the last several decades and whenever I hear the voices of criticism of globalisation and open trade – and it distresses me immensely that both of the candidates in the United States appear to have turned their backs on the Trans Pacific Trade Partnership, something that would involve the economies of 60 per cent of the world, and the United Sates has been so often the standard bearer, the great clarion crier, when it comes to trade expansion and trade growth. We should never, let me say again, lose sight of what globalisation and competitive capitalism have done for the poor of the world.

Edmund Burke's life reminds us, as does his example as a member of parliament, that politics above everything else is a battle of ideas. It is not a public relations contest. And when I think of those towering figures of world conservativism, Margaret Thatcher and Ronald Reagan, you are instantly reminded that theirs were lives committed to the great battle of ideas. When Ronald Reagan told his speech writers that he was going to deliver a speech calling on Mr Gorbachev to tear down that wall (the Berlin Wall), they shuffled their feet and many of his foreign affairs advisers said, well, maybe, it is not quite the right time to say that.

The wall had been up for a few years by then. It was erected in 1962 if my memory serves me correctly. But he went ahead and he did it and he was an exemplar of a person who understood that, at crucial moments in the history of his own nation and of the world, there was a time to stand against any tide of nervous public opinion in favour of principle and, as far as he was concerned, there was a great principle involved.

We all know, as a consequence, not just of that, but of the special partnership forged between him and Margaret Thatcher with a magnificent moral contribution of leadership from Pope John Paul II, that great product of a proud Polish state, we eventually saw the collapse of the Soviet Union.

And, in your own country, the example of Margaret Thatcher stands with equal height. There was never any doubt that she saw politics as a battle of values and ideas. There was never any doubt what her values and what her ideas were. She was not always right. Nobody in politics is, but she was right about the big things. And the successful political leaders of the world are those who get the big things right. Political leaders who try as hard as they can never to make a mistake will never get any big things right because, in the end, it is getting the big things right that really matter.

Burke also reminded us of the importance, as Jesse [Norman] did tonight, of the political party as a core unit of advancement and activity and we should not, in reflecting on that, feel in any way complacent about the state of party politics around the Western world. Political movements today are not the mass movements they were 40 or 50 years ago. Their memberships are no longer as representative of the generality of the people who vote for them as they used to be. They are far more prone to falling into the hands of factional operators than used to be the case. And it is very important that we understand that we are dealing with an electorate that is more prone to approaches not based on principle but based on what I regard as the insidious rise of identity politics – identity politics whereby you seek to gather the support of a group based on what that group has in common, not the support of that group for a common principle which might gain acceptance throughout the entire community. That is not a healthy development.

It is also important to remind ourselves – and this is perhaps the one comment that I might make on your recent referendum on membership of the European Union – that, despite what we are frequently told by many, we still live in a world of the nation-state. It is still a Westphalian world. It is still a world where the key organising principle of world affairs is relations between nations. That is not a call to move away from international cooperation, it is simply a recognition of what the nation-state can achieve. And as I have moved around the region in which my own country is geographically located, I am constantly reminded of the great admiration held for Lee Kuan Yew, the founder of the state of Singapore. He is a classic modern example of somebody who recognised the power of the nation-state and his ability to build this wonderful country from so little and in such adverse circumstances.

Finally, I think Burke would want us to understand how fundamental to the sort of society he helped bequeath to this and other generations is the importance of defending free speech. I have often argued that you do not need – and it remains my very passionate view – a Bill of Rights. Bills of Rights restrict rights. They do not expand them. If you have a robust parliamentary system, if you have a completely free media and you have an incorruptible judiciary, you have the elements of a free society. You have the basics.

But we do live in an age where there is a creeping political correctness which is restricting free speech. I can think of two quite egregious examples of that: one in my own country and one in yours. Recently, a well-known cartoonist in *The Australian*, Bill Leak, published a brilliant cartoon which depicted an Aboriginal policeman holding an Aboriginal boy and confronting the father of that boy and saying to the father, "it's about time you taught him about personal responsibility", and the father, holding a can of beer, said, "righto, what's his name then?" It was a brilliant, perceptive cartoon that made the point, and I think it was a point that was applauded around the community, not just in relation to the Aboriginal community where failed fatherhood is a problem but to other communities where failed fatherhood is also a serious problem. And yet, for his pains, Bill Leak and his newspaper is being dragged before the Australian Human Rights Commission and asked to explain. That is a terrible assault on free speech. Burke would have been appalled and rightly so.

And Burke would be appalled about what I might loosely call the baker's case in Northern Ireland where a baker who has a view about same-sex marriage, which he is entitled to have, which other people do not have. But that is not the point. The point is he is prosecuted for refusing to place a statement on the icing of a cake that does not reflect his own personal view. And the man ends up being dragged before the courts. I do not condemn the judge. The judge was enforcing his interpretation of the law.

But if we really live in the shadow of Edmund Burke and we revere him and we value his principles, then surely we would look at those two examples of the way in which a creeping political correctness and the manner by which anti-discrimination laws have been carried to almost demented lengths and we would express our concern and our alarm at those developments.

Tonight is a special occasion for me and I know I speak for Janette in saying how moved we are to see so many old friends in a room in the capital of a nation for which I have deep affection and which has contributed so much to the things that we hold dear and, through the centuries, has stood against tyranny, supported always by my own country and by our friends in other parts of the world, particularly across the Atlantic. And to say to all of you that the legacy of Burke is a precious one.

It informs, as Daniel[13] said, my own party which I have always described as a broad church of classical liberals and conservatives. It is a great heritage and you have all, in different ways, fought to defend it. I thank you for that.

And in accepting this Award with great gratitude I want to salute Daniel and you, Jan [Zahradil], and your friends for the way in which you carry the torch for the right kind of conservatism, of that great blend of preserving what is good until it is proved bad. And preserving a fundamental belief in the importance of individuals, the need to limit the role of government, of faith in markets, and a belief in the right of people

---

[13] Daniel Hannan is a Peruvian-British journalist, author and member of the European Parliament for South East England since 1999 for the Conservative Party. Jan Zahradil, a member of the Civic Democratic Party, was elected to the European Parliament in 2004.

to accumulate private property, to make money, to be successful in life, providing they do it honestly, and they pay through taxation their due contribution to caring for those in the community who, through no fault of their own, have fallen through the cracks. I know everybody in this room stands for that kind of society and, to the extent that I have helped in my own political life to build it in my own country, I am grateful to have had the opportunity.

# II

# Governing for all Australians

## Howard's Philosophy and Approach to Government

# The Role of Government

## 1995 Headland Speech
## Canberra – 6 June 1995

Shortly after resuming the leadership of the Parliamentary Liberal Party on 30 January 1995, John Howard delivered a series of "Headland" Speeches on such topics as "the Role of Government", "Fair Australia" and "National Identity". In these addresses, the then Leader of the Opposition outlined major challenges facing Australia and the approach he would take to them as prime minister. In so doing, he sought to present the Australian public with a decidedly alternative vision for the nation from that offered by the Labor Government during the previous twelve years.

In this speech on the "Role of Government", Howard reflected that there was palpable disillusionment amongst the Australian mainstream that government in recent years had turned its back on the interests and aspirations of ordinary people to serve, instead, powerful, vested interests. Determined to arrest this development, the aspiring prime minister outlined his vision for a government which would work for the common good and serve the interests of all Australians. To accomplish this mission, government needed to embrace a four-pronged objective to "lead and unite", to "secure", to "expand choice" and to "care". In accordance with his Liberal philosophy, Howard maintained that the role of government should always be strategic yet limited.

The Liberal tradition has always held that ideas are not political ends in themselves, but the basis for developing practical policies that work for the common good. ...

The prevailing mood towards governments around the world today is one of mistrust. There is intense cynicism, especially amongst the young, towards most aspects of government. There is a widespread belief that governments have few answers for contemporary problems. They are variously seen as the puppets of special interests or composed of people bent on self-promotion rather than the enhancement of the national interest.

This harsh judgment has a strong resonance in Australia. Numerous surveys have revealed public indifference towards, even disdain for, the political process. The reasons for this malaise are complicated. In part it is due to the perceived inability of governments to solve basic challenges and to cure the many social ills, and arrest the processes of disintegration which have overtaken so much of Western life in past decades. ...

There is a frustrated mainstream in Australia today which sees government decisions increasingly driven by the noisy, self-interested clamour of powerful vested interests with scant regard for the national interest. The power of the mainstream has been diminished by [the Keating] Government's reactions to the force of a few interest groups. Many Australians in the mainstream feel utterly powerless to compete with such groups, who seem to have the ear completely of the Government on major issues.

This bureaucracy of the new class is a world apart from the myriad of spontaneous, community-based organisations which have been part and parcel of the Australian mainstream for decades. These trends reflect a style of government which will change profoundly under the Liberal and National parties. Under us, the views of all particular interests will be assessed against the national interest and the sentiments of mainstream Australia.

For the past 12 years Labor has governed essentially by proxy through interest groups. Identification with a powerful interest group has been seen as the vehicle through which government largesse is delivered. Increasingly Australians have been exhorted to think of themselves as members of sub-groups. The focus so often has been on where we are different – not on what we have in common. In the process our sense of community has been severely damaged.

Our goal will be to reverse this trend. Mainstream government means making decisions in the interests of the whole community, decisions which have the effect of uniting, not dividing, the nation, drawing upon the numerous community-based organisations which are the natural expression of the sense of neighbourhood which so many Australians have.

It is undeniable that a major cause of the reduced respect for government, specifically in Australia, has been the deterioration in the simple trust and confidence which used to exist between people and their governments. Although Federal politics in Australia has been relatively free from corruption, the same cannot be said of State politics. These breaches of fundamental ethics have added massively to the disrepute of governments.

But particularly at the Federal level, exaggerated election promises, followed by seemingly guiltless repudiation shortly after an election, have also fuelled growing cynicism and resentment. To many Australians the apotheosis of this behaviour was reached by the Prime Minister [Paul Keating] with his blatantly cynical grabbing back – after the [1993] election – of the so-called L-A-W law tax cuts, his indirect tax hikes in the 1993 budget, despite having campaigned against a Goods and Services Tax, his latest broken promise on the Medicare levy, and his recent budget decision to lift company tax, despite having previously proposed a cut in company tax as the main element of his business policy for the 1993 election.

Many of the so-called true believers harbour deep resentment towards both a Prime Minister and a Treasurer who induced Australians to buy shares in the Commonwealth Bank on the back of a solemn promise that majority government ownership of the bank would be retained, only to find their Labor leaders subsequently jettisoning that promise when it was politically expedient to do so.

As well, honesty is being swamped by cynical election campaigns based on fear, or the big scare, or the massive lie.

## *Rebuilding Trust in Government*

Any intelligent examination of the role of government in modern Australia must start with a firm commitment to restoring a proper sense of trust and confidence between the people and their government. Rebuilding that trust will not be achieved speedily. Moreover, it will require action on a number of fronts. I intend to introduce many improvements which in the end will clean up government and clean up Parliament itself. That must start with economic honesty, where people can have an honest account of the state of the nation's finances and the plans the Government has for the future.

Both Peter Costello and I are committed in government to introducing a charter of budget honesty. We will take the people into our confidence on our fiscal policy intentions, set benchmarks against which fiscal performance can be assessed and make it easier for people to follow the budget papers. We will minimise the scope for budget fiddles and accounting tricks and there will be no more fiscal sleight of hand. We will separate clearly the recurrent and capital sides of the budget. We will tackle debt levels and achieve an appropriate balance between operating revenue and operating expenditure.

This approach will provide a degree of predictability about the level and stability of tax rates for future years.

A Commission of Audit will be appointed immediately after the election to report on:

- the contingent liabilities of the Commonwealth;
- the impacts of demographic change on Commonwealth outlays and how to make provision for them;
- the preparation of a full Commonwealth Balance Sheet;
- the state of Commonwealth infrastructure and the private and public measures required to restore it to levels required for the next decade;
- financial performance targets for Commonwealth departments; and
- the level of duplication between Commonwealth and the

States in the delivery of services and the measures necessary to promote more efficient delivery.

This commitment is a practical gesture towards the broader goal of rebuilding confidence in the annual accounting process, via the Federal budget, to the Australian people. Care and responsibility in the making of election promises will be a key element in rebuilding trust.

It is neither the time, nor does Australia have the resources and economic infrastructure, to underwrite the huge fiscal shifts which would be involved in massive election promises. The Australian public, now long accustomed to its expectations being disappointed, would greet such an approach with deserved cynicism and contempt.

I would rather promise half of what people might want and honour 100 per cent of it than commit myself to everything and deliver only half of it. That does not mean we will be saying nothing new or not offering substantial improvements in various areas. We will. But they will be affordable, achievable commitments…

### *The Liberal Tradition*

In sketching a contemporary approach by the Liberal Party to the role of government, it is first desirable to say something of the special character of the Liberal Party of Australia. The Liberal Party, unlike the Labor Party, is not beholden to any one sectional interest group. It is a party made up of people from all walks of life and it is one which governs for all Australians. The Liberal Party is not shackled by any ties which could inhibit responsible decision-making.

Atypically, of centre right parties, the Liberal Party of Australia is a blend of classical liberalism and conservatism. We are the custodians of both traditions in the Australian polity. We have been distinguished for our long commitment to individual rights and beliefs, but have also fought to preserve those traditions and characteristics of our past which remain relevant for the present, and continue to serve the national interest.

The art of good statecraft has always been to preserve from the past that which continues to serve the national interest, whilst discarding the tired and the failed.

Both traditions of the Liberal Party of Australia are on display at present. It is the Liberal Party which is resisting current assaults on free speech by the Labor Government, which is the dangerously imprecise proposal to jail journalists who publish certain material.

On the subject of constitutional reform, the Liberal Party is not saying that our Constitution is immutable. We do, however, advocate an effective mechanism to ensure that if change is to occur it will only be because the Australian people believe our quality of government will be enhanced as a result of that change.

I have never seen economic rationalism, economic efficiency – call it what you will – as an end in itself or a stand-alone political credo. Sound money, responsible budgets and efficient markets are nothing more than the mechanisms to deliver rising living standards and stable employment, which are so necessary for united families and communities.

Australian Liberals are not blindly hostile to government but they are profoundly suspicious about what governments can achieve and are concerned about the concentration of power now in the hands of government. For Liberals the role of government should always be strategic and limited.

## The Responsibilities of Government

In expounding on the role of government, we must not only delineate its responsibilities but also define its limits. A proper balance must be struck between a healthy scepticism about what governments can achieve, and the Australian tradition of believing that there is a role for government which goes beyond its being a mere keeper of the ring.

Australians may not want government out of their lives, but they do want it off their backs.

Most political reflections on the role of government approach the issue only in a quantitative sense. It is either a matter of expanding or reducing government's percentage share of GDP. This must always be an integral part of any Liberal approach. Liberals will always remain committed to restraining the role of government in people's lives.

However, as well as the purely quantitative approach there is a need, frequently overlooked, to address the role of government, and that is to define what ought essentially to be the responsibilities of government in the modern Australian context. We need to address the quality of government as well as the size of government. The modern responsibilities of government in Australia essentially fall into four categories. They are:

- To lead and unite
- To secure
- To expand choice; and
- To care

The leadership role includes the responsibility of government to address the principal economic and social problems, to define future challenges and goals for our nation and to unite Australians by engendering a sense of common purpose and community co-operation.

The security role covers the responsibility of government to maintain effective defence against external attack, and to preserve internal law and order.

The choice role involves the responsibility of government to expand and enhance individual liberty, freedom, opportunity and choice, to help people help themselves.

The caring role is that real responsibility of government to ensure that there is a fair safety net for those in the community who, through no fault of their own, require special assistance.

### *The Leadership role of Government*

The first responsibility of any government is to unite the community and to provide leadership to the nation. A conspicuous feature of Labor government during the past 12 years has been the way in which it has deliberately pursued policies which have divided rather than united the Australian community.

Central to my beliefs about the Australian character and the way in which Australia should be governed is the simple proposition that those things which unite us as Australians are infinitely greater and more enduring than the things which divide us.

Most Australians believe that as we approach the Centenary of Federation and a new millennium, we could all do with a heavy dose of those things that unite us and bind us together, and not those things which pull us apart. When I speak of the things that unite us, I have my own idea of the Australian dream:

- I have in mind our great commitment to personal freedom and liberal democratic values;
- I have in mind that all Australians should enjoy equality of opportunity and social mobility, that we live out the great Australian inheritance of a classless society;
- I have in mind the critical importance of strong family life to the Australian community;
- I have in mind a decent social security safety net, a strong health system and expanding educational opportunities;
- I have in mind giving people incentive to take risks and display business flair;
- I have in mind restoring a sense of progress, where our children are better off than we are, that once again our standard of living will be amongst the highest in the world;
- I have in mind a nation continually renewed by our vibrant cultural and artistic life;
- I have in mind a united community, not an aggregation of separate interest groups with little in common;
- I have in mind taking the best of our past, our identity and our traditions and blending them with the challenges of the next century to produce a prouder, stronger nation.

There are three paths that leadership in modern Australia can take. It can take the path of blind economic efficiency for its own sake. It can take the path of social and political change for their own sakes, inevitably promoting the current fad of the time and adopting the agendas of vociferous interest groups.

Or it can choose the path which sees leadership as uniting the strengths of the Australian people to a common purpose, and which recognises that good government is always about achieving a synthesis between the best of our past and the desirability of positive change for the future, between the imperative of a modern globalised economy and the innate belief of Australians in a fair go for all.

I want a nation of caring achievers, a nation based on hope, reward and incentive for the individual, confident of its history and its place in the world and determined to extend practical mateship to those in need....

## The Security Role of Government

The responsibility to provide both external and internal security ought to be accepted as a prime responsibility of government – probably the prime responsibility – without comment or debate. That means ensuring we have a Defence Force ready to support Australia's security objectives, nurturing traditional alliances, forging co-operative defence arrangements with regional powers and focussing our foreign policy to meet our security and economic interests.

Internal security or, as most Australians would describe it, law and order, is overwhelmingly a State government responsibility. That is not to say the Federal Government does not have a major role through its Customs surveillance, anti-terrorist personnel and international crime prevention links.

While the day-to-day management is plainly a State one, there is clearly a leadership role for the Federal Government in harnessing community resources to help combat some of the real causes of crime, such as high unemployment, family breakdown, drug abuse, a lack of support systems, a sense of desperation and helplessness and a loss of self-esteem and confidence.

Let me say that in the ebbing and flowing debate on the availability of weapons, I am firmly on the side of those who believe that it would be a cardinal tragedy if Australia did not learn the bitter lessons of the United States regarding guns. I have no doubt that the horrific homicide level in the United States is directly related to the plentiful supply of guns. How else does one explain the simple fact that in the United States the murder rate is 10 per 100,000, against one per 100,000 in England and Wales and 2.0 in Australia.

Whilst making proper allowance for legitimate sporting and recreational activities and the proper needs of our rural community, every effort should be made to limit the carrying of guns in Australia.

## The Role of Government in Enhancing Choice

The next great responsibility of government is to expand and enhance freedom of individual choice. So often government has been looked at in the light of whether or not its powers should be used to curtail individual liberty or choice in the presumed common good. There has been far too little focus on what governments can do to expand individual choice, freedom and opportunity.

It has always been part of the Liberal tradition in Australia to expand the horizons of individual choice. One of the great legacies of the Menzies period was the massive contribution made in the early 1960s in expanding freedom of choice in education.

The decision of the Menzies Government in 1963 effectively to introduce direct government assistance for independent schools not only helped to demolish almost a century of sectarian division, but also struck a mighty blow for freedom of parental choice.

In so many areas, the divide between Labor and Liberal in the 1990s surrounds individual choice. The essence of the Coalition's industrial relations policy is an unswerving belief that individuals should have the right to decide. They should be free to join or not to join a union. They should be free to choose their own workplace arrangement. They should be free to conduct any negotiations on workplace arrangements themselves or to have someone do it on their behalf. If they decide to join a union, they should be free to join the union of their choice. Moreover, any group of employees should have the right to form a union centred on their workplace if that is their choice.

These ought to be simple unarguable rights in a free society yet, incredibly enough, advocating such basic freedoms continues to draw fierce resistance. That is because there are some who still believe there should be no choice. They think that the only way is the union way.

The philosophical underpinning of the Coalition's industrial relations approach is its staunch commitment to individual freedom and choice. The policy is not driven by hostility to unions. Trade unions will be welcome participants in the industrial relations system of tomorrow, provided they play by the rules applicable to all other participants. They will not be disadvantaged players. However, their capacity to thrive and succeed will be determined by the quality of the services they offer to their members and not by a special privilege conferred by law. ...

## The Caring Role of Government

Caring for the genuinely disadvantaged, the unlucky and the under-privileged is the fourth great area of government responsibility.

Despite noisy rhetoric to the contrary, the gap between rich and poor has widened dramatically in Australia in recent years.

Recently, for example, the Bob Gregory/Boyd Hunter ANU study found that since the mid-1970s the average real household income of the poorest five per cent of suburbs dropped 23 per cent, while the richest five per cent increased their incomes by 23 per cent. The income gap has widened 92 per cent, or $20,000 in 1995 dollars. In particular, males in the poorest half have lost jobs or been forced to take low paid ones and the proportion of working women from poor areas has slumped 40 per cent. There are now substantial areas of non-employment. Worryingly, higher levels of education are now needed to get the same income or a given level of education brings a lower income. ...

64

Support for a decent, fair social security safety net is a bipartisan given in Australian politics today.

The Australian ethos is one of caring for the less fortunate. It is an extension of our great tradition of fairness and mateship. Many of the great social welfare initiatives in the post-World War II period have come from the Liberal and National parties … the Coalition is committed to the maintenance of a proper safety net and recognises that the fundamental causes of the blow-out in Australia's welfare budget have been due not to massive extortion of the system but rather to economic and social breakdown. …

## *The Role of Parliament*

No address on the role of government can ignore the role of Parliament itself and the community's view of the institution, particularly since the televising of Parliament.

No person who holds parliamentary sovereignty dear could be other than disturbed at the steady decline in both the actual power and the reputation of the parliamentary institution. …

Question Time has been debased, Parliament relegated to second best through major statements often made outside Parliament even when in session. …

Reversing this trend uniquely lies within the power of the government of the day. Our party system dictates that if the Executive has a will to bypass Parliament, only a major revolution from within the government party – which might imperil the government's very existence – can prevent that occurring.

For that reason I wish in advance of the election of a Coalition government to commit the next government of this country to a series of reforms which will restore greater authority, dignity and meaning to our parliamentary institutions. The Coalition will seek to invest the Speaker of the next parliament with greater independence, similar to his or her counterpart at Westminster. This will require the positive response of the Labor Party. For our part the commitment is genuine and on-going. …

We will establish a completely independent Auditor-General so that a fearless and authoritative surveillance of government departments can occur without intimidation from the Executive…Under the Coalition the Auditor-General will be an officer of the Parliament. He will be funded from the Appropriation for the Parliament.

## The Federal System of Government

Our highly successful Constitution, which incidentally was both written and approved by Australians and not by the British Colonial Office – was and remains a unique blend of practice drawn from many sources.

The Federal system of government has been well-suited to our first century as a nation. Yet even the most benign observer must concede that it is not functioning as freely and as fully as it might…

I do not have false hopes about what can be achieved on this front. I do, however, have a strong commitment to a more rational revenue-sharing approach. In government the Coalition will allocate a fixed percentage of tax revenue to the States. We will revert to the practice of former Coalition governments of winding back section 96 for specific purpose grants to the States. That will mean States themselves will have greater freedom of choice when deciding their programmes and priorities.

It will be a specific brief of the Audit Commission, to be established upon the Coalition's assumption of office, that it examine existing areas of duplication between the Commonwealth and the States. Few will dispute the proposition that duplication of functions between the various levels of government in Australia is costing our taxpayers dearly.

## Conclusion

This address represents a framework for a future Coalition Government.

Our goal will be to end the drift, the division, the favouritism and the peripheral agendas which have been hallmarks of the past 12 years. The enduring strength of the Liberal Party has always been its capacity to include and represent all Australians. We have never been a party of privilege, of sectional interests or narrow prejudice.

More than at any time in our nation's recent history the people of Australia want a government that unites them in the common purpose of building a stronger, more secure and more prosperous society – a society built on individual effort, business flair and the incentive to achieve, yet a society which cares for the less fortunate.

With energy, unity and commitment the opportunity to deliver that goal is ours.

# Vision for National Government

## Sir Thomas Playford Memorial Lecture
## Adelaide Town Hall – 5 July 1996

Just two months after he took office as Prime Minister, John Howard was invited by the Liberal Club at the University of Adelaide to deliver the 1996 Sir Thomas Playford Memorial Lecture. The lecture series was established to honour the life and achievements of South Australia's longest-serving Premier, Sir Thomas Playford (1896-1981). A contemporary of Menzies, Playford had served as Premier of South Australia from 1938 to 1965 when he presided over the State's strong economic growth and development. In paying tribute to Playford, Howard believed that the Premier's lengthy administration was aided by its adherence to a consistent set of values and priorities, an attribute he sought to emulate in his own Government.

Accordingly, in this lecture to canvass the philosophy and approach he would bring to governing Australia, Howard told his audience that whilst his Government would be guided by clearly-stated values and aspirations, it would not be driven purely by ideology but would seek to reflect the interests and priorities of mainstream Australia. In the tradition of Menzies, his liberal philosophy of government would "march down the middle of the road" to avoid the two extremes of state paternalism and *laissez-faire* libertarianism. In short, Howard believed not so much in getting government out of people's lives, as getting it off people's backs.

I am delighted to be with you tonight to honour the contribution of a great Australian, Sir Thomas Playford, to the development of our country and of this State of South Australia....

In defining a vision for national government … it is as important to govern by a consistent set of values and priorities as it is to implement an appropriate mix of policies.

Back on Election night, on 2 March 1996, I emphasised two of the guiding principles for the new Coalition Government. I committed the Government to govern for all Australians. The right to govern is always an ongoing gift from the people, and there is an accompanying responsibility for any government to unite rather than to divide the community.

I also resolved to be true to the values, priorities and policies we had spelt out in the lead-up to, and during, the Election campaign. I made it clear on Election night that "we have not been elected to be just a pale imitation of the Government that we have replaced".

Those two principles have guided us as a Government since Election day, and they will continue to guide us into the future.

We are a Government with clearly stated values and priorities which reflect those of the great mainstream of Australian society. We are not a Government beholden to political correctness but one committed to broad community values and practical outcomes on both economic and social issues.

We are not a Government of economic rationalism in the popular sense of that term. We are a Government of economic common sense. We seek greater economic efficiency, more responsible budgets and more effective markets, not as ends in themselves, but as means for achieving rising living standards, expanding employment opportunities and an effective safety net.

We are not a Government of ideology. We are a Government of ideas and ideals. And in responding to the scale of social, economic and political change I have outlined, it will be the ideal that will motivate us and the ideals to which we aspire, rather than any pursuit of narrow ideology, that will take us forward.

We are, however, a Government with some fixed goals and strong commitments. In the economic area, for example, it would be a great mistake for anyone to underestimate the strength of my commitment to achieving labour market reform and a profound enhancement of the conditions in which small business operates in Australia.

Freeing Australia's arthritic labour markets is indispensable to securing stronger growth, greater competitiveness and, over time, an improvement in Australia's current account deficit. We seek labour market reform because it will provide greater freedom for individuals and more rewarding outcomes for both employers and employees. It is the absolute cornerstone of the reform plan that the Coalition has for the Australian economy. Without it our prospects will remain dented and future economic growth needlessly enfeebled.

Likewise, on the social horizon, we are steadfast in our determination to strengthen the role and place of the family unit within society. This goal will be the axis around which policies in many areas such as taxation, industrial relations and social welfare will rotate. ...

In addition to restoring a relationship of trust between Australians and their national government, another of the ideas which motivates us is to give practical policy effect to our belief that it is individuals who matter more than governments, bureaucracies and vested interests. That is why the Government is committed to making choice for individuals the golden thread running through all our policy initiatives: choice in the labour market, choice to join or not to join a trade union, choice in education, choice in telecommunications, choice in retirement income, and choice in a whole range of other policy areas.

It is why we are committed, in this period of rapid change, to strengthening the family unit which has proved itself over time as the source of the most effective emotional support for individuals and as the best social welfare system that any society has ever devised.

Our policy priorities are also motivated by a commitment to achieve a practical balance between the limits of government and the limits of markets. We believe in getting government, not out of people's lives, but off their backs.

That is why we are committed, as a Government, to maximising individual decision-making, promoting private enterprise and limiting the power of the state over its citizens. We will continue to pursue those goals through guaranteeing the separation of powers, through greater choice, diversity and competition in the provision of goods and services, and through sensibly and sensitively limiting the claims that are made on the state.

In recognising the proper limits, of government, we also recognise the practical limits of markets. That is why we do not believe in complete laissez-faire government. It is why we do not see markets as ends in themselves. We do, however, see markets as delivering superior outcomes to state-determined allocations. Governments have a proper and necessary role to guarantee a fair safety net for those who, through no fault of their own, require special assistance. Governments also have a responsibility to encourage self-sufficiency among those who are capable of it.

The safety net guarantee, however, is critical if individuals are to have the opportunity to develop their full potential. Without such a guarantee, the liberal concepts of a free society and equality of opportunity lose their meaning.

We are also motivated by a commitment to meet the challenges of globalisation while continuing to assure the Australian birthright of a fair go for all. That means achieving progress in the reform area where Labor failed so dramatically – reforms such as fiscal repair, labour market freedom, micro-economic reform, a more internationally competitive infrastructure and financial system, higher productivity and less foreign debt. They are all reforms which are necessary if Australia is to harness the process of globalisation for its own advantage. And they are all reforms which are necessary to ensure that Australia participates fully in the dynamic economic growth of the Asia-Pacific region.

In addition to the ideas for enhancing choice and freedom that motivate our policy-making priorities, we are also a Government with a clear set of ideals to which we aspire and from which we will not be diverted.

We will continue to meet the true tests of national leadership. That is why we will continue to be straight and direct with the people on major national issues (such as gun control, the Budget deficit and the imbalance in our immigration programme), and on our strategy to address them. It is why we will continue to set a clear course for the future based on consistent values and priorities in areas such as fiscal strategy, job growth, infrastructure reform, environmental protection and resource development.

And it is why we will continue to be committed to building a sense of common national purpose rather than papering together an amalgamation of special interests. We will not be swept off-course from our commitment to pursue economic reform policies aimed at freeing up the labour market, building savings and investment, creating jobs, developing export- and import-competing industries, and boosting productivity and living standards.

We will remain rock solid in our commitment to strengthen the decentralised networks of family, workplaces and communities as more effective guarantors of choice and freedom than the centralisation of political power. That is why we will be acting to reduce the economic pressures on low and middle income families, and especially those with dependent children (through tax, health care and other reforms).

It is why we are moving to implement our enterprise-based workplace reforms.

And it is why we will continue to support the great voluntary associations that are so central to the strength of local communities.

We will remain unshakeable in our resolve to reward hard work, initiative and "get up and go". That is why we regard our policy agenda to restore small businesses as the great generators of jobs, national wealth and individual opportunity as central to our whole purpose in government.

And we will remain absolutely committed to interacting more extensively and cooperatively with the countries of our region at the same time as we continue to develop our important and long-standing relationships with traditional friends. We will do so confident of whom we are and what we stand for, and confident of the important regional contribution we can make as a democracy, as an advanced and innovative economy and as a force for security and stability.

The values and priorities we have set for our Government are clear. They are relevant to the forces of both change and continuity in our society. They are also relevant to the challenges we face as a nation into the twenty-first century.

We aim to pursue those values and priorities with the same consistency, the same commitment and the same community-mindedness with which the great leaders of the Liberal tradition in Australia, such as Tom Playford, pursued the values and priorities which they judged to be right for their own time.

Few political leaders acquire the status of an institution in their own lifetime. Tom Playford was one such leader. We have much to learn from the Playford era and from the integrity of the leader who presided over it. I am pleased to have been able to play some part in honouring his memory tonight.

# Allowing our Democracy to Flourish

## Closing Address to the Constitutional Convention
## Canberra – 13 February 1998

On behalf of the Coalition, John Howard promised in 1995 that if elected at the next election, the Australian people would be given an opportunity to vote for a republic in a referendum before the turn of the century. In the lead up to the vote, he also promised to hold a Constitutional Convention to discuss various proposals for an Australian republic to be put to a referendum. Held from 2-13 February 1998 at Old Parliament House, the Convention comprised 152 delegates from all Australian States and territories. From both the pro-monarchy and pro-republican sides, 76 delegates were elected whilst 76 other parliamentary and non-parliamentary delegates were appointed, including current State and territory leaders. Chaired by Ian Sinclair of the National Party and Barry Jones of the Labor Party, the Convention debated a range of positions from maintaining the constitutional *status quo*, to minimalist republican models and more radical, direct-election proposals.

The Convention adopted the minimalist "Bipartisan Appointment of the President" model for a republic to be voted upon at a referendum in 1999. Whilst the Prime Minister had firmly supported the existing constitutional arrangements, he accepted the outcome of the Convention and praised the delegates for the good nature in which they had conducted the debate. Whatever way the Australian people decided to vote at the referendum for a republic, he reminded the delegates

that Australia had much to celebrate as it approached
the Centenary of Federation.

I ask myself what have I learnt out of this last two weeks? I have
learnt something that I was not so sure of at the beginning, and that is
that I have no doubt that Australia can conduct a referendum on this issue with vigour, with passion and with meaning, and yet in a way that
does not undermine or fracture the essential values of our society.

I have learnt out of this Convention that this Australian way we have
of doing things is special and is unique. I have not experienced anything
like this in all the years I have been in public life. The bringing together
of so many people in different ways, with different backgrounds, with
different contributions, with different views was something that at the
beginning one might have thought was fraught with danger, that anything could have happened, that anything could have emerged.

In terms of the positions that were taken, I suppose, at various stages,
that appeared possible. But in a great display of civility and good humour,
and with great integrity in many areas, it was possible for us to really let
out what has been a moment in Australia's history and a moment that I
am sure that everybody has treasured. I have been a member of this Federal Parliament since May 1974 and I have been immensely privileged to
come to the highest-elected position in this country and to be given the
greatest honour that can ever become the lot of any Australian man or
woman, that is, to be the Prime Minister of our wonderful country.

I would have thought therefore that the sense of excitement and exhilaration is something that I had already enjoyed. But there was something about this gathering and the look on people's faces, and I share
Geoffrey Blainey's response to the look on the faces of those like Malcolm Turnbull[14] and Neville Wran[15] and Janet Holmes à Court,[16] not
people who on this issue I identified with very closely, but obviously

---

[14] Malcolm Turnbull served as chairman of the Australian Republican Movement (ARM)
from 1993 to 2000 and represented the ARM at the Constitutional Convention.
[15] Neville Wran served as the Labor Premier of NSW from 1976 to 1986 and represented the
ARM at the Constitutional Convention.
[16] Janet Holmes à Court is a Perth-based businesswoman and philanthropist who represented
the ARM at the Constitutional Convention.

you have an enormous enthusiasm for it and felt a sense of exhilaration and happiness that what they had worked to achieve had in fact been achieved.

Could I also pay particular tribute to Lloyd Waddy and to Kerry Jones as the leaders of Australians for Constitutional Monarchy. I know the difficulties that they have endured in putting forward a cause which, for a long time, received very little support or recognition in commentaries on this issue. I know their lack of resources. I know what was said and suggested at the beginning about their propensity to vote strategically. I salute their immense integrity in the way in which they have handled themselves throughout this entire debate.

The reason that this has been a success and the reason why it has captured, to a very significant degree, the interest and the imagination of the Australian people, is that despite our differences we all smell the same Eucalypt, we all know the same dust and we all feel the same salt in the same ocean. Those things that are dear to one side of the argument are equally dear to others. And what has struck me more than anything else about this whole Convention and about the whole debate is the integrity of the Australianism that has been expressed by all the delegates. And I will go away from this Convention an even more idealistic Australian, one with an even greater passion to allow our democracy to flourish.

We will have a vote next year. The Australian people will decide the outcome of that. And we will all accept the verdict of the Australian people with grace and goodwill, all of us, whatever the result may be.

Can I say that it was always my fervent wish that this issue could be resolved in the sense of its not being on the agenda when we celebrated the Centenary of our Federation. If Australia is to become a republic, it ought to be become a republic on 1 January 2001. If Australia is not to become a republic at that time, let it be off the agenda for the celebration of the Centenary of our Federation so that we can share together the jubilation and the gratitude and the affection that we feel for what this country has meant to us over the last 100 years.

That does not mean that the issue, if it is rejected next year, will not necessarily return. It is in the nature of a democracy that it is always open to the people. But the focus for now will be on the celebration of 100 years of the Australian nation, with all its achievement and acknowledging all of its blemishes. Can I also say on that point, that one of the things which have enriched this Convention has been the contribution of representatives from the first Australians, the Indigenous people.

And I hope in a small way, to you, Lois[17] and Gatjil[18] and Nova[19], and to Pat[20] and George[21] and to Neville,[22] and to David,[23] I hope that this is in some way a sign and a signal from all of us that you do occupy a very special place in our community.

We can look forward, with great hope and in a very positive way, to the conduct of this referendum. This Convention has spoken very clearly. It will be the intention of my Government, if it is returned at the next election, to hold the referendum before the end of 1999. In the meantime, in the nature of things, other issues will flood back to the stage of public debate and I imagine that there will be a period in which the debate on this issue might go slightly on to the backburner, particularly so far as some of the more active political players are concerned. But that, once again, is in the hands of the Australian public…

It has been a very special experience. I have loved every minute of it. I feel privileged to have been the Prime Minister who brought it about and I think it has brought us all together as Australians, whatever the outcome of the referendum may be, in a very, very special way.

---

[17] Lois (Lowitja) O'Donoghue (1932- ) is an Aboriginal leader and former chairperson of the Aboriginal and Torres Strait Islander Commission (ATSIC) who represented South Australia at the Constitutional Convention.

[18] Gatjil Djerrkura (1949-2004) was an Aboriginal elder and an appointed delegate to the Constitutional Convention for the Northern Territory.

[19] Nova Peris (1971- ) is an Aboriginal athlete who represented Western Australia and the Northern Territory as an appointed delegate at the Constitutional Convention.

[20] Pat O'Shane (1941 - ) is an Aboriginal Australian jurist and activist who represented A Just Republic at the Constitutional Convention.

[21] George Mye (1926-2012) was a Torres Strait Islander elder who represented Queensland as an appointed delegate to the Constitutional Convention.

[22] Neville Bonner (1922-1999) was the first Indigenous Australian MP, serving as a Liberal Senator for Queensland from 1971 to 1983. He represented Australians for a Constitutional Monarchy (ACM) at the Constitutional Convention.

[23] David Curtis was an Indigenous leader and ATSIC Commissioner who represented the Northern Territory as an elected delegate at the Constitutional Convention.

# Keeping Institutions which Continue to Work

## Constitutional Referendum on the Republic Statement in Support of the "No" Case
### Sydney – 27 October 1999

As the Australian people prepared to cast a vote in the 6 November 1999 referendum on whether Australia should become a republic, the Prime Minister issued a public statement on how he intended to vote and why. While Howard's support for the existing constitutional monarchy was already on the public record, he believed that this was a timely opportunity to explain, publicly, his reasons for voting "No" on the question of establishing an Australian republic.

In this statement, his principal argument against change was that the existing constitutional system had delivered consistently sound and stable government to Australia. While he had always held the Queen and the royal family in high esteem, his stance against a republic was based less on royalist sentiment than on his conservative instinct to preserve an institution that had worked well for Australia. Having given serious consideration to the "Bipartisan Appointment of the President" model, the proposed republic to be voted on, the Prime Minister identified what he regarded as some of its serious flaws. These included the lack of public participation in the appointment of a president and the ease by which a president could be summarily dismissed by the prime minister. In addition, Howard argued that an Australian republic would do nothing to enhance Australia's independence or its reputation on the world stage, particularly its standing in the Asia-Pacific. Accordingly, he expressed his desire to see Australians reject the republic at the ballot box.

## *Introduction*

On 6 November [1999] Australia will vote on two constitutional proposals – one on a republic and another on a preamble to the Constitution.

The people of Australia are entitled to know how I intend to vote and why.

The referendum on the issue of a republic fulfils a promise I made to the Australian people, on behalf of the Coalition, before the 1996 election and before I became Prime Minister.

As Leader of the Opposition, I promised that if elected the Coalition would hold a Constitutional Convention and, furthermore, give the people of Australia a vote on the issue before the turn of the century.

At the Convention, held in February 1998, I said that if clear support for a particular republican model emerged then the Government would put that model to the people at a referendum. Clear support for the model now proposed did emerge from the Convention. In fulfilment of our pledge, the referendum is now being held.

I have never disguised my personal views on this issue. I have been completely consistent. I told the Australian people prior to both the elections of 1996 and 1998 that I supported current constitutional arrangements. At the Constitutional Convention, I voted in favour of our present system.

## *Why I will vote "No" to a Republic*

I will vote "no" to Australia becoming a republic because I do not believe in changing a constitutional system which works so well and has helped bring such stability to our nation. The changes being proposed would not make Australia's Constitution or system of Government any better or more effective. They are not as simple or as minuscule as their proponents would like people to believe. There are no demonstrated benefits from the proposed changes. They would add nothing to the already democratic character of Australia.

They will not enhance our independence.

There is nothing to be gained from tampering with a system of government which has contributed to our country being one of only a handful of nations which has remained fully democratic throughout the 20th century.

Some of the checks and balances in our present system would be weakened under the republic being proposed. The president could be less secure in his or her position, than is the Governor-General. This in turn could, among other things, affect the appropriate exercise of the reserve powers by a president in a future republic.

### An Australian Head of State

The main argument advanced by republicans is that our head of state should be an Australian.

The Queen is Queen of Australia. However, under our present Constitution, the Governor-General is effectively Australia's head of state. The only constitutional duty performed by the Queen relates to the appointment of the Governor-General which must be done on the recommendation of the prime minister of the day.

Since 1965 every Governor-General of Australia has been an Australian. It is inconceivable that any future occupant of that office would be other than an Australian.

The circumstances of history have given Australia a very stable and workable system of government. Executive political authority is vested in the prime minister and other members of the Cabinet who must always come from the majority party in the House of Representatives. The essentially ceremonial functions of government are separated from the day-to-day executive responsibilities.

A fundamental characteristic of our system is not only the separation of the ceremonial and executive functions of government, but also that the person discharging the formal or ceremonial functions is so politically neutral – both in reality and perception – that he or she can act as the ultimate defender of the constitutional integrity of the nation.

I do not believe that the republican proposal would be as effective as present arrangements in delivering that outcome.

The Governor-General is the ultimate constitutional umpire. He exercises the reserve powers of the Crown, completely free of any interference from anyone. His powers flow from the Australian Constitution. They do not flow from the Queen. He acts in accordance with the Constitution of Australia. Although he is the Queen's representative, he does not take instructions from her.

He acts in accordance with the powers given to him by the Constitution as well as the conventions of the Crown which have been developed and distilled through hundreds of years of constitutional practice. That is one of the reasons why our system of government is so stable. It has evolved over a long period of time. Its history is a strength not a weakness. We should not lightly put aside something which has worked so well and helped give us such stability.

That the Governor-General is the effective head of state of Australia and must act in accordance with the Australian Constitution was clearly illustrated in November 1975. After the Governor-General had withdrawn Mr Whitlam's commission as prime minister, the House of Representatives passed a vote of no confidence in the caretaker Fraser Government.

The text of that resolution was sent to the Queen with a request that she intervene. The reply on her behalf was as follows:

> …the Australian Constitution firmly places the prerogative powers of the Crown in the hands of the Governor-General… and the Queen has no part in the decisions which the Governor-General must take in accordance with the Constitution… it would not be proper for Her to intervene in person in matters which are so clearly placed within the jurisdiction of the Governor-General by the Constitution Act.

In other words, the matter was to be resolved by Australians under the terms of the Australian Constitution which, incidentally, had been assented to by Australians before it came into effect in 1901.

## *An Independent Nation*

Australia is a fully independent and sovereign nation. Even staunch republicans like the former Prime Minister Mr Gough Whitlam acknowledge this. The 1988 report of the Hawke Government's Constitutional Commission, of which Mr Whitlam was a member, found that "Australia had achieved full independence as a sovereign state of the world" sometime between 1926 and the end of World War II and was so recognised by the world community.

Despite this some argue, including the former Prime Minister Mr Keating, that Australia must become a republic to demonstrate to the world, and especially to the Asian-Pacific region, that it is a truly independent nation.

This is a shallow argument with no merit or substance. Mutual respect is the basis of good relations between nations.

Just as Australia does not seek to tell other nations how to arrange their constitutions, so it is that our friends in the region and elsewhere do not seek to tell us what form our Constitution should take.

This reality was best captured by the Senior Minister of Singapore, Mr Lee Kuan Yew, probably the elder statesman of Asia and certainly a good judge of the mood of the region. Addressing the National Press Club in 1994, he said: "I don't think Asia understands what the argument is about. Australia would not generate greater esteem in Asia as a republic than it does with its present constitutional arrangements."

Moreover, my experience from all the negotiations in which I have been involved concerning East Timor in recent months is the strongest evidence to me of how empty and transparent is the proposition that Australia must become a republic to demonstrate its independence to the world.

Those negotiations were as intense and as high level as any negotiations in which any Australian prime minister has been involved since World War II. They involved frequent discussions with the leaders of many of our regional neighbours, the President of the United States, the Prime Ministers of New Zealand, Canada, Portugal and Japan and the Secretary-General of the United Nations.

They led to Australia, for the first time in her history, being asked to lead a multinational force.

To suggest that I came to those negotiations otherwise than as the prime minister of a completely independent nation is ludicrous. It would be equally ludicrous to suggest that the outcome of those negotiations would have been either different or better if Australia had come to them as a republic.

This "independence" argument is one of the poorest of all advanced in favour of a republic.

### A directly elected President?

I will vote "no" because I support the present system, not because I prefer some other kind of republic than the one on offer.

I do not support a directly elected presidency. This would produce rival power centres in our political system.

Under such an arrangement both the prime minister and the president would claim popular mandates. Even if the president's powers were carefully laid out in the Constitution, the adversarial nature of Australian politics would ensure that tension between the two would arise.

### Flaws in the republican model

Although my principal reason for voting "no" is that I support the present system, I am obliged to point out that there are flaws in the republican model that people are being asked to support. This is due in no small measure to the fact that it is a compromise model designed to attract the support of direct election republicans for an appointment process which gives the power to appoint the president to the members of the Commonwealth Parliament. In the process the worst of both worlds has resulted.

Final power to choose the president rests with parliament and not the people. This is undoubtedly unsatisfactory to those who want a direct election for the president.

Under the republican model being proposed, public nomination for the presidency would be called for by a committee comprising 32 people, half of them chosen by the prime minister and the other half serving members of the Commonwealth and State parliaments and the Territory legislative assemblies.

This committee would recommend a short list to the prime minister who would then propose a candidate of his choice to the Parliament. He would not, incidentally, be obliged to nominate a person from the short list.

This is a "Clayton's" public consultation process. It is designed to placate the direct election republicans with the illusion of public involvement in the selection process. But it is without one of the advantages of a pure parliamentary appointment model (where there is no such public consultation process) which is that, in practice, the full range of talented Australians would be available for the post of president – as is the case now with the appointment of the Governor-General.

Under the republican proposal being put at the referendum many Australians holding prominent positions might not submit themselves to the nomination process either because of the embarrassment at not being short listed or chosen, or through a fear that their rejection, or the possibility of public knowledge that they were under consideration, might reduce their capacity to discharge their current duties. Would, for example, a High Court judge, or even an eminent businessman or community leader allow their names to go forward if they feared that their involvement in the nomination process might compromise the performance of their current duties?

Australia has been extremely well served by its Governors-General. If the republic is supported at the referendum then I do not believe that the pool from which a future president would be drawn will be as deep as the one now available for the Governor-General.

### Dismissal of a President

There has been much debate about whether, or not, the president in the proposed republic would be more or less secure in his or her office than is the Governor-General under the present Constitution. I believe that, on balance, the Governor-General has greater security of tenure. Let me state why.

Under the proposed republic, the president can be summarily dismissed by the prime minister by notice in writing at any time without reason or appeal. The requirement that the dismissal be approved by the House of Representatives within thirty days adds little to the president's security of tenure.

The government party, with a majority in the House of Representatives, would scarcely repudiate their own prime minister's action in dismissing the president. Even if it did, that would not reinstate the president. His or her removal would be final and absolute.

No Australian Governor-General has been dismissed from office. If, in the future, a prime minister did wish to have a Governor-General dismissed, it would almost certainly be for a political reason and any action taken to secure the dismissal would be highly controversial.

In those circumstances, a recommendation from the prime minister to the Queen to remove the Governor-General would be seen to involve her directly in a political dispute.

Although a future prime minister might be willing to do this, a natural reluctance to involve the monarch very directly in a political dispute could act as a constraint on a prime minister recommending removal of a Governor-General. However, under the conventions of our system the Queen would be bound to accept the advice of the prime minister to remove the Governor-General. The very requirement of formal advice to the Queen, together with the formal consideration by her and the time taken, however short this may be, could act as a valuable additional check against totally arbitrary removal.

I therefore find it difficult to accept the argument advanced by some that the president in the proposed republican model would have greater security of tenure than the Governor-General. As I say, I believe that, on balance, the reverse is the case.

## Reserve powers

Under the model it is not proposed to specify the reserve powers of the Governor-General. It is commonly believed that the reserve powers relate to appointing and dismissing the prime minister, refusing to dissolve the Parliament and forcing a dissolution of the Parliament.

Any lessened security of tenure which has come about by the more arbitrary process laid down for the dismissal of a president could also influence him or her in the appropriate exercise of these reserve powers.

## Another referendum?

Recently the Leader of the Opposition, Mr Beazley, and others, have raised the possibility of another referendum being held, if the republic wins on 6 November, to give Australians the chance of deciding whether or not they wish to directly elect the president.

This is a stunt to entice direct election republicans into supporting the "yes" case.

If the republic wins on 6 November there will not be a referendum for a directly elected president. The republicans will have got what they wanted.

Almost all of the prominent politicians who support the "yes" case for the referendum are in favour of the members of Federal Parliament choosing the president. Few of them are direct electionists.

In addition, the majority of those Members of Parliament who advocate a "no" vote are just as opposed to a directly elected president as they are to the model being proposed.

If the referendum wins, therefore, these two groups will make common cause to oppose a direct election option being put to the people.

I do not agree with those who want a republic in which the people directly vote for a president. Their cause is not my cause. I oppose any change to the present system.

I do, however, understand why so many of them are advocating a "no" vote on 6 November.

If the republican model on offer, whereby the president is chosen by two-thirds of the members of the Commonwealth Parliament, wins on 6 November, it will be there forever.

## *Conclusion*

The current Federal Government is the first since Federation to give Australians a choice between retaining their form of Government under our Constitution or changing to a republican alternative.

Consistent with our great democratic traditions the result, whatever it may be, should be embraced by all Australians.

My support for a constitutional monarchy is not based on nostalgia. Rather, it is based on a belief that we will not give ourselves a better system of Government if Australia becomes a republic and, in all prob-ability, will give ourselves a less effective one.

I am more ready than most to argue the cause of change when I be-lieve that it is in the national interest to do so.

On issues such as industrial relations and taxation reforms as well as privatisation, I have been willing to advocate the need for fundamental reforms, even in the face of fierce opposition, because I have seen such reforms as being in Australia's interests.

On other issues, however – and the constitutional change to a re-public is one of them – I will staunchly oppose change because I do not think it will benefit Australia. Not all change is for the better; I cannot support change for change's sake.

Prudent nations elect to keep those institutions which continue to work, and discard those which do not.

Not even the most zealous republicans in our midst would claim that our system has broken down, that the constitutional monarchy in Austra-lia is in a state of crisis. In fact, republicans have paid a massive compli-ment to the present system by continually arguing that the change they want is minuscule, that it is virtually no change at all.

Some republicans imply that it is almost un-Australian not to want a republic. Such an attitude is offensive. There are passionate and deeply patriotic Australians on both sides of this debate.

As I move around Australia I find no great groundswell for change. Intense debate is confined to the deeply committed on each side.

Even amongst many who intend to vote "yes" there is a ready acknowledgement that there are far more important issues on the national agenda.

In these circumstances Australians are right to be sceptical about the need for change. I hope they reject the republic. It will not produce a better Australia.

# Reflections on Australian Federalism

## Melbourne – 11 April 2005

Invited by the Menzies Research Centre to address the subject of Australian Federalism, the Prime Minister defended the existing Federal system of government but observed that traditional State loyalties had been largely eclipsed by localism on the one hand and a maturing national Australian identity on the other. He stressed that the States had the potential to diffuse power throughout the Commonwealth but was not oblivious to the fact that these same State governments could also impinge upon the autonomy of local communities through bureaucratic over-reach, particularly in fields such as education and town planning.

While accepting that the Federal system had generally served Australia well, the Prime Minister recognised that it was in need of continuing reform for it to deliver sound government and essential services to the people. In particular, he identified industrial relations and the overlapping role of the Commonwealth and States in the realms of health and education as areas where the Australian Federation could work better. In keeping with his conservative-liberal instincts, he argued that future approaches to reforming the Federal system needed to be incremental and always considered.

In addressing the condition of federalism in Australia let me make it clear at the outset that the federal structure of the Australian nation will remain. The responsibility of all of us in government is to make the federal system work better for all the Australian people. If we had our time again, we might have organised ourselves differently. Perhaps many of us have had those thoughts – I certainly have on numerous occasions – but they are only thoughts. Thoughts can be beautiful but they are only thoughts and there is not much point in indulging ourselves in theorising.

In that context there has been a little bit of commentary of late that my Government has discarded its political inheritance in a headlong rush towards centralism. Ironically, this charge has arisen just as the Commonwealth is being urged, often by the same people who make these comments, to assume more and more responsibilities – especially in areas of economic and social infrastructure traditionally owned and run by the States.

Let me say at the outset that these fears of a new centralism rest on a complete misunderstanding of the Government's thinking and its reform direction. Where we seek at present a change in the Federal-State balance, our goal is to expand individual choice, freedom and opportunity, not to expand the reach of the central government.

Let me illustrate in a policy area very close to my heart and close to the hearts of many in the audience, that is the issue of industrial relations. The desire to have a more national system of industrial relations is driven by our wish that as many businesses and employees as possible have the freedom, the flexibility and the individual choice which is characteristic of the Government's philosophy in the area of workplace relations. And this can only be achieved at present by removing the dead weight of Labor's highly-regulated State industrial relations systems.

The goal is to free the individual, and not to trample on the States. We have no desire at all to take over functions that are being properly discharged by the States and the territories. On the contrary, through the introduction of the Goods and Services Tax, the Government has delivered the most important federalist breakthrough since the Commonwealth took over income tax powers through the exercise of the defence power during World War II. But nor will we shirk our responsibility to seek the best possible outcomes for the nation and to extend Australia's economic prosperity through this century.

I am, first and last, an Australian nationalist. When I think about all this country is and everything it can become, I have very little time for vestiges of State parochialism. This Government's approach to our Federation is quite simple. Our ideal position is that the States should meet their responsibilities and we will meet ours. And our first impulse is to seek State cooperation with States and territories on national challenges where there is overlapping responsibility. But I have never been one to genuflect uncritically at the altar of States' rights. Our Federation should be about better lives for people, not quiet lives for governments.

Australian Liberalism has always been a highly optimistic creed. It values freedom and initiative above compulsion and conformity. And the golden thread of this inheritance is to trust the choices of the Australian people. It is a philosophy that we bring to areas such as education, healthcare, workplace relations and helping parents find the right balance between work and family responsibilities. It is a philosophy that has a timeless quality in a world of constant change. And I believe that part of that change, especially in the last 10 to 20 years, has been the greater focus by the Australian people on ties to nation and to their local community, and less on traditional State loyalties.

What I call the nationalisation of both our economy and our society can be seen very clearly over time. When I was a young solicitor in Sydney in the early 1960s, our legal firms were confined exclusively to State capitals. A Sydney law firm like the then Allen Allen and Hemsley, now Allens Arthur Robinson, would, for example, have Victorian agents for its business in Melbourne. The very expression, Victorian agents, sounds quaint, even old fashioned in the world of the 21st century. Today that is no longer the case and the same trend has occurred across all sectors of the Australian economy.

Think, too, of something really important and that is the nationalisation of our football codes. Once upon a time, someone following the Victorian Football League would have been an oddity in Sydney or Brisbane. Today, we all put in our footy tips for the AFL every Friday, in many codes in the case of prime ministers. And who would have thought a few years ago that Melbourne would for a time hold the record for the largest Rugby crowd in Australian history?

In the vital area of education, the increased mobility of our population means that no fewer than 80 000 Australian students move from one

State or territory to another each year. And against this backdrop of the nationalisation of our economy and our society there is understandable frustration, even anger, among the Australian people at what they see as the constant buck-passing in our federal system and a failure to achieve uniformity when that uniformity will deliver obvious benefits.

Too often we talk about cost-shifting. All Australians hear is blame-shifting. As societies change and attitudes change, so there are inevitable pressures on political structures and parties to change as well. I am reminded especially of this when I think of our Party's conversion to the cause of industrial relations reform. For many years, the Liberal Party was more than comfortable with the old system of centralised wage-fixing and arbitration. I well recall Menzies praising the system's contribution to industrial peace and productivity in writings after his retirement. Like many others, he saw any move towards workplace bargaining as leading inevitably to strikes and industrial dislocation. This is not a view that many Liberals would hold today. And nor is there any desire within the Australian community, in a more entrepreneurial and self-reliant nation, to turn back the clock to what we would now see as a highly illiberal industrial relations system.

Similarly, my own attitude towards our federal system has evolved over a life in politics. Like other Liberals, I am a strong constitutionalist. The dispersal of power that a federal system promotes, together with its potential, and I stress potential, to deliver services closer to peoples' needs, are threads of our political inheritance that I have always valued and greatly respected. The trouble is that, in practice, there is often less to these arguments than meets the eye. For instance, the view that State governments have benign decentralist tendencies has always been something of a myth. At various times, State governments of both persuasions have found occasion to trample over local government decision-making.

Without passing judgment on particular cases, it does expose the selective indignation of the States when it comes to the virtues of decentralisation. And a State education bureaucracy can appear pretty remote if you are a parent in Mount Isa or Kununurra struggling to make sense of your child's unintelligible report card. This indifference to localism can apply to metropolitan areas as well. In recent years, in both New South Wales and Queensland, government schools wishing to expel students under a strict anti-drugs policy have been overruled by State bureaucracies, to the understandable chagrin of parents and teachers.

But the major source of discontent with Australia's federal system today must turn on the underwhelming performance of current State governments following the introduction of the Goods and Services Tax. Those who argue that my Government has embraced centralism are suffering from a severe case of historical myopia. Our decision five years ago to grant every last dollar of the GST to States and territories was the greatest vote of confidence in the federal system in the Liberal Party's history. For years, literally for years – first as Treasurer and then as Prime Minister – I sat across the table from premiers of both political persuasions who pleaded for access to a growth tax. These calls came as strongly from Charles Court and Joh Bjelke-Petersen and Jeff Kennett as they did from Neville Wran and John Cain and Steve Bracks. They said, in effect: "Give us a growth tax and we will leave you alone. We will get on and deliver the services like public hospitals, public transport, police and government schools which are the core responsibilities of State governments". We delivered with the GST. And it liberated the States from their dependence on inefficient financial taxes and from general revenue assistance grants provided by the Commonwealth.

No government in 60 years has given the States more fiscal autonomy to fulfil their constitutional responsibilities. In March 2000, we calculated that States and territories would benefit in the first eight years by $3.7 billion over and above the previous revenue sharing arrangements. In fact, the latest estimates suggest that that benefit has climbed to almost $10 billion. Over the next five years, States and territories collectively will be $16 billion better off than they would have been under the arrangements that I inherited when I replaced Mr Keating as Prime Minister. In that time, the windfall to Victoria alone will be approximately $3.2 billion.

All the Commonwealth asks now is that the States make a determined effort to meet their responsibilities and obligations. Part of that bargain was to reduce the burden of State taxes. Peter Costello has outlined a plan which would cut indirect taxes by $8.8 billion by 2009-2010 and still leave the States better off by around $7.5 billion. This targets inefficient, nuisance taxes on business, especially a range of stamp duties. Abolishing these taxes will help Australian firms to compete in a tough, competitive world. It is not centralism to want to cut taxes. It is liberalism.

Looking across our federal system, we do find areas where the Federation works well, areas where the case for rationalisation is strong, and areas where a more incremental approach is the best way to proceed. Co-operation between the Commonwealth and the States on water reform is a good example of how the federal system can work for Australia's betterment. While the States have a constitutional responsibility for water management, a national approach was needed to deal with what I have called the great conservation challenge of our age. The greatest of Australian river-systems, the Murray-Darling, flows from Queensland to South Australia. What happens in one State directly affects irrigation and the environment downstream in another State. Farmers need to have secure access to water, our scarcest resource, on a sustainable basis. The Commonwealth therefore led the development of the National Water Initiative and has now established the National Water Commission, with the cooperation, I am pleased to say, of most State and territory governments. ...

In other cases, however, the existing structure of Federal-State responsibilities has run its course. Soon, my Government will unveil a new round of industrial relations reforms to bring Australia's workplace relations system finally into the 21st century. Reform is vital if Australia is to further consolidate the transformation of its economy to one where wages are based on the capacity of firms to pay and on the productivity of individual workplaces. We made very good progress towards a more flexible and competitive system with the passage of the *Workplace Relations Act* in 1996. But, as many of you know, important reforms in areas such as unfair dismissals and improved flexibility in agreement making have been blocked repeatedly in the Senate. ...

I want to remind you, however, that those areas where the Commonwealth seeks to cover the field in our federal system will always be very rare. In most cases, making our Federation work better will rely on an incremental approach. Incremental reform usually gets a bad press, especially from editorial writers accustomed to dispensing advice in 800 words or less. But incremental or piecemeal reform is in fact the kind of reform that liberals and conservatives invariably are most comfortable with. Indeed, as Karl Popper taught half a century ago, it is often the most rational approach, especially if the alternative is utopian social engineering.

Health and education are two areas where overlapping roles and responsibilities are built into our federal system. Despite problems that arise from time to time, I am not one who regularly denigrates our health and education systems. They are among the best in the world. And I had a vivid reminder here in Melbourne in visiting that wonderful bionic ear centre of the sheer excellence and world class of the medical science that this country has produced. Among comparable countries, our health system ranks highly: third for people's life expectancy; sixth for healthy life expectancy; and third in the OECD for overall health system effectiveness. Our education system is also rising to the challenge. According to the most recent data, Australian 15-year olds are performing well against benchmarks for reading, mathematics and science when compared with their counterparts elsewhere.

There will always be great room for improvement and the Australian Government has a particular responsibility to promote choice and to ensure high national standards in both areas. But I am not persuaded by some of the options for radical reform that are often canvassed. In particular, I am not persuaded that the effectiveness or efficiency of healthcare in Australia would be improved by the Commonwealth assuming responsibility for public hospitals. Any possible gains would be outweighed by the disadvantages to local hospitals and their communities of management by a more distant health bureaucracy. And it is unlikely that consensus could be achieved for the necessary overhaul of Commonwealth-State financial relations that would follow such a transformation. ...

We do need to look carefully at the respective roles and responsibilities of Commonwealth, State and territory governments for health, aged and disability care. We do so with only one intent: to make life easier for older people, those with disabilities and those who care for them. We are also looking at ways to drive reform in a targeted fashion in vocational and technical education. Australia currently enjoys the lowest unemployment rate for 30 years. And this has created skills shortages in parts of the economy and, as a result, in the 2004 election campaign we made far-reaching commitments to boost opportunities in traditional trades.

I have said many times before, and I repeat, that this nation made a cultural error a generation ago when we embraced uncritically the notion that the highest path of success for a young person was to go to university. This did a huge disservice to the 70 per cent of young people who do not go direct from school to university. And it reflected an intellectual failure to understand the continuing needs of our economy. ...

Can I conclude with some broader reflections? Australians are a non-ideological, pragmatic and empirical people. They want governments to deliver outcomes and not make excuses. They want governments that take responsibility, not states of denial. Now and in the future, my Government stands ready to cooperate with States and territories on Australia's great reform challenges. And we will continue to err on the side of cooperation.

But while ever the States fail to meet their core responsibilities, there will be inevitable tensions in our federal system. With the GST, the States no longer have an alibi. There are times when tensions can arise within Australian Liberalism's traditional commitment to limited government. This Government recognises that dispersal of power is basic to our philosophy. But so is leaning against an over-governed Australia, something that can become all too apparent in a federal system with eight Labor governments.

We resolve this ultimately by pursuing policies that spread power, freedom and opportunity to the suburbs, workplaces, towns and farms right across our nation. In the end, we approach the challenges of Australian federalism as we approach other challenges, not by walking away from our political inheritance, but by seeking to extend it.

# Keeping Faith with Our Common Values

## 2008 Irving Kristol Lecture
## Washington DC – 5 March 2008

Shortly after leaving the prime ministership, John Howard was invited by the Washington-based American
Enterprise Institute to deliver the 2008 Irving Kristol
Lecture. Named in honour of an American public intellectual who championed conservative values, the lecture provided a platform for Howard to deliver a compelling exposition of the liberal-conservative philosophy
he brought to government in his almost twelve years as
prime minister. Defending his legacy, he told his audience that his Government had pursued a mutually reinforcing blend of economic liberalism and social conservatism. At the same time as reinforcing the traditional
values of Western civilisation such as patriotism, the
Judeo-Christian ethic and the importance of the natural
family, his Government had embarked on bold reforms
to modernise Australia's labour market, taxation system and trade policies to position Australia as a strong
economic player in the Asia-Pacific. Howard believed
that this approach had ultimately made Australia a
more bold and outward-looking country yet one that remained in touch with its national identity and heritage.

I thank you for the honour you have given me in asking me to deliver
the 2008 Irving Kristol Lecture.

The American Enterprise Institute, over the years, has consistently
defended fundamental freedoms, both personal and economic. It has
stoically resisted the insidious tide of political correctness in so many
facets of our daily lives.

It has frequently displayed great policy courage – often facing a chorus of ridicule and dissent. This was recently the case regarding the surge in Iraq, a subject to which I will return later.

Most prominently, though, this Institute has always understood the relentless force of ideas and values in shaping societies.

Written in 1973, Irving Kristol's words have a timeless relevance to all of us who strive in different ways to build better societies and nations. He said then:

> I know that it will be hard for some to believe that ideas can be so important. This underestimation of ideas is a peculiarly bourgeois fallacy, especially powerful in the most bourgeois of nations, our own United States. For two centuries, the very important people who managed the affairs of this society could not believe in the importance of ideas – until one day they were shocked to discover that their children, having been captured and shaped by certain ideas, were either rebelling against their authority or seceding from their society. The truth is that ideas are all-important. The massive and seemingly-solid institutions of any society – the economic institutions, the political institutions, the religious institutions – are always at the mercy of the ideas in the heads of the people who populate these institutions.

To achieve success, governments need a guiding philosophy; not a zealous ideology which is insensitive to political compromise, but a directional touchstone which provides overall consistency through the years. In other words, ultimately they must be ruled by values and ideas and not only by an instinct for political survival–necessary though that is.

It is good to be back in Washington, a city which I visited many times as Prime Minister of Australia. I was here on that fateful September morning in 2001 having, only the previous day, met the President for the very first time.

To experience the shock and disbelief of a free and generous people being subjected to an unprovoked and evil attack left me with a feeling which I have retained to this day.

The long friendship between Australia and the United States has grown deeper and stronger as we have responded to the threats of these past years. It is a powerful testament in the modern world that the values which unite nations create the most enduring bonds of all.

Australia has been beside the United States in every military conflict of consequence in which your country has been involved since our soldiers first fought together at the Battle of Hamel, in France, on 4 July 1918.

Important though that history of military cooperation may be, important though our political, economic and cultural ties might be, they are dwarfed by the commonality of the values that we share. They are the values of personal liberty and individual freedom, the belief that decency and hard work define a person's worth, not class or race or social background, and the confidence that all of the peoples of the world will embrace democracy if they are given the opportunity to enjoy its benefits.

To make that friendship even stronger was a cornerstone of the foreign policy my Government pursued. I speak to you as an unapologetic and continuing advocate of the broad conservative cause, restlessly conscious, as you are, that the battle of ideas is never completely won and must always command both our attention and our energy.

The former Australian government, which I led, was accused of many things, but never of betraying its essentially centre-right credo. We pursued a blend of economic liberalism – in the classical sense of that term connoting, as it does, a faith in market forces and social conservatism. So far from being in conflict, the one reinforced the other. ...

From our election in 1996 we pursued reform and further modernisation of the Australian economy. On the social front we emphasised our nation's traditional values, sought to resurrect greater pride in her history and became assertive about the intrinsic worth of our national identity. In the process we ended the seemingly endless seminar about that identity which had been in progress for some years.

When we left office in November 2007 Australia was a stronger, prouder and more prosperous nation than it had been twelve years earlier. ...

In this lecture I wish to touch on some of the values and responses which, in the world we now inhabit, are important for today's conservatives.

Whilst the intrinsic worth of values never changes, their relative importance and the tenacity with which they are applied by societies will always be determined by contemporary threats and challenges.

Today's world remains confronted by the ongoing threat of Islamic fascism, a new and quite unfamiliar assault on our values and way of life. It relies on indiscriminate terror without regard to the identity or faith of its victims. It also calculates that it is the nature of Western societies to grow weary of long struggles and protracted debates. They produce, over time, a growing pressure for resolution or accommodation.

The particular challenge posed by extremist Islam means, therefore, that more than ever before, continued cultural self-belief is critical to national strength.

Ronald Reagan and that other great warrior in our cause, Margaret Thatcher, taught us many things.

One of them was to remain culturally assertive, to understand always the importance of self-belief in the psyche of a nation; to be willing to stand against the fashion of the time. …

In the protracted struggle against Islamic extremism there will be no stronger weapon than the maintenance by Western liberal democracies of a steadfast belief in the continuing worth of our own national value systems. And, where necessary, a soaring optimism about the future of freedom and democracy.

We should not think that by trading away some of the values which have made us who we are will buy us either immunity from terrorists or respect from noisy minorities. If the butter of common national values is spread too thinly it will disappear altogether.

We should not forget that it is the values of our societies that terrorists despise most. That is why we should never compromise on them.

It is not only their intrinsic worth that should be staunchly defended. It is also because radical Islam senses – correctly – that there is a soft underbelly of cultural self-doubt in certain Western societies.

There are too many in our midst who think, deep down, that it is really "our fault", and if only we entered into some kind of federal cultural compact, with our critics, the challenges would disappear.

Perhaps it was this sentiment which led the Archbishop of Canterbury[24] to make the extraordinary comment, several weeks ago, that in Britain some accommodation with aspects of sharia law was inevitable.

It is fundamental to the continued unity and purpose of a democratic nation state that there not only be respect for the rule of law but the state have but one body of law, to which all are accountable, and from which all are entitled to an equal dispensation of justice.

Economically, the world faces both some new challenges as well as the possible re-emergence of some old foes.

The economic difficulties which have quickly become apparent in recent months will provoke intense debate about the right responses.

Competitive capitalism within free markets remains the most effective economic paradigm, both domestically and internationally. ...

The right responses will be grounded in free-market orthodoxies. We should avoid resort to re-regulation. We should preserve the independence of central banks. We should maintain open and free labour markets. We should continue cutting taxes where possible and we should seek to increase savings.

If individuals will not save, then governments must add to public savings by running budget surpluses or significantly reducing budget deficits.

Above all, there must be no return to protectionism. Freer world markets, particularly, but not only, in agriculture are essential. For certain poorer nations the dismantling of trade barriers by developed nations will be far more helpful than foreign aid....

A conservative edifice must always have at its centre, the role of the family and what Americans call faith-based organisations in maintaining and strengthening social infrastructure. Despite the repeated attempts of some social engineers to suggest that traditional family arrangements

---

[24] John Howard was referring to Rowan Williams, Archbishop of Canterbury from 2002 to 2012.

are no longer needed and that they are, in any event, headed for extinction, the field evidence suggests that united, functioning families remain not only the best emotional nursery for children but also the most efficient social welfare system that mankind has ever devised.

Holding families together in preference to picking up the pieces when they fall apart must always be the major driver of social welfare policy.

It remains a reality in Western societies that two of the greatest contributors to poverty are joblessness and family breakdown. We should maintain a cultural bias in favour of traditional families. That does not mean discriminating against single parents but it does mean ceaselessly propounding the advantages for a child of being raised by both a mother and a father.

Marriage is a bedrock social institution – with an unmistakable meaning and resonance. It should be kept as such. Taxation laws should promote, not penalise, marriage. The taxation system should generously recognise the cost of raising children. This is not middle class welfare. It is merely a taxation system with some semblance of social vision. The tax payment system must also support choice for parents about who cares for their children.

When a parent elects to withdraw from the workforce, either wholly or partly, to care for a child, that decision must be supported by the taxation system. What we sought to do in government was to promote the principle of choice when it came to the caring arrangements parents made for their children and the attendant career decisions involved for those parents. ...

Maintaining a cultural bias in favour of families also means that governments should reinforce the role of parents in choosing what form of education their children receive.

Australia has largely succeeded in maintaining a good quality, publicly-funded education system.

Parallel with that there has always been a robust non-government school sector. In the last dozen or so years in Australia there has been strong growth in that area. Now some 33 per cent of Australian school children are educated at independent or non-government schools, the great bulk of which have a religious affiliation.

There is no constitutional barrier in Australia to governments giving direct help to schools with a religious affiliation provided there is no discrimination between religions. Most schools receiving this help are Christian denominational schools. Jewish and Muslim schools receive similar help. All of these schools must adhere to curricula laid down by State education authorities. ...

The former government in Australia gave faith-based groups direct involvement in policy-making and execution, adding to their traditional roles of relieving distress and providing spiritual support. Let me illustrate. Until 1996, unemployed Australians seeking work registered with a government agency which kept a list of available jobs given to it by employers seeking workers.

This system had essentially been in operation in that form for decades. It always received very mixed reviews.

In our first budget (1996) we privatised the employment service, ending the government monopoly and replacing it with a job network open to private providers. The new job network attracted participation from the employment arms of some of the largest religious-based charities in Australia such as the Salvation Army and Wesley Missions.

This quite radical policy change has been a success. The significant involvement of faith-based organisations has been a major feature. Private enterprise providers have also been successfully involved.

I am not aware of any system quite like it elsewhere in the world. I am sure that the new job network has played some part in reducing Australia's unemployment rate.

I mention this example of the successful (to date) involvement of church-based organisations in the coal-face delivery of social services. Such groups bring two priceless assets to the delivery of human services. The first is genuine compassion. The other is a hard-headed approach to money. Hardened by years of ceaseless fund-raising, most religiously based charities or organisations spend their money far more carefully than do bureaucrats. ...

Those who hold to conservative values continue to face a major ideological battle. The left-liberal grip on educational institutions and large, though not all, sections of the media remains intense.

Global warming has become a new battleground. The same intellectual bullying and moralising, used in other debates, now dominates what passes for serious dialogue on this issue.

That having been said, the past twenty-five years have seen striking conservative gains. It was Ronald Reagan's strength and determination, nourished by his positive and optimistic view of freedom and American life, that brought down the evil empire.

The left-liberal view then was one of great power accommodation, tinged on occasions with moral equivalence.

Margaret Thatcher's transformation of Britain was, ironically enough, to be vindicated by Tony Blair's embrace of her changes to Britain's labour laws.

He confronted his nation's unions and his own party with the news that those changes had to stay. Britain then learnt that the old "beer and sandwiches at No 10" approach to resolving industrial disputes, when union leaders and government ministers met to decide how many more hundreds of millions of pounds of taxpayers' money would be poured into the latest failing nationalised industry, had gone forever.

On a smaller scale, in my own country, a number of the more conservative social policies of my government have been endorsed by the new Australian government. The sincerity of its conversion will be tested by experience of office.

But our strongest grounds for optimism lie in something that Peggy Noonan drew attention to in her tribute to William Buckley in last Friday's *Wall Street Journal*.

She reminded us that the conservative values we hold to are grounded in the unshakeable realities of life. Governments serve people, not the reverse, that freedom is good and must be defended against all assaults, whether from those of communism in earlier years or Islamic fascism today, and that strong competitive markets produce the best economic results.

# III

# Watershed Events
# and Policy Reforms

# A Government for all Australians

## Sydney – 2 March 1996

On the Saturday evening, 2 March 1996, John Howard
entered the Wentworth Hotel in Sydney to claim victory
to a jubilant throng of supporters. After thirteen years in
the political wilderness, Howard had led the Coalition
back to government with a decisive majority of 45 seats
over the Labor Party in a House of Representatives of
148 seats. Some of the biggest swings towards the Coalition had occurred in the traditional Labor heartland
of western Sydney. The 1996 election represented only
the third time that the Coalition had won government
from Opposition since the Second World War. The
swing to the Coalition was clearly greater than Howard
had anticipated. The Prime Minister-elect acknowledged
that the deepest emotion he felt was "humility". Echo-
ing Menzies almost half a century earlier, he promised
to govern for Australians who had voted against him
as well as those who had voted for him. Determined to
place his stamp on the ensuing governance of Australia, he made it clear that his government would not be
a "pale imitation" of the one it had just replaced. In concluding, the Prime Minister-elect pledged to "advance
the welfare of all the Australian people".

Can I say to you, and my first words are addressed to all of the people
of Australia, that I am very conscious of the enormous responsibility
that has been placed upon me and upon my colleagues by the verdict of
the Australian people today.

I feel many emotions tonight, but the deepest emotion of all I feel is
that of humility that the Australian people have given me the privilege
of leading the Government of this country.

I want to say that the Government that I will lead will be a Government not only for the people who voted for us but also for the people who voted against us.

Nine years ago, when I was unsuccessful in an election, I said in my concession speech that the things that united Australians were infinitely more important and more enduring than the things that divided Australians. That has always been my political credo and it will be a political credo that I will carry forward in the governance of this country over the next three years.

I want to thank Paul Keating for his gracious words. I want to wish Paul Keating and Annita and their family good health and happiness in the future. Can I say that although we have been vigorous opponents he has been a great warrior for his own political cause and, despite our differences, that is something that I recognise.

I owe thanks to many people and I will come to that in a moment. I want to make it clear that although uniting the Australian people will be the cornerstone of my approach in government, we have been elected with a mandate, a very powerful mandate. And whilst I will seek, at all times, unity and a common point of view, we have not been elected to be just a pale imitation of the Government that we have replaced.

We have been given this emphatic mandate tonight because there have been many things that have been left undone that need to be attended to and addressed. We need to implement the programme on which we were elected and I want to make it very clear that there will be an absolute determination with fairness and understanding to do that and to do it with resolution and without qualification.

I want to thank all my colleagues and I especially wish to thank Tim Fischer and the National Party. I will lead a Coalition in Government as I have led a Coalition in Opposition, and I look forward to working very closely with Tim Fischer as the Deputy Prime Minister of Australia. To all of my parliamentary colleagues, I say thank you. I particularly want to extend my thanks to the Liberal Party organisation; to Tony Staley, the Federal President; to Andrew Robb, the Federal Director; and Ron Walker, the honorary Federal Treasurer; and the many other members of the organisation who have worked so tirelessly.

Can I say it is an immensely proud moment for me tonight to lead the Liberal Party of Australia back into government. We have endured sixteen years without a Federal election victory and tonight is an immensely proud and wonderful moment.

In celebrating the miracle of democracy that we can peacefully and respectfully transfer power through the ballot box, and through no other device, let us also as Liberals and as Liberal supporters celebrate the magnificent win that we have had tonight. It is a victory for those who voted Liberal in the past and for those who are by habit swinging voters, and it is a victory that has also embraced many traditional Labor Party areas of Australia.

When you look at the swings in western Sydney and in some of the traditional Labor areas of Sydney and when I think of the magnificent result in Queensland, that wonderful result in South Australia, and the way in which the Liberal Party held its very high proportion of seats in Victoria and the early returns in Western Australia are very encouraging. It is a comprehensive endorsement of the philosophy and the approach of the Liberal Party.

To all of you who have endured the barbs and the insults and you have heard your Party being written off, I want to say to the rank and file of the Liberal Party, you have endured far too many years in the political wilderness. Tonight it is a victory that we all share. It is not mine alone, it is mine because I was given, from the moment I became the leader of the Liberal Party just over a year ago, the most magnificent loyalty and support by my parliamentary colleagues and all of the members of the organisation. I say from the bottom of my heart how grateful I am for that support and that loyalty because that has given us the victory that we have tonight.

I said when I launched our campaign only a few weeks ago that one of the great features of the Liberal Party is that it was owned by no section of the Australian community, and our only obligation is to give good government to all of the Australian people. It will be my intention and my commitment that from now, I and my colleagues will devote our all to delivering good government, to doing good things, and to delivering the maximum degree of unity and cohesion to the Australian people.

There is something special about being an Australian. Today, along with everybody else, I had to queue up to cast my vote and the bloke in front of me turned around and said, " Oh, hello". He had a Labor Party how-to-vote ticket, he did not have a Liberal one, and he said, "It's nice to meet you but I'm not going to vote for you!" And that is, can I say, a celebration of what Australia is all about.

The very last thing that I want to say is a special word of thanks to some people who have been very close to me over the past months. I want to thank my own personal staff. The personal staff of a party leader carry enormous burdens and responsibilities. I am personally very, very grateful to all of my staff for the magnificent job that they have done. They have shared the disappointments and, tonight, they share the exhilaration of this remarkable victory.

Lastly, can I say to my wife Janette, and to my three children, Melanie, Tim and Richard, of all the things, these four people in the world, they have kept me going and they have sustained me and they have shared the difficulties as well as the successes of politics. Anybody in public life should always remember the contribution of their families and I unhesitatingly express not only my affection, but also my enormous gratitude to my wife and my three children for what they have done for me and what they continue to mean to me.

My very last words are to all of the people of Australia. To my fellow Australians, I am both deeply moved and I understand very deeply and very profoundly the responsibility that has been given to me tonight. I can but make a simple promise and a simple commitment, that from now on I will do all I can to advance the welfare of all of the Australian people.

I will focus on those things that bind us together; I will focus on our strengths; I will defend the interests and the values and the principles of this country both domestically and internationally. There is something very special, there is something unique about our nation and about being Australian and I commit myself and my future Government to the service of all the Australian people.

# Gun Control

## House of Representatives – 6 May 1996

On the 28 April 1996, the usual tranquillity of the colonial-era settlement of Port Arthur, Tasmania, was shattered when a lone gunman shot dead thirty-five people in a murderous rampage that shocked Australia and the world. Later describing the massacre as contributing to a "loss of Australian innocence", the recently-elected Prime Minister resolved to take action to avoid repetitions of such a tragedy on Australian soil. With the gunman having used two semi-automatic weapons to lethal effect, it gave added urgency for John Howard to reiterate his original call in June 1995 for Australia to adopt tougher gun laws.

Now, as the Prime Minister, Howard told the House of Representatives that he would work closely with the Attorney-General and his State/territory counterparts to introduce a proposal for tighter firearms laws. Among other things, these would include a total prohibition on automatic and semi-automatic weapons; a more rigorous control of firearm imports into Australia and an effective system of national registration. Despite vehement opposition from some parts of the Coalition's rural constituency, the Howard Government was determined to "seize the day on guns" and the new legislation was passed in 1996 with the support of the Labor Party and other non-government parties.

The new gun laws were a difficult issue for the Prime Minister because their stringent regulation of personal firearms grated with his Liberal instinct for greater individual liberty. At the same time, he affirmed that these new laws were necessary for the broader national and

human interest in public safety. He also anticipated
Australia's new gun regime to be something of a cultural watershed in preventing the nation from spiralling
down the American path of gun violence.

Mr Speaker, the purpose of my speaking tonight is to briefly outline
decisions that have been taken by the Government in relation to a proposal to be put to the police ministers meeting in Canberra on Friday to
significantly strengthen laws relating to gun control in Australia. Every-
one is aware of the circumstances which have finally brought to a head a
drive in the community for strong and effective gun control laws.

As I have said in other places and on other occasions in the Parliament, it would be wrong to simply see a response to what happened in
Tasmania last week as being found in tougher gun control laws. The
causes of that dreadful event lie deeper than simply the inadequacy of
our gun control laws. They go to aspects of the kind of society we are.
They go to issues concerning violence on the screen and in videos. They
also, in the view of many of my colleagues on this side of the House –
they are views that I share – raise legitimate questions about contemporary attitudes towards the treatment of mental health problems.

I want to make it clear to the House that, whilst I do not form any
summary judgments, if we are as a community to seriously examine the
causes and provide a range of responses, then we have to go beyond
issues of gun control legislation. We have to go to an examination of
some of those other matters. I can assure the House that, in a sensible,
measured way, the Government will be doing precisely that.

As to the question of gun control laws, the Government is strongly of
the view that we need effective, uniform legislation. We need to achieve
a total prohibition on the ownership, possession, sale and importation of
all automatic and semi-automatic weapons. That will be the essence of
the proposal that will be put by the Commonwealth Government at the
meeting on Friday. We need an effective registration system and we will
be pushing very strongly for that.

This decision, if it is supported by all of the States, will inevitably
cause inconvenience and present some difficulties for tens of thousands

of law-abiding people throughout this country. I think particularly of Australia's rural community, a community that, more than many others, always matches the national need and rises to the occasion in times of national difficulty. I want to say to those many tens of thousands of people who may not find the Government's position a palatable one, that it is only being done because of an overwhelming view on the part of the Government that there is a broader national interest in having a very extensive prohibition.

People will argue that you can draw the line between one particular style of weapon and another. I do not parade expertise in this area, but I have some understanding of the depth of community feeling on this issue and a desire, as I find it amongst my fellow Australians, to grab this very tragic moment to bring about a profound cultural shift in the attitude of this community towards the possession and the use of destructive weapons. Perhaps if we do that, as a community, we can avoid some of the trauma experienced almost as a daily fact of life in the United States. I would hate to contemplate the future of this country if we went willy-nilly down the American path when it comes to gun violence.

I think we do have an opportunity at this moment to do something to turn that around. It will involve difficulty. Part of the Government's proposals is to have a six-month amnesty period during which people will be invited to surrender their guns and full and proper compensation will be paid. That will involve a cost, and ultimately that cost will have to, as it properly should, be borne by the entire community and not just by the people who are being encouraged to surrender their weapons.

The Attorney-General (Mr Williams), as the responsible minister, will be releasing the document in the course of the next day or so. I will ensure that the Leader of the Opposition (Mr Beazley) gets a copy of the document as soon as it has been finally settled, and I want to take this opportunity of thanking the Leader of the Opposition for the very constructive and positive way in which he has responded so far. I make no judgments about the future. He, as the leader of the alternative government, has his political rights, as I had my political rights as the former leader of the alternative government.

This issue, above most issues that I have encountered in my years in politics, has demanded, as best we can provide in this place, a bipartisan response. The decisions that the Government has taken will not be universally popular—I accept that—and there will be people who will argue that they represent unacceptable infringements of individual rights.

It is not an issue that is new; it has been around for quite some years. Those who might argue that in some way what the Government is doing is a knee-jerk reaction have forgotten the extensive public debate that occurred after the Hoddle Street and Strathfield massacres. I ask those who argue, and who will be told over the days and weeks ahead, that what you need is further discussion and debate and deliberation, to see that discussion for what it is. It is inevitably a code for doing nothing in the hope that the immediate anger in the aftermath of last weekend will in time subside and that nothing will change.

In a sense it is always a sombre moment in a country where you ask the people who have done the right thing to put up with inconvenience because a limited number of people have done the wrong thing. But that is the nature of a democratic society. As somebody who is a fervent opponent of regulation, I always feel uncomfortable in responding to a problem with new laws. I think that this is an occasion when, if we did not, we would not be matching the national concern or the national need.

I should say to the House that I have had the opportunity over the weekend of having some very positive and helpful discussions with leaders of some of the farming bodies, and their attitude does not surprise me. As I said a moment ago, they usually respond in a very positive fashion to national issues. Their reaction has been one of understanding the dilemma that the Government faces.

In essence, our proposal involves a total prohibition on automatic and semi-automatic weapons; a strengthening of the import regime; the seeking of an effective system of national registration; a tightening of the criteria under which people can be given licences, which I think picks up a point that was made by the Opposition; and the commitment of funds for an education campaign; a six-month amnesty period, and after that a descending order of penalties including, potentially, a mandatory gaol sentence for the possession of the more high-powered destructive weapons, including those that were used in the Port Arthur massacre and which have been used on other occasions.

It gives me no pleasure to make this statement because it does involve an infringement of individual liberty by the state, which is never something I like. But there is a broader national and human interest involved, and I hope it is an approach that will win the support of all members of the House of Representatives and the Senate. I hope that the State governments—they will all be represented at the meeting on Friday—will find themselves able to respond. This is not an issue where I have sought some kind of aggregation of power to the Commonwealth. If it can be achieved through cooperation by the States, that is infinitely to be preferred, and that is what I will seek.

It does involve an acceptance by the whole community and ultimately, if it becomes necessary because of the cost involved in compensation, the Government will be seeking a contribution from all members of the community to cover the cost of that compensation because all members of the community will benefit. I commend the statement to the House.

# Tough on Drugs

## Education, Law Enforcement, Treatment
## Melbourne – 18 March 1999

Illicit-drug taking and the high rate of youth suicide were two social problems in the Australian community that troubled John Howard as Prime Minister. Conceding that he needed no encouragement to embrace a zero-tolerance approach to illicit drugs, the Prime Minister resolved to introduce what he would term a "Tough on Drugs" strategy to curb illicit drug use with its disastrous consequences. As with his social welfare approach to tackling poverty, the Prime Minister sought to mobilise a social coalition of government agencies, churches, charities, community groups and businesses to confront the scourge of illicit drug activity. In 1997, he assembled these groups into a new body, the Australian National Council on Drugs, to provide advice on drug policy and strategy.

In this address to Anglicare at its Victorian headquarters, Howard announced that his Government's campaign against drugs would enlist the frontline experience of welfare organisations to tackle the problem at the coalface. This would be accompanied by provision of resources to educate the community about the perils of drugs, and to support rehabilitation services to help people overcome their drug addiction. The Prime Minister saw his "Tough on Drugs" strategy as critical not only to sparing young lives, but integral to his vision for a safer Australia where citizens could walk the streets and dwell in their homes without the threat of drug-induced violence and crime.

I would first of all like to thank Anglicare for the opportunity of launching this second round of Federal Government financial support for treatment programmes here at its Victorian headquarters.

Anglicare is one of the major frontline welfare organisations in Australia. It is an organisation which is an important part of the social coalition needed in Australia to deal with difficult welfare issues and to tackle major social problems. I use the expression, social coalition, very deliberately to underline the point that no one section of the community is adequate to the task of dealing with underprivilege, or adequate to the task of dealing with a challenge such as drug abuse.

The Government alone cannot beat the drug problem. Individuals alone cannot beat the drug problem. Families need help to tackle the drug problem and we need, as individuals, as family members and as leaders of the Government, we need to enlist a frontline experience and support of organisations such as Anglicare. That is why it is entirely appropriate that on the day in which I announce a further Commonwealth financial commitment to the treatment programmes which are an important part of our tough on drugs strategy, I do so here – at the headquarters of one of those organisations that is an important element in the fight against drugs and, indeed, the general campaign to deliver a fairer, more decent, and just society.

The drug problem has been very much in the news in recent weeks. Not because it is something that has suddenly arrived but, through a combination of circumstances, there has been a level of public preoccupation with and concentration on it that I do not think I have experienced at any time since I entered Parliament almost 25 years ago.

I do not pretend for a moment as Prime Minister that what my Government has done has provided all the answers. It is not essentially an issue that should be divided on party political lines. There are people who are deeply concerned about this issue and have something to contribute on this issue from all strands of political life in Australia, both State and Federal.

I would hope, to the maximum degree possible, that the effort at a government level to deal with the problem should be on a bipartisan basis. That will certainly be the approach that I will take as Prime Minister to the Premiers' Conference on 9 April when this issue will be the main business of the afternoon session of that particular conference. I have said before, and I repeat it, that I will work as freely and willingly with a Labor premier of any of the States of Australia as I will with a Liberal or National Party premier.

The Government's "Tough on Drugs strategy" which involves the expenditure of about $290 million, is in dollar terms the largest commitment by any Federal government to such a strategy. I do not say that to score a point but merely to record a fact and I appreciate the fact that, on a number of issues, I have received public support and endorsement from the Leader of the Labor Opposition in the Federal Parliament [Kim Beazley].

The "Tough on Drugs" strategy recognises that action is needed on three levels. We need to continue to commit further resources to law enforcement. Some of the evidence of the benefit of the additional resources committed by the Federal Government to both Customs and Federal Police, with the stationing of officers of the Australian Federal Police in source countries and countries through which drugs have passed from their original source, has already begun to pay dividends. Once again I do not overplay that but equally we should not understate it.

It is true that it is a very difficult fight and it is easy for people to despair, it is easy for people to throw up their arms and say: we have not solved the problem, we appear to be losing ground. We can be cast around in the mistaken belief that by abandoning everything that has been done thus far; we will be suddenly more successful in dealing with the problem in the future. It is a battle of attrition and it is a battle of attrition which requires, of all sections of the community, a determined commitment both of human resources and also of financial resources from both the State and Federal governments. Part of that is obviously law enforcement, and part of it must be continued co-operation between not only the Federal agencies, such as Customs and the Federal Police, but also the maximum co-operation between the Federal Police and the police of the various States. The success that has been achieved in relation to heroin and cocaine seizures in recent months has very much been a consequence of enhanced and more effective co-operation, between the law enforcement agencies of the Commonwealth and the law enforcement agencies of the States' polices.

The second component is education. There can be no limit to the requirement that people, particularly young people and children, be educated about the drug menace. There should be, in my view, and I make no apology for saying this, absolutely no reluctance at any level to pursue as vigorously as possible the "Tough on Drugs" message within our schools. I cannot think of a higher priority, I cannot think of something where we should have a less complicated and a less uncompromising approach than the absolute determination to pursue the drug menace within our schools.

So, therefore, the second and equally important element of our campaign is to provide resources to educate the community against the menace of drugs. We have set aside about $17.5 million for a plan to campaign at a Federal level against illicit drugs in schools, and to send the strongest possible message to school students about the danger and the threat posed by drugs, not only to the young but to the community generally. In a sense, it is unfortunate that so much of the debate in recent weeks has focused on whether or not there should be a heroin trial. In the process, I think the community has lost sight of, or perhaps not given enough attention to, the very real progress that has been made, at both a State and a Federal level, in improving the resources for education, and also the plans; some of which have been announced and some of which I am to announce this morning, for committing further resources to treatment facilities.

Part of the campaign, and the third and most important part of the campaign, as far as my announcement this morning is concerned, is the treatment of people who are addicted, not only to heroin but to other substances which they are abusing. It is fair to say that there is nothing more distressing in this whole campaign, in this whole issue, for somebody in my position than to be on a radio programme, as I have been on two occasions here in Melbourne in recent weeks, and to speak to the despairing mother of somebody who says that she cannot get her daughter or her son into a treatment programme because there are no places available.

Whatever views people may hold about heroin trials or, indeed, any other aspect of this whole debate, there ought to be no argument that the community has an overwhelming responsibility to provide more resources for those people who are trying to beat their addiction, and for those people who are trying to break the habit. Surely there can be an across-the-board view within the Australian community that this is unarguably one of the major priorities that we must address our attention to.

So it has been that we have, in the "Tough on Drugs" campaign, made major announcements last year which involved the provision of about $30 million in our first round of grants to fund 24 communities and 68 non-government organisations for innovative community education programmes and new treatment services. Examples of that first round included $1.5 million for the Ted Noffs Foundation to establish a new non-residential treatment service in Sydney for 12 to 18 year-olds, and $1.5 million to the Salvation Army in Preston here in Victoria for a residential rehabilitation facility for women and their children.

Today I want to announce a further round of grants totalling approximately $20 million for over 50 groups Australia-wide to boost treatment and counselling services. This funding will make a further contribution to the cause of providing increasingly greater treatment facilities for people who are trying to break their habit. Examples of the projects being funded in this round include $750 000 to youth off the streets in Ultimo in Sydney for an intensive two to four week residential service for young adults with a history of drug abuse; $375 000 to the Salvation Army in Adelaide to employ two Aboriginal workers for a 25 bed sobering-up unit for Aboriginal people; and $474 000 to Anglicare in Lilydale here in Victoria for support training and treatment for illicit drug users and their families.

These announcements that I have made this morning represent a further down-payment, if I can put it that way, on the Government's 290 million "Tough on Drugs" strategy. I do not represent to you; I do not pretend to you that by this announcement we have found some new and revolutionary response to the problem. It is just another contribution towards making it easier for some in the community who do have a drug problem to do something about it. It is a further contribution on the part of the Commonwealth to encouraging the volunteer sector in the tremendous work that they do in providing relief within the community.

I will be talking to the State premiers about some further proposals in relation to the nation-wide campaign against the drug problem. I do regard this as a national issue. I do believe it carries national responsibilities and it therefore commands the attention of the national Government. But it can only be done effectively if we, all of us, work together. If we focus on those areas of the fight against drugs where we have common ground, we can maximise our efforts in relation to those areas. We must continue to see it very much as something that involves compassion for the victims of drug abuse, as well as a total intolerance and a detestation of those who would profit from their misery and profit from the trafficking in drugs.

Those two words, zero tolerance, have been much used and, perhaps, over-used in this debate in recent times. I want to make it clear that I do not think there is anybody in the Australian community who has anything other than maximum contempt and zero tolerance for those in our community who would seek to make money out of human misery and human suffering.

Like any other member of the Federal Parliament or, indeed, member of a State Parliament who has done his or her job in recent years, I have confronted the experience of discussing with parents left distraught by the loss of children through the scourge of drugs. I have spent much time listening to some of their harrowing stories and, as a parent myself, I can try to understand the sense of loss and frustration and disillusionment and despair and anger and all of the other human emotions that a parent must go through when they experience that particular happening. I can only say to them that the Government is trying.

I do not pretend that we have all of the answers. I do not think anybody has the monopoly of wisdom in this area. We are committing more resources. We do listen to the advice of people who are affected. One of the problems is that for as many parents affected in the ultimate way by this problem who may, for example, support one course of action, there are just as many who are violently opposed to that course of action. The idea that there is one sort of universal, coalface view about something like, for example, a heroin trial or, indeed, anything else that is controversial, is totally mistaken. That is part of the dilemma that this particular issue throws up.

I have not come here pretending that I have provided, or can provide, all of the answers. I have come here because I am personally committed to trying to make a difference in this area. I am personally very concerned about the impact of drugs, not only on the lives which are devastated by them, but also the way in which it feeds into crime activity. The way in which it makes our streets less safe, the way in which it makes our homes more vulnerable to burglaries, the way in which it makes our elderly people feel more threatened as they go about doing things that for generations have been taken for granted, that you can peacefully and safely do within the Australian community. Every time an elderly lady's handbag is snatched in a busy suburban street in Australia, nine times out of ten that can be related to the drug problem.

All of these things collectively impose on all of us a huge responsibility. I thank the welfare organisations for what they are doing. I also want to thank the other members of the National Council on Drugs, a number of whom who are here today. It is a very broadly-based Council. It is an organisation that represents the many points of view that ought to be represented on this issue because there is no one single right or correct solution. However, there is one single resolve, I hope on the part of the Australian community, remembering difficult though the problem is, that the perspective should be kept that some two per cent of the Australian community have in some way been directly involved in hard drugs.

We must keep a sense of perspective about it whilst recognising it is a long and difficult campaign ahead of us. But I am encouraged by the level of public support for doing something about it. I am encouraged by the fact that on other occasions, Australia has faced enormous problems of this magnitude and it has been able to respond effectively. If we continue to have the co-operation of State and Federal governments of both political persuasions, indeed, of all political persuasions; of the various welfare organisations, many of whom are represented here today; and also of individuals within the community who have been affected by this issue and touched by it, then I think we really can make a difference.

"Tough on Drugs" is about trying to help the people who are addicted to drugs, understanding in a compassionate way, the emotional devastation that that brings to their families. It is about opposing, in the most unrelenting fashion, the criminal behaviour of those who seek to profit from it. It is about providing decent treatment for people who want treatment. It is about educating in a quite uncompromising, uncomplicated way, our young against the dangers of drug taking, and that is tremendously important. It is about doing all of those things. It is not about one to the exclusion of the other. It is not about one in priority to the other two. It is about a three-pronged approach – education, law enforcement, treatment. They are the three things that we have to balance in our campaign against drugs and I hope that today's announcement has made an important practical contribution to realising that goal.

# Defending what is Right

## INTERFET (East Timor) Welcome Home Parade
## Sydney – 19 April 2000

Reflecting on his prime ministership in 2010, John Howard cited Australia's liberation of East Timor as one of his Government's greatest achievements. Supporting the small, former Portuguese province's struggle for independence from Indonesia in the late 1990s proved a complicated issue for the Howard Government, especially in light of Australia's interests in maintaining cooperative relations with Indonesia.

While President B.J. Habibie of Indonesia had announced in January 1999 that East Timor would be offered the choice of immediate independence, the tumultuous journey of the province towards nationhood was fraught with civil unrest and violence from pro-Indonesian militia groups. After the people of East Timor voted overwhelmingly for full independence in a referendum in August 1999, the turmoil escalated to the point where the United Nations deemed it necessary to send peace-keeping forces to bring order to the emerging nation.

After talks with the UN, the Howard Government agreed to send an INTERFET peace-keeping force of Australian troops to East Timor under the Command of Major-General Peter Cosgrove. This decision was widely supported by the Australian public who took great pride in the pre-eminent role their nation played in liberating the people of East Timor. Conscious of indifferent treatment of Vietnam War veterans, Howard pledged that the troops who had served in East Timor would be welcomed home as patriots. At this welcome home parade in Sydney for Australia's INTERFET forces, the Prime Minister expressed the nation's gratitude for the role they played in bringing peace, stability and freedom to the fledgling nation. In so doing, he said they had continued the great Australian tradition of fighting for freedom and peace.

Today is an opportunity in a very public fashion for a group of Australians to express their thanks, their gratitude and their respect to the men and women of the Australian Defence Force, as well as the men and women of the Australian Federal Police, for the remarkable job that they did in bringing peace, stability and freedom to the people of East Timor.

In doing what they did, they followed in a great Australian military tradition – a tradition that does not seek to impose the will of this country on others, but rather to defend what is right and to uphold the opportunity of people to live in freedom and in peace. Of all the great privileges that have come my way as prime minister of this great country of ours, none has been more moving and more important than the opportunity I had to say goodbye to the men and women who were going to East Timor, understandably feeling a sense of trepidation and concern about the future, but nonetheless determined and resolved in a quiet professional way to do their duty by their profession and by their country. Then the further opportunity to visit them in Dili and elsewhere in East Timor, to see the magnificent way in which they interacted with the people of East Timor and the quiet professionalism that they were displaying.

So can I say on behalf of everybody gathered, to the men and women who served Australia so well, who went abroad not in the name of one particular point of view in Australia, but went abroad in the name of Australia, representing all of us, to do a duty, to pursue a mission, to protect the people and to bring peace in accordance with the great traditions for which Australia stands.

To you, Major-General Cosgrove,[25] for your splendid inspiring command, you have won the respect and the affection of the entire nation. To

---

[25] Peter Cosgrove was an army officer and Vietnam War veteran who, as a major-general, led INTERFET in a peace keeping mission to East Timor in 1999.

Superintendent Alan Blake, and Superintendent Donovan of the Australian Federal Police, you should also feel very content and proud of the tremendous role that you discharged in great danger and in accordance with the best traditions of the professional police force to which you belong.

This is a proud day, not only for the people of Sydney, but also for the people of Australia. We say thank you to the men and women of our forces for a magnificent job done in our name which has brought great credit to you and, through you, great credit to our nation.

# Showcasing Everything Good about Australia

## House of Representatives, Canberra – 3 October 2000

In 1993, Australia had won the right to host the 2000 Olympic Games, the XXVII Olympiad, in Sydney. It was the second time that Australia had hosted the Games, the previous occasion being Melbourne in 1956. Featuring glittering opening and closing ceremonies, the Sydney Games took place from 15 September to 1 October 2000 with teams from 199 countries competing. The host nation performed well, winning 58 medals in a well-received tournament that attracted universal acclaim from around Australia and the world.

As Prime Minister, John Howard was an enthusiastic supporter of the Sydney Games, frequently attending numerous events to cheer on the home side. Two days after the closing ceremony, the Prime Minister rose in the House of Representatives to reflect on the nation's pride in hosting the 2000 Olympics. He remarked on how the sportsmanship of Australia's athletes and the dedication of the Olympic volunteers had brought great credit to the nation. Paying tribute to the efforts of all those involved in the successful staging of the Games, he acknowledged that they had "showcased everything that was good about Australia".

I do not think there is any doubt that the entire nation feels a great sense of pride with what has occurred over the past 2½ weeks. I think we can best sum up the national mood by saying that these Games have brought enormous credit to the entire nation. The people who, above all, have made the Games a great success are the people who have been mentioned in this motion.

But, above and beyond that, I think we should acknowledge, as the elected representatives of the Australian people, the enormous contribution made to the success of the Games by the attitude and the spirit of the entire Australian nation during the currency of the Games, because on display throughout the entirety of the Olympic Games was the sportsmanlike spirit of all Australians. Australians cheered endlessly for competitors from all Australian teams and, when Australians were competing in individual sports, on no occasion were there any displays of bad sportsmanship in relation to victories by athletes from other countries or teams representing other nations.

I think it reflects very great credit on the people of Australia—no one section but on all the people of Australia—that there should have been such a sportsmanlike approach. I would especially like to record the respect and admiration I have, and I know that all Australians have, for the members of the Australian Olympic team. It was without doubt the most successful team across a range of sports of all the teams that Australia has sent to the Olympic Games. Australia is one of only three countries since 1896 to be a consistent participant in the Games. Across a whole range of sports, Australia had very strong representation in these Games and a very wide range of success.

I would like to congratulate, as the motion does, all of those associated with the organisation of the Games and particularly the members of the Sydney Organising Committee for the Olympic Games. I record, in that context, my congratulations to the chairman of that committee, Mr Knight. I also record my congratulations to the Minister for Finance and Administration [John Fahey] and to the member for Cook [Bruce Baird] for the role they played in winning the Olympic bid back in 1993. I also record my congratulations to the member for Lindsay, the Minister for Sport and Tourism and the minister who so ably assisted me in the build-up to the Olympic Games.

Most importantly of all, I congratulate the people who were involved in the Games: the athletes, the organisers, the volunteers and those responsible for the design and the construction of the facilities; all of them deserve the respect and the thanks of the Australian people and of this Parliament.

It was a great event. It showcased everything that was good about Australia: our openness, our friendliness, our sense of fun in sport and relaxation, and our capacity to compete very strongly and very effectively on the sporting field and in other sporting arenas. No person who visited Australia during the Games went away with other than a very positive and powerful impression of the modernity, the sophistication, the capability, the friendship, the good humour and the hospitable disposition of the Australian people.

All of us, whatever our politics are, whatever our sporting tastes may be, and even those of us who have no disposition towards following sport, no matter who you are, have every right as Australians to feel very proud of what has been done and of what has been achieved. I think we should in a very unconditional, open-hearted, bipartisan fashion convey through this motion our immense respect for those who made this possible, our gratitude to the athletes, our thanks to the volunteers and a sense of well-deserved pride and satisfaction at what our nation has done and the credit it has won in the eyes of the world.

# A Massive Assault on Free Men and Women

## House of Representatives
## Canberra – 17 September 2001

On the morning of 11 September 2001, John Howard was in Washington as part of an official visit to the United States to mark the 50th anniversary of the historic Australia, New Zealand and United States (ANZUS) Treaty. As the Prime Minister took his customary morning stroll on what was a sparkling autumn morning in the United States capital, he heard word of the shocking terrorist attacks on the World Trade Center towers in New York; the Pentagon in Washington was attacked shortly afterwards. After emergency briefings with the acting Australian Prime Minister, John Anderson, Howard immediately dictated a letter to US President, George W. Bush, expressing "Australia's resolute solidarity with the American people at this most tragic time".

Having felt especially privileged to have been in the capital of the United States to convey, personally, the sympathy and support of the Australian people, the Prime Minister, while returning to Australia, invoked the ANZUS Treaty. Shortly afterwards, on 17 September, he moved a motion in the House of Representatives to express Australia's sympathy and support for the United States. Speaking on the motion, he decried the terrorist attacks as "a massive assault" on the values of the free world and observed that they had "touched many Australian homes" with grief and sadness. Again, he affirmed Australia's unbreakable friendship and soli-

darity with the American people as they came to terms
with the enormity of this tragedy on their home soil.

In the 27 years that I have been privileged to be a member of this Parliament, I can think of no more sombre occasion than the circumstances under which this House meets today. We have had tragedies of a national and international kind before. We have been touched by the poignancy of the deaths of people. We have confronted significant moral and national challenges, but none matches in depth, scale and magnitude the consequences of what the world must now do in response to the terrible events in the United States.

In sheer scale, the death and destruction are almost incomprehensible in a time not regarded as a time of war. It would appear that more than double the number of Americans who died at Pearl Harbor have died in New York City and Washington as a result of these terrorist attacks. The death toll could easily be more than the entire American battle losses on the first day of the Normandy invasion in June of 1944. They dwarf, of course, the terrible loss inflicted by Timothy McVeigh's act of madness on the federal building in Oklahoma some six or seven years ago. So it is in every sense a tragedy and an obscenity of an appalling and repugnant magnitude.

It goes beyond the death so cruelly inflicted without warning, without justification and without any skerrick of moral authority on innocent people merely going about their daily lives; its context represents a massive assault on the values not only of the United States of America but also of this country – the values of free men and women and of decent people and decent societies around the world. It is an act of terror. It is an act which is repugnant to all of the things that we as a society believe in. On occasions like this, those things that divide us in this Parliament, those things that we might bicker and quarrel over as a people, as we go about our lives, are so suddenly and so quickly put into perspective.

I remember the morning in Washington – as the House knows, I had been in the United States. I had been for an early morning walk. It was a beautiful Washington morning— there was just a touch of autumn. I had walked past the Lincoln Memorial and many of the other great memorials of that great nation which stood between us and tyranny on one critical occasion in our history. I, like millions of other Australians, was deeply moved and distressed. I felt an enormous sense of empathy towards the American people who had suffered this awful deed.

Out of that tragedy have come, as always, great stories of the spirit and the heroism of men and women in circumstances of disaster and tragedy. As much as we are devastated and distressed by what has happened, and as much as we feel repelled by the belief that there should be people on our Earth who would want to plot for years to undertake such attacks, as always the events that followed these attacks have given us a source of great hope and faith in the resilient spirit of men and women who face moral and physical danger and challenge. The stories of heroism that have come out of these events are a tribute to the spirit of the American people and a tribute to the spirit of resilient men and women around the world. Who will ever forget the story of that wonderful Father Mychal Judge, the chaplain of the New York Police Department, who remained behind to deliver the last rites of the Catholic Church to a dying fireman, or the immense courage of those three people on the plane that crashed in Pittsburgh who, knowing they faced certain death, decided to tackle the terrorists in the cockpit, perhaps averting even further destruction being rained on either Washington or New York?

As we struggle as Australians and as we struggle as citizens of the world to come to terms with what has happened, it is certain, as others have said, that the world has changed. We are all diminished, we are all changed, and we are all rather struggling with the concept that it will never be quite the same again. This is no isolated act of terrorism: this is the product of years of careful planning, it is the product of evil minds and it is the product of an attitude of a group of people who in every sense invoke those very evocative words of Winston Churchill when he said that those responsible for the Nazi occupation of Europe should be regarded in their brutish hour of triumph as the moral outcasts of mankind.

This is a tragedy which has touched many Australian homes. There is grief and sadness in hundreds of Australian homes at present. The sheer scale of the loss of life suffered by our American friends has perhaps dwarfed the realisation that up to 80 or 90 Australians have lost their lives. There will be many in this House who will know somebody or who will know the family of somebody who died in New York or in Washington. Moreover, we will know people who, simply as a result of the lottery of life, escaped death. In my own case it is a former Treasury official and economic adviser of mine employed by Morgan Stanley, a firm which had 3 500 employees in that building. But for the happy circumstance for him of being on parental leave for the birth of his second child, he would have been in the building. Two hundred of his work mates are yet unaccounted for. That story can be repeated time without number.

The number of Australians who have died is a reminder of just how interconnected we all are. This attack has brought home to us many things. It has brought home to us the global character of our world. I suppose in their evil disposition those who launched this attack had that precisely in mind. When you think about it, it was an outrage to attack buildings in a city which is a monument to inclusion. There is no more multiracial city in the world; there is no city in the world that has more generously welcomed people from around the globe than the city of New York. When you go through those poignant photographs of those who died, so many of them tragically young, you have white faces and black faces; you have smiling Irish-American faces, you have Asian faces and you have Hispanic faces; you have bearded faces and you have clean-shaven faces. I have no doubt that amongst those who died were many Americans of the Islamic faith, and that is an issue to which I will return in a moment.

In the wake of this tragedy, we express our unstinted admiration for those who risked their lives. The tragedy upon tragedy of an event like this is that people such as firemen and policemen, whose sworn duty in life is to help others, often in the process risk their own lives and pay a greater price.

The world will think and ponder and react in different ways. In reacting to what has occurred, it is important to do so with calm and steely determination. Justice, decency and humanity require that no effort be spared to bring to justice and to punish unconditionally those who have been responsible for these deeds. Because I was in Washington I had the opportunity to express immediately to the US administration the willingness of the Australian Government to work with the Americans in responding. I take the opportunity of thanking the Leader of the Opposition for the way in which he has associated the Australian Labor Party with the response that I have made to the administration.

These events do bear very much upon the relationship between our two great societies. The World Trade Center itself was a centre for many activities and many activities in which Australians and Americans worked together, and it is therefore with symbolic as well as practical resonance that any response that is undertaken, if we are asked and within the limit of our capability, will have the involvement of the United States.

I did have the opportunity when I was in Washington the day after the attack to visit Congress to hear the resolution passed by the House of Representatives and then to go onto the floor of the Senate and particularly to personally extend my condolences to Senator Clinton and Senator Schumer, the two Democrat senators representing the State of New York in the United States Senate. The bonds between our two nations run very strong and very deep. They present themselves and manifest themselves in many ways, but none more so than in our shared commitment to liberty, our shared commitment to peace.

The President said a few days ago that the American people are peaceful people. So, indeed, are we. We have a great peace-loving tradition. Also, when we think of our military tradition, we think of it not in terms of seeking to inflict our views and our will on others but rather seeking, when required, to stand up and fight for the things that we really believe in. Standing up and fighting for the things that we believe in over the months and perhaps the years ahead in the wake of these terrible events will require perseverance. There is united, righteous, deep, seething anger around the world at present. But, as the months go by and as perhaps the early dividends of retaliatory action

133

are not ready and not apparent, some of that anger may subside; and some may argue that the extra miles that are required to be travelled are not really worth it. But, if those who died last Tuesday are not, in the judgment of history, to have died in vain, there is an obligation on all of us to persevere, to travel the distance, to persist and to root out the evil that brought about those terrible deeds.

But, in the process of responding, we must do so with care as well as with lethal force. We should understand that barbarism has no ethnicity and evil has no religion. Both around the world and within our own society, we should take pause lest we engage in the evil of scapegoating individual groups within our society. I have said on a number of occasions that I know that my fellow Australians of Islamic faith are overwhelmingly as appalled about what happened as I am, as an inadequately practising Christian. This is an assault on values common to all the great religions of the world, and it is also an assault on the values of many people who profess no religion.

I say to my fellow Australians of Islamic faith or of Middle Eastern descent that I extend to you the hand of friendship. You are part of our great society; you are part of the fabric of the great, decent, freedom-loving, fair-minded Australian nation; and you are as entitled to share my outrage, my sorrow, my anger and my sadness as are others within our community – because wouldn't it be a terrible, tragic, obscene irony if in responding, however we do it as individuals or as nations, to these terrible terrorist attacks we forsook the very things that we believed had been assaulted last Tuesday in New York?

It has been said many times in the wake of these attacks that words are inadequate to express how you feel. Nobody is ever really prepared for personal tragedy. Nobody is ever really prepared for the sudden death of a wife, a husband, a son, a daughter, a sibling or another loved one, or a close friend. No nation is ever ready or ever prepared to respond to a tragedy of this order and of this magnitude and, in the end, the quality of our people and the quality of our society will be judged by how we respond: we will be judged very harshly in the eyes of those left bereaved by the people who died if we do not respond effectively and to the full measure of our capability but we will be also judged very critically if we respond in a careless or an indiscriminate fashion.

Finally, the experience of being in the American capital at the time enabled me to feel a sense of the despair and the desolation of the American people but also a sense of their great spirit, their great resilience, their great faith and the depth of their belief in the inherent decency of their society. The wonderful words spoken by the United States Ambassador at the memorial service earlier today beautifully evoked the spirit of a people who have carried heavy burdens, a people who have suffered a great deal and a people who have been joined to this country in every major conflict of the last 100 years.

In every way, the attack on New York and Washington and the circumstances surrounding it did constitute an attack upon the metropolitan territory of the United States of America within the provisions of articles IV and V of the ANZUS Treaty. If that treaty means anything, if our debt as a nation to the people of the United States in the darkest days of World War II means anything, if the comradeship, the friendship and the common bonds of democracy and a belief in liberty, fraternity and justice mean anything, it means that the ANZUS Treaty applies and that the ANZUS Treaty is properly invoked.

As a proud, patriotic Australian, I was literally moved to tears by what occurred in the United States. I was filled with admiration for the spirit of the American people. I can with genuine affection and fondness say that their behaviour in the wake of those events and their determination to respond appropriately, to heal the wounds and to help those who mourn and grieve demonstrates very powerfully that the American people do live, in the words of their wonderful national anthem, "in the land of the free and the home of the brave".

# We Gather Here in Sorrow

## Bali, Indonesia – 17 October 2002

On 12 October 2002, the buzzing tourist district of Kuta on the Indonesian island of Bali suffered a terrorist attack. Members of the violent Islamist group, Jema'ah Islamiya, had detonated three bombs near the popular Paddy's Pub and Sari nightclub, killing 202 people including 88 Australians. Given the proximity of the attack to Australian shores and the high number of Australian casualties, the tragedy shook the nation with widespread reactions of shock and mourning.

Acutely touched by this national grief, the Prime Minister travelled to Bali and delivered this heartfelt and poignant speech at the Australian Consulate. After denouncing the wanton barbarity of the terrorist attacks, he expressed Australia's solidarity and empathy with the Balinese people reeling from the enormity of this attack on their own soil. With generations of young Australians flocking each year to revel in the island paradise of Bali, the Prime Minister appreciated the depth of mutual goodwill between the two peoples and this was something he desired to nurture and strengthen in the wake of the tragedy. Refusing to yield in the face of terrorism, the Prime Minister defiantly affirmed that "the Australian spirit would not be broken" and that it would continue to reach out to the nations of the world in a spirt of peace and cooperation.

As the sun sets over this beautiful island, we gather here in sorrow, in anguish, in disbelief and in pain. There are no words that I can summon to solve in any way the hurt and the suffering and the pain being felt by so many of my fellow countrymen and women and by so many of the citizens of other nations. I can say, though, to my Australian countrymen and women that there are 19.5 million Australians who are trying, however inadequately, to feel for you and to support you at this time of unbearable grief and pain.

The wanton, cruel, barbaric character of what occurred here last Saturday night has shocked our nation to the core. I know the anguish that so many are feeling, the painful process of identification which has prolonged that agony for so many, the sense of bewilderment and disbelief that so many young lives with so much before them should have been taken away in such blind fury, hatred and violence.

I can on behalf of all of the people of Australia declare to you that we will do everything in our power to bring to justice those who were responsible for this foul deed. We will work with our friends in Indonesia to do that and we will work with others to achieve an outcome of justice.

Can I say to our Balinese friends, the lovely people of Bali, who have been befriended over the decades and the generations by so many Australians who have come here, we grieve with you, we feel for you, we thank you from the bottom of our hearts for the love and support that you have extended to our fellow countrymen and women over these past days.

As the Chaplain said, there will be scars left on people for the rest of their lives, both physical and emotional. Our nation has been changed by this event. Perhaps we may not be so carefree as we have been in the past, but we will never lose our openness, our sense of adventure. The young of Australia will always travel. They will always seek fun in distant parts. They will always reach out to the young of other nations. They will always be open, fun-loving, decent men and women.

So as we grapple inadequately and, in despair, try to comprehend what has happened, let us gather ourselves around each other. Let us wrap our arms around not only our fellow Australians but our arms around the people of Indonesia, of Bali. Let us wrap our arms around the people of other nations and the friends and relatives of the nationals of other countries who have died in this horrible event.

It will take a long time for these foul deeds to be seen in any kind of context. They can never be understood. They can never be excused.

Australia has been affected very deeply, but the Australian spirit has not been broken. The Australian spirit will remain strong and free and open and tolerant. I know that is what all of those who lost their lives would have wanted and I know it is what all of those who grieve for them would want.

# Dealing with a Dictatorship of a Particularly Horrific Kind

## Address to the Nation – 20 March 2003

As Australia prepared to join the Americans and the British in the military operation against Saddam Hussein in March 2003, the Prime Minister addressed the nation in what he described later as "the most controversial foreign affairs action" of his government. Well aware that his decision to commit Australian forces to a US-led coalition was deeply unpopular amongst sections of the community, with many naturally fearing the likelihood of human casualties and the international repercussions of such an action, he nonetheless affirmed that the strike on Iraq to topple the regime was a legitimate and justifiable act of anticipatory self-defence against future assault. Given the Iraqi regime's brutality towards its own citizens, its track-record of regional aggression, its support for global terrorist activities and its violation of past UN Security Council resolutions, the Prime Minister believed it was beyond reasonable doubt that the rogue regime possessed weapons of mass destruction that needed to be summarily dealt with to avert any future catastrophic strike.

In this televised address to the nation, he told the Australian people that such weapons would pose a direct, undeniable and lethal threat to Australia and its people. For this reason, Australia needed to act in Iraq to prevent the spread of chemical and biological weapons. In addition to ensuring the safety of Australia and the free world, the removal of Saddam Hussein would also lift the burden of terror from the Iraqi people who had suffered so much under his dictatorship. Whilst admitting that it was a difficult decision for the Government, he told his fellow Australians that it was ultimately good for Australia's "long term security and the cause of a safer world".

The Government has decided to commit Australian forces to action to disarm Iraq because we believe it is right, it is lawful and it is in Australia's national interest.

We are determined to join other countries to deprive Iraq of its weapons of mass destruction, its chemical and biological weapons, which even in minute quantities are capable of causing death and destruction on a mammoth scale. Iraq has been an aggressor in the past against its neighbours and even its own people. If Iraq is allowed to keep these weapons not only might she use them again but, moreover, other rogue countries will copy Iraq knowing that the world will do nothing to stop them.

And the more countries that have these weapons – countries run by despotic regimes – the greater becomes the likelihood that these weapons will fall into the hands of terrorists. If that happens, can anyone doubt that the terrorists will use them whatever the cost might be?

The attacks on 11 September 2001 and in Bali showed that international terrorists have no regard for human life no matter what the nationality of their victims may be. Iraq has long supported international terrorism. Saddam Hussein pays $25 000 to each family of Palestinian suicide bombers who wreak such murderous havoc in Israel. He has sheltered and sponsored many terrorist groups.

International terrorism knows no borders. We have learnt that to our cost. Australia and Australians anywhere in the world are as much targets as any other Western country and its people. Therefore the possession of chemical, biological or, even worse still, nuclear weapons by a terrorist network would be a direct undeniable and lethal threat to Australia and its people.

That is the reason above all others why I passionately believe that action must be taken to disarm Iraq. Not only will it take dangerous weapons from that country but it will send a clear signal to other rogue States and terrorists groups like Al-Qaeda which clearly want such weapons that the world is prepared to take a stand.

There is also another reason and that is our close security alliance with the United States. The Americans have helped us in the past and the United States is very important to Australia's long-term security. It is critical that we maintain the involvement of the United States in our own region where at present there are real concerns about the dangerous behaviour of North Korea.

The relationship between our two countries will grow more rather than less important as the years go by. A key element of our close friendship with the United States and, indeed, with the British, is our full and intimate sharing of intelligence material.

In the difficult fight against the new menace of international terrorism there is nothing more crucial than timely and accurate intelligence. This is a priceless component of our relationship with our two very close allies.

There is nothing comparable to be found in any other relationship – nothing more relevant, indeed, to the challenges of the contemporary world.

I know that some people are saying that what we have done makes it more likely that terrorists will attack Australia. Australia has been a terrorist target at least since 11 September 2001.

Australia is a Western country with Western values. Nothing will or should change that. That is why we are a target. Remember that bin Laden specifically targeted Australia because of our intervention to save the people of East Timor. Does any Australian seriously suggest that if bin Laden's warning had come before the East Timor action we should have caved in and changed our policy. That will never be the Australian way.

We believe that so far from our action in Iraq increasing the terrorist threat it will, by stopping the spread of chemical and biological weapons, make it less likely that a devastating terrorist attack will be carried out against Australia.

I want to assure all of you that the action we are taking is fully legal under international law. Back in the early 1990s resolutions were passed by the Security Council authorising military action against Iraq. That action was only suspended on condition that Iraq gave up its weapons of mass destruction. Clearly we all know this has not happened. As a result the authority to take military action under those earlier resolutions has revived.

America's critics both here and abroad have been both opportunistic and inconsistent. They know and admit that weapons inspectors only returned to Iraq because of the pressure of the American military build-up. Yet they have persistently criticised American policy. Apparently they believe that a quarter of a million American, British and, indeed, Australian troops should stay in the desert doing nothing indefinitely. We all know that if the troops had been withdrawn Iraq would have immediately stopped its minimal co-operation with the inspectors.

Another point I would make to you very strongly is that we are not dealing here with a regime of ordinary brutality. There are many dictatorships in the world. But this is a dictatorship of a particularly horrific kind.

His [Saddam Hussein's] is an appalling regime: its torture, its use of rape as an instrument of intimidation, the cruelty to children to extract confessions from parents. It is a terrible catalogue of inflicting human misery on a people who deserve much better. This week, *The Times* of London detailed the use of a human shredding machine as a vehicle for putting to death critics of Saddam Hussein. This is the man, this is the apparatus of terror we are dealing with. The removal of Saddam Hussein will lift this immense burden of terror from the Iraqi people.

Our argument is with Saddam Hussein's regime. It is certainly not with Islam.

Australians of an Arab background or of the Islamic faith are a treasured part of our community. Over the weeks ahead and beyond we should all extend to them the hand of Australian mateship. To those in the community who may not agree with me, please vent your anger against me and towards the Government. Remember that our forces are on duty in the Gulf in our name and doing their job in the best traditions of Australia's Defence Forces.

Can I say something that I know will find an echo from all of you, whether or not you agree with the Government. And that is to say to the men and women of the Australian Defence Force in the Gulf – we admire you, we are thinking of you, we want all of you to come back home safe and sound. We care for and we anguish with your loved ones back here in Australia. Our prayers and our hopes are with all of you.

We now live in a world made very different by the scourge of international terrorism. This has been a very difficult decision for the Government but a decision which is good for Australia's long term security and the cause of a safer world.

# Responding Swiftly and Generously to Heartbreaking Tragedy

## Address to the Nation – 9 January 2005

On Boxing Day 2004, South Asia was rocked by one of the deadliest natural disasters in recorded human history. A severe 9.1 earthquake off the west coast of Sumatra triggered a series of devastating tsunamis, decimating entire coastal settlements and killing up to 280 000 people in fourteen countries. The country hardest hit was Indonesia, followed by Sri Lanka, India and Thailand. As Australia saw its northern neighbour suffer yet again, after the brutal terrorist attacks on Bali in October 2002, the response of both the Australian Government and the general public was swift and generous. At a time of year when Australians are typically immersed in the carefree, summer holiday fun of cricket and the beach, the nation joined the world in rallying to the plight of its tsunami-stricken neighbours with personal donations and the deployment of emergency relief efforts on the ground.

Moved by the response of his fellow Australians, the Prime Minister addressed the nation in the New Year to thank those involved in the relief efforts and to express Australia's resolve to provide practical aid and assistance to the victims of the disaster. A centrepiece of the Howard Government's response was provision of $1 billion over five years in both grants and loans to assist the Government and people of Indonesia in the immense reconstruction task that lay ahead. The Prime Minister saw the package as not only a response to a massive humanitarian crisis at hand, but a practical step in further developing the Australia-Indonesia partnership.

Tonight I want to report to you about Australia's response to the Asian tsunami disaster which has decimated the lives of so many people across the nations of our region.

More than 150,000 people have been killed, while millions more are injured or homeless. Whole communities have been washed away. And we are in a race against time to prevent further deaths from water-borne diseases such as cholera.

This has been one of the greatest natural disasters in modern history.

At this stage the final number of Australians who, tragically, have been killed or injured remains unclear. We are working as fast as possible with the identification of victims and to ascertain the whereabouts of those Australians originally reported as missing.

I know that the thoughts and prayers of you all are with those who have lost loved ones or endure the terrible agony of waiting for further news.

The response of the world community – and, not least, Australia – to this heartbreaking tragedy has been swift and generous. Along with other governments, international agencies and non-government bodies, Australians are now playing a leading role in one of the biggest humanitarian aid operations since World War II.

I express the thanks of the nation to the many Australians working night and day to provide relief to victims. I especially thank the men and women of the Australian Defence Force, officers of the Australian Federal Police and their State colleagues, medical workers, staff from the Department of Foreign Affairs and Trade and many other Australian Government departments and agencies who have come together in a great national effort. This crisis has seen the Australian Public Service working at its dedicated and professional best.

Thanks also are due to the large number of Australians working for non-government relief organisations, often as volunteers.

The Government's initial response was to provide emergency aid of $60 million and to send medical relief teams and defence personnel into badly affected areas, particularly Indonesia but also the Maldives and Sri Lanka.

A tragedy of this magnitude, however, requires a long-term commitment of resources if shattered communities are to be rebuilt and survivors provided with some hope for the future. The loss of life and destruction in Indonesia, our nearest neighbour, has been truly staggering. At least 110,000 people have lost their lives in Aceh alone. The recovery challenge facing this developing country is immense.

The Government has therefore decided to commit $1 billion over five years in both grants and highly-concessional loans to assist the Government and people of Indonesia in the mammoth task of recovery and rebuilding. This will be the largest individual aid package in Australia's history.

Under a plan to be called the Australia-Indonesia Partnership for Reconstruction and Development, this $1 billion amount will go directly to areas of need through programmes that must be approved by the Australian Government, in conjunction with the Government of Indonesia. This process will ensure that resources go where they are most needed.

As well as being the right response to an immediate humanitarian crisis, this Partnership is an historic step in Australian-Indonesian relations. Australians were the first foreigners on the ground in Indonesia after the disaster – a fact gratefully acknowledged by President Yudhoyono during our recent meeting in Jakarta. We will stay as long as we are needed.

Our nation will continue to help other affected countries. For example, Australian police officers are playing a leading role in identifying victims in Thailand and arrangements are in hand to send school teachers to the Maldives and scientific experts to help in repairing the damage to that country's coral reef system.

The spontaneous outpouring of generosity from individual Australians in the last two weeks should be a source of pride to us all. Well in excess of $100 million has been pledged by individuals and companies in a great expression of the decency and good heart of the people of our nation.

The events of last Boxing Day and their aftermath have brought tragic loss and grief to many Australians. We have all been touched in different ways. Next Sunday, the 16th of January, will be a national day of mourning and reflection for the victims of the tsunami. I ask all Australians to mark this occasion in the way they think fit.

This catastrophe has brought the world closer together in a spirit of common humanity. It has been a brutal reminder of the force of nature but also of the inspiring capacity of mankind to ease the suffering of others in their hour of need.

Australia, in its distinctive practical way, will remain in the forefront of helping those who have lost and suffered so much.

# Making Every Drop Count

## Great Hall, Parliament House
## Canberra – 25 January 2007

Recognising the long-term implications of climate change for a warm, dry and drought-prone continent such as Australia, John Howard believed that practical new policy measures were essential for the nation to rise to this challenge. In particular, the Prime Minister argued that Australia needed to rethink its water policy and how this most precious resource could be harnessed for the benefit of the nation's primary industries and food supply. To this end, the Prime Minister and his government had established the National Water Commission to help formulate water policy. One of the Commission's primary tasks was to advise on the allocation of a $2 billion water fund established by the Federal Government for investment in water use and conservation projects, largely put forward by the States, on a shared-funding basis.

Drawing on the work of the Commission and identifying the Murray-Darling as one of Australia's pre-eminent river systems and sources of fresh water, the Prime Minister devised what became known as the "Murray-Darling Rescue Plan". In this address at the National Press Club to launch the landmark initiative, Howard announced that the Commonwealth would spend some $10 billon over a number of years to improve water efficiency and to address the over-allocation of water in rural Australia, particularly in the Murray-Darling Basin. As part of the project, the Government would embark on the largest modernisation of irrigation infrastructure, both on and off-farm, ever undertaken in Australia's history. For the Prime Minister, this policy was all about Australia taking the necessary action to overcome the handicap of drought so it could emerge as a global supplier of food and raw materials in the coming decades.

Today I want to address in a very direct and detailed fashion one of the great challenges of our time and that is water security....

Water has always been at the very heart of the existence of the Australian nation. It influenced the life and the activity of the first Australians. It determined that the British settlement would occur at Port Jackson rather than at Botany Bay, and the great Federation drought of 1892 through to the early part of the next century inspired Dorothea Mackellar to pen those immortal words about droughts and flooding rains. As we grew and prospered as a nation after World War II, we placed heavy demands on our water resources, but that was a time when we invested heavily in infrastructure.

We built the great Snowy Mountains Scheme, we invested heavily in dams and other ways of ensuring that our water resources were there and were available. But, by the time of the 1980s, policies began to change. Governments, for a combination of reasons, in some cases of misguided implementation of environmental policies, became reluctant to invest in construction of water conservation infrastructure, particularly dams. And that created understandable concern about the availability of water to look after us in the years ahead.

In the last decade or so, we have begun to turn this around. Billions of dollars both at the State and a Federal level have been set aside for individual projects. Our own $2 billion Water Fund is leveraging major investments in every State. And through the Living Murray Initiative, we are on the way to restoring six iconic environmental sites in our greatest river system. And with the National Water Initiative, a long-term framework is finally in place to increase the efficiency of water use, to service the needs of communities, and to return our river and groundwater systems to environmental health.

Despite this, the current trajectory of water use and management in Australia is not sustainable. In a protracted drought, and with the

149

prospect of long-term climate change, we need radical and permanent change. I regard myself as a climate change realist. That means looking at the evidence as it emerges and responding with policies that preserve Australia's competitiveness and play to her strengths.

There does appear to have been a contraction to the south in the weather systems which traditionally brought southern Australia its winter and spring rains. Our rainfall has always been highly variable. The deviation around average rainfall is enormous. And it seems to be getting bigger. We need, so to speak, to make every drop count, on our farms, in our factories and in our homes. Our water management systems must be geared not to a world of steady averages that rarely materialise, but to the variability that has been part of Australia's climate since time immemorial.

Water solutions will vary from place to place. The truth is, as I said last July [2006], we have the capacity to drought-proof our large cities. What is needed is more investment, sensible pricing and an end to State governments using water utilities as cash cows. Our water scarcity problems are bigger in rural Australia given the drought and unsustainable water use in many places.

Against this backdrop, I announce today a $10 billion, 10-point plan on a national scale to improve water efficiency and to address the over-allocation of water in rural Australia, particularly in the Murray-Darling Basin.

The plan has the following quite specific elements:

- Number one, a nationwide investment in Australia's irrigation infrastructure to line and pipe major delivery channels.
- Number two, a nationwide programme to improve on-farm irrigation technology and metering.
- Number three, and very importantly, the sharing of water savings on a 50/50 basis between irrigators and the Commonwealth, leading to greater water security and increased environmental flows.
- Number four, addressing, once and for all, water over-allocation in the Murray-Darling Basin.

- Fifth, a new set of governance arrangements for the Basin.
- Number six, a sustainable cap on surface and groundwater use in the Basin.
- Number seven, major engineering works at key sites in the Murray-Darling Basin such as the Barmah Choke and Menindee Lakes.
- Number eight, expanding the role of the Bureau of Meteorology to provide the water data necessary for good decision-making by governments and industry.
- Number nine, a taskforce to explore future land and water development in Northern Australia.
- Finally, completion of the restoration of the Great Artesian Basin.

This 10-point plan opens a new chapter of national water management in Australia. It is a large but prudent investment, especially given the importance to Australia of the Murray-Darling Basin, and the scale of the water crisis that confronts it. The Basin accounts for the vast bulk of irrigated agricultural production in Australia and roughly 85 per cent of our irrigation water use. It has a population of two million people, and another one million people in South Australia are heavily dependent on the system for their water.

The last five years have been the driest in the Basin since records began. As a result, the operation of the River Murray remains, in the words of the Commission, on a "knife-edge". In 2006, the inflows into the Murray were only 40 per cent of the previous all-time low. Water security will remain an enormous challenge in the Basin. Indeed, it could get worse.

The CSIRO estimates that by 2020, average annual flows could decline by about 15 per cent due to climate change, recovery from bushfire, farm dam and plantation expansion and increasing use of groundwater. All parties must recognise that the old way of managing the Murray-Darling Basin has reached its use-by date. The tyranny of incrementalism and the lowest common denominator must end.

I will therefore be writing to all relevant State and territory leaders requesting that they refer to the Commonwealth their powers of water management over the Murray-Darling Basin. The $10 billion plan I have just outlined will only work if the governance arrangements for the Basin are put on a proper national footing. The proposal is conditional on this occurring.

In a normal year, irrigated agriculture uses about 14,000 gigalitres of water, that is roughly 70 per cent of all water used in Australia. This water is not used as efficiently as it should be. A huge amount, up to 30 per cent, is lost transporting the water, through leakage, seepage and evaporation.

To increase the efficiency of water use, and to maximise future water security, the Government will embark on the largest modernisation of irrigation infrastructure, both on- and off-farm, ever undertaken in Australia's history.

At a cost of almost $6 billion, works will include the lining or piping of major delivery channels, improved metering and the installation of drip systems. When complete, these investments should save more than 3,000 gigalitres of water – equivalent to an efficiency gain of more than 20 per cent in Australia's irrigated water use, or about 17 times the city of Adelaide's annual water use.

Many of our largest irrigation districts – such as Murray, Murrumbidgee and Goulburn-Murray irrigation areas – offer significant potential for water savings. Districts such as the Burdekin in Queensland and Harvey Irrigation Area in Western Australia will also be able to significantly improve the efficiency of water use.

The Commonwealth will be contributing about $3 billion to this phase of our plan, with irrigation companies expected to contribute $750 million. 50 per cent of the water savings will be retained by irrigators and 50 per cent held by the Commonwealth will go to enhancing water security and to sustaining river systems and wetlands. We also need a radical transformation in on-farm water efficiency. At the moment, up to 20 per cent of water delivered to the farm gate may be lost in on-farm distribution channels. And roughly 10 to 15 per cent of water applied to crops is lost through over-watering.

The Government will invest $1.5 billion nation-wide to raise on-farm water efficiency. Farmers will be expected to provide significant contributions to achieve a step-change in on-farm technology. This will lift the productivity of large parts of our farm sector through the ability to deliver water on demand and better match water application to crop needs. A further $225 million will be invested in accurate meters at the farm gate to increase transparency of use within irrigation systems.

To accrue the benefits of this multi-billion dollar infrastructure investment, farmers and irrigators will need to meet strict new conditions. These include full compliance with the National Water Initiative, acceptance of mandated metering standards, including the metering of all bores and a new metered regime for stock and domestic use in priority catchments and acceptance of an enforceable regime on the building of new farm dams.

To complement these measures, the Government will invest a further $500 million to improve the efficiency and effectiveness of river operations and storages. This is especially important in the Murray-Darling Basin where large-scale engineering works are required to improve water use efficiency and water trading options. At the Barmah Choke, for example, there is an urgent need to alleviate channel capacity constraints to enable more effective delivery of irrigation and environmental water, a fact acknowledged only two days ago Mr John Thwaites, the Deputy Premier of Victoria.

As well as improving water efficiency, we need to confront head on and in a comprehensive way, the over-allocation of water in the Murray-Darling Basin. We must strike a sustainable balance between the demands of agriculture, industry and towns, on the one hand, and the needs of the environment on the other.

Therefore I announce that the Government will allocate up to $3 billion to adjust water entitlements in the Murray-Darling Basin. This is the Commonwealth assuming responsibility for a problem created by the States. We are willing to address the chronic over-allocation of water in the Basin and to carry the entire cost of doing so....

Governments have a role in helping communities adjust, but we must also make sure that we have strong, efficient markets to continue this process once a sustainable base of water allocations has been established.

Australia has an enormous opportunity if we take the right action now to expand our role as a global supplier of food and fibre in coming decades. We live in an increasingly urbanised world whose population is expected to reach 8 billion people by 2030. These people will continue to demand food and clothing....

Australia's water scarcity problem also requires that we measure our water resources and our usage of them far more accurately. You cannot manage what you cannot measure. At the moment in Australia, water information is dispersed across more than 100 agencies. To facilitate more accurate and timely water decisions, I announce today that a sum of $480 million will be invested in a significant upgrade in the role of the Bureau of Meteorology. And that will provide comprehensive water resource assessments, rigorous and nationally-consistent water usage measurements, greatly improved access to water information and much greater independence and transparency.

Armed with better information, we will be able to make sensible long-term decisions for future land and water use and, not for the first time in our history, water scarcity in southern Australia has spurred interest in further developing the water resources of northern Australia....

Today I have outlined the biggest and most costly and boldest plan to tackle Australia's rural water challenge. 70 per cent of Australia's water is consumed in rural Australia. We cannot solve the problems unless we do two things. We invest heavily and on an unprecedented scale in irrigation infrastructure, both on and off farm, and we have the courage as well as the financial commitment to tackle the problem of over-allocation. The plan I have outlined today is detailed, it is costed. It has been in preparation for some time, it represents a fundamental response to the greatest environmental challenge of our time and that is of water security.

It is conditional upon improving the governance arrangements. But we do not come to this debate unwilling to commit the financial resources of the Commonwealth. Those financial resources are available because, let me remind you, in a sense concluding where I began, they are available because of the sound economic management of the past decade which has taken this country out of debt, into surplus, which has delivered us the most consistently strong economy that we have had since World War II, a generationally low level of unemployment and a sense that optimism and hope that about the future that imbues the whole country.

Tackling Australia's water security is an immense challenge. It requires a comprehensive, bold plan. It requires a commitment of resources and, above all, requires people to think as Australians above any other parochial identification or consideration.

I commend this plan not only to you and to my fellow Australians, but I commend this plan to all of those around the nation who have responsibility in government. This is our great opportunity to fix a great national problem. It can only be solved if we surmount our parochial differences, it can only be realised if, above all, we think, as we should on the eve of Australia Day, overwhelmingly as Australians.

# IV

# Building a Stronger Economy

## Economic and Industrial Relations Reform

# Waterfront Reform

## Sydney – 3 April 1998

Notwithstanding his reputation as a traditionalist, particularly on social and cultural matters, John Howard was also a keen reformer and moderniser who affirmed the necessity for change to make Australia's economy more open, productive and prosperous. This formed the context of a major address, marking the second anniversary of his Government's election, to the New South Wales Division of the Liberal Party,

For Prime Minister Howard, there were few areas where reform was more needed than the Australian waterfront which he saw as beholden to archaic industrial relations arrangements that had stymied Australia's export performance and economic growth. He diagnosed Australia's wharves as "notoriously deficient". According to one operator, the ports of Melbourne were only 39.9 per cent as efficient as Antwerp and 66 per cent as efficient as Auckland.

After discussions with responsible ministers, John Sharp (Transport) and Peter Reith (Employment and Workplace Relations), the Prime Minister proposed reforms to the Australian waterfront to bring it into line with international competitive standards. These would entail an end to compulsory unionism; giving operators power to manage their own enterprises and breaking the monopoly of the powerful waterfront union, the Maritime Union of Australia (MUA). Despite fierce resistance from unions, the reforms prevailed and their boost to Australia's export capacity soon became apparent. Container movements per hour on the waterfront improved from 17.6 in 1998 to 27.5 by 2003. The

Prime Minister observed that as a result of the reforms, "many of the old and odious work practices had been eliminated, productivity levels were markedly higher and waterfront remuneration more in line with community averages". For Howard, the achievement of a more efficient and productive waterfront was a critical breakthrough in maximising Australia's export performance and economic growth.

… I came into the prime ministership and my Government came into office with a number of quite basic guiding principles. I have always had a strong personal philosophy about the quality of government in this country that essentially says that the art of good statecraft as we come towards the end of this century and approach the third Christian millennium, the art of good statecraft is really to strike a balance between preserving those values of our past and those values of our culture and our history that continue to serve us well and continue to remain relevant for our future, and to be willing to defend those values and those cultures with great tenacity. But, by the same token, to be ready to challenge and to change, fundamentally if necessary, those practices and those attitudes that really have no place in the future Australia that we want to build into the 21st century....

Just as I believe that there are many things about Australia that have been part of our past, that we should fight with passion to defend as we go into the future, there are some things about our past that we should fight to get rid of because they are holding us back. One of those things is the industrial relations system which has its origins back in pre-World War I days, built on some rather unsound notions, coming out of the decision of the old Arbitration Court in the now almost infamous Harvester case. Over the years, that award-driven system has weakened Australia economically and one of the things we resolved to do in 1996 was to change that forever. At first, some of the changes we made were seen with suspicion, even by some of our friends and supporters as perhaps not going far enough, as perhaps being weaker than they would have liked.

But those critics were wrong and those suspicions were misplaced because we have brought about fundamental change in the industrial relations area and we have been able to do it without industrial turmoil. We were told before the last election that if we tried to do what we had in mind there would be industrial strife. The reality has been completely the opposite. It may stagger some of you to know that in 1997, Australia recorded the lowest number of days lost to industrial disputes for 85 years. In other words, we had to go back to World War I days to find such an impeccable industrial record.

What we have done with those industrial relations changes is to build a framework and a basis for one of the most defining industrial challenges that this country has faced and that of course is fundamental reform of the industrial relations of Australia's waterfront. We all know that Australia has an inefficient waterfront. We all know that the unproductive practices of the waterfront, and the activities of the Maritime Union of Australia and its predecessors, are almost legend in the industrial relations folklore of Australia. We all know that it is one of the things that stands between Australia and the full realisation of her potential as a modern, competitive, highly productive and highly successful nation. It is one of those things that continues to deny us the full realisation of the potential that the rest of the world has always seen in our country. And, at long last, we have that intersection of circumstances.

We have a government which has had the courage to change the law of this country, to break the monopoly of the Maritime Union on the supply of labour. We have, in the National Farmers' Federation, a very courageous organisation of men and women who are seen as an integral part, not only of the history and the backbone of this country, but also of its export capacity and its export future. We also see in the Patricks company, led by a person who I think has conducted himself with great courage and great commitment, Mr Chris Corrigan, people who are prepared to use the tools provided by the changes to the law that my Government has made.

Now this is a defining moment. It is a defining dispute in the industrial relations history of Australia. We do not seek an argument with any union in this country. We have no enduring quarrels with any union. We do not wish to destroy unions, we do not wish to destroy unionists and we do not wish to destroy unionism. There is a place for both union and non-union labour on the waterfront of Australia just as there is a place for union and non-union labour on any factory floor and in any office in this country.

It is a question of personal choice. Over a period of time, union membership has declined and I guess that process will go on. But that is a matter of individual choice. But what we are determined to see changed, because it is important for the generation of jobs and the earning of export income for this country, are the practices on the waterfront that have damaged this country's interests over such a long period of time.

So it is an important dispute. It is a crucial issue. It is one of those defining moments in the industrial relations experience of any country and it will be important that those who want the goals that we have talked about for so long in this area to be achieved and realised over the months ahead. It will be important that you continue to give us and those involved in these events your wholehearted support because Australia's export income future is at stake. The potential jobs of thousands of Australians are involved and the economic reputation and the reliability of this country, as seen by the rest of the world, are very much involved.

# Calling it for Australia

## Campaigning for Re-election, 1998
## Parramatta, NSW – 20 September 1998

In his campaign for re-election of the Government at the 1998 general election, the Prime Minister appealed to the electorate to accept his bold plans to modernise the Australian economy for the 21st century. The centre-piece of his second-term agenda was implementation of a new taxation system to help make Australia the economic hub of the Asia-Pacific region. Entailing the introduction of a 10% Goods and Services Tax, the new system sought to reduce the existing burden of income tax and to make Australian industries and businesses more competitive. As well as cutting personal taxes by $13 billion a year, the tax reforms would remove uncompetitive taxes at a State level, remove $10.5 billion of costs from business and take $3.5 billion off the cost of fuel whilst guaranteeing protection for pensioners and low income earners. To enhance the functioning of the Federation, the tax system would also seek to resolve many revenue disputes between the Commonwealth and the States. Reminding his audience that Australia's greatness lay not simply in its material prosperity, Howard urged fellow Australians to cherish and embrace their traditions of personal freedom, enterprise, class-lessness, racial harmony, compassion and generosity.

… Election campaigns are never held in a vacuum. They are not dry comparisons of neat policies, be they economic, taxation or otherwise. They are an opportunity for a nation collectively to take stock, ask what Australia stands for and to ask what we want it to stand for in the future.

Election campaigns are an opportunity for alternative leaders to present their values and their priorities to their fellow Australians. It is impossible as an Australian, as we come to the end of this century, not to feel an immense sense of surging excitement about the opportunities that lie in front of us. There is no nation on Earth that has been gifted with the special combination of such assets. We are in every sense of the word a projection of Western civilisation in this part of the world. We have taken the good things from Europe, the liberal political traditions, the civility of our public life and, thankfully, we have rejected the bad things of Europe, the stultifying class divisions built on tribal prejudice.

We retain uniquely great and enduring links that give us influence with the most powerful democracy in the world, the United States of America. But here we are in the Asia-Pacific region, uniquely at an intersection of geography, history, economic opportunity and cultural diversity. And we alone have an opportunity to draw on that special combination of talents, to make our mark not only in this region but in the wider world.

So, therefore, it is with a sense of great excitement that I look forward, and all Australians should look forward, to the 21st century. We have the opportunity to leave a mark as the Australian people in the 21st century that history has given to us....

I said when this election campaign was called that the major issue was that of economic competence. The major question to be asked was which side of politics was better able to manage and lead the Australian economy in these difficult times into the 21st century. And nothing, my friends, has changed that as the central, most important issue of this election campaign. Economic competence is relevant not only as to what it says about past performance and past comparison. It is also relevant as to what it says about future courage and future commitment to the changes that are needed for the Australian community....

But economic competence is also about the courage, the political courage, you are prepared to summon for the future in front of us.

There is no doubt, my fellow Australians, that this country desperately needs a new taxation system. We may differ and quarrel about the detail but one thing unites all of us except for the purposes of this election campaign, the Leader of the Labor Opposition, Mr Beazley, and his Deputy, Mr Evans. And that is that the present Australian taxation system is broken, it is failing the Australian community and unless it is renovated and changed we cannot deliver a stronger Australia for the 21st century.

Our tax reform plan is good for Australia, because removing $10.5 billion of costs from business will make businesses more competitive and they will be able to generate more jobs. Because removing $4.5 billion from exports will make us more competitive on world markets, and that will mean more jobs because we will sell more goods overseas and we will need to employ more Australians in order to service the burgeoning markets overseas.

Tax reform is good for Australia because it will bring massive relief to many of our farmers and many of our fellow Australians who live in the bush. It will take $3.5 billion off the cost of fuel in this country. It will be the greatest single economic blow against what Geoffrey Blainey described so eloquently as "the tyranny of distance", which has so long dogged the experience of all Australians.

Taxation reform will also enable us, because of the removal of so many inefficient, uncompetitive taxes at a State level, to reach our dream, our goal, of becoming a major financial centre in the Asia-Pacific region. There is no reason at all, ladies and gentlemen, why by the year 2030, the Wall Street of the Asia-Pacific region should not run slap bang through the central business district of a major Australian city.

Our tax reform plan is good for Australia because we are going to cut personal taxes by $13 billion a year. Our tax plan is good for Australia because, under it, 81 per cent of Australian wage and salary earners will be on a top marginal rate of only 30 cents in the dollar. And that will mean that if your boss asks you, and you are on $30,000 a year, and there are millions of Australians on that level of income, to work some overtime, you can earn up to $20,000 more overtime without going into a higher taxation bracket.

We reward effort and hard work. The Labor Party envies it and pe-nalises it. Our tax reform plan is good for Australia because it further recognises the costs that people incur when they have and raise children. And our tax plan gives to the parents of Australia effective choice for them, and them alone, to decide their child-caring arrangements. Our tax reform plan is also good for Australia because it will end for all time the undignified wrangles between the Commonwealth and the States at annual Premiers' conference meetings. Under our plan, we are going to dedicate all the revenue coming from the Goods and Services Tax to the States of Australia. As a result, we will be able to guarantee growing levels of revenue flows to all of the States. What that means is that the States will be able to find a secure funding base to provide the schools, the police services, the hospitals, the roads, and all of the other day-to-day services that all Australians, wherever they live, have a right to expect.

And it is only through having a Goods and Services Tax as part of our plan that we can actually guarantee the levels of government services and the levels of welfare support that all decent minded Australians believe should be available in a modern, civilised and compassionate Australian community.

My friends, our tax reform plan is also good for Australia because it will balance fairness and incentive. The present taxation system is unfair: too many people can dodge it. The cash or the black economy runs rampant. Introduction of a Goods and Services Tax will drag the cheats into the net. It will make it harder for the dishonest to prosper and it will reward the honest, law-abiding citizen. That is the fairness and the justice of our system.

A Goods and Services Tax will sweep away the ten inefficient Commonwealth and State taxes we now have. The wholesale sales tax will be completely abolished, and all of those unfair, troublesome, burdensome, State taxes such as the bed tax, the tax on stamp duties, the tax on business conveyances, the bank account debits tax, the financial institutions duty, the tax on share transfers: the list goes on and on. It is part-and-parcel of our system that every last one of those taxes is totally abolished when our new plan comes into operation.

Our plan is fair because it will guarantee protection for pensioners and those on low incomes. Under our plan, those on the pension will always be one-and-a-half per cent in real terms ahead of any cost of living impact. Always one-and-a-half per cent ahead of any impact from the cost of living. And our plan is good for Australia because it will reward those who have already taken out private health insurance for the confidence and the commitment they have shown towards private health insurance over the years. And it will also provide a new incentive for more Australians to take out private health insurance because we are going to give to everybody, irrespective of income, a 30 per cent tax deduction on payment off the total cost of their private health insurance premiums.

Those, my friends, are some of the benefits of our tax plan. They are some of the reasons why it is good for Australia. They are some of the reasons why I believe in my heart that this is the most important reform that I have ever committed myself to in public life. I have now been a member of the Commonwealth Parliament since 1974. I have watched and I have participated in many great debates about economic and other issues. I have seen political courage displayed on issues, I have seen political cowardice displayed on other issues. I have had the great privilege over the last two-and-a-half years of occupying the position of Prime Minister of our nation. And a greater privilege could not come the way of any human being. …

This is an election campaign, more than most, where we clearly have to call it for Australia and not for a selfish, sectional interest. And so, as I move to some other issues that I want to dwell on for a moment, I leave you with that very, very simple thought that the Australian national interest overwhelming demands and calls for and requires a fundamental reform to our taxation system. Risky though it is to propose it from government before an election, it is nonetheless the right thing to do for our country. And I have never, in 24 years of public life, been more certain than I am today that I am doing the right thing by Australia in pursuing the cause of taxation reform. …

One of the philosophical principles that have been at the heart of the policies of our Government over the last two-and-a-half years has been the principle of mutual obligation. And what that says is that, as a decent, compassionate, caring community, we look after those who, through no fault of their own, cannot find a job or who cannot care for themselves. We are not a society that will allow people literally to beg in the streets for survival. That has never been the Australian way, and under the Coalition it will never in the future be the Australian way.

But we also believe that if people are supported by their fellow Australians, and they are able to do so, they should provide something in return for that support. And we have put that into practice with our Work for the Dole scheme. Our Work for the Dole scheme introduced, against the cynical opposition of the Australian Labor Party, a scheme that would undoubtedly be removed and destroyed if Labor were to win in October. Described as a "Mickey Mouse" scheme by Martin Ferguson, it has brought the work ethic and the habits involving the work ethic to many tens of thousands of Australians. Work for the Dole is a practical expression of the principle of mutual obligation. And because of its success and the contribution that it is making to helping young people, I am announcing today that a re-elected Coalition Government will fund $100 million over four years to further expand the Work for the Dole scheme to ensure that all school leavers within three months of leaving school who are not in education or training must be involved in a Work for the Dole scheme.

Strong education facilities are vital for the future of any nation. And Australia has strong and rich educational traditions. Over the last two-and-a-half years we have particularly responded to a growing concern in the Australian community about some quite appalling standards of literacy and numeracy amongst many young Australians who have left school. And we have put hundreds of millions of dollars into that programme. And today I am announcing that we will further extend our drive for higher standards of literacy and numeracy by spending an additional $112 million over three to four years to further improve literacy and numeracy standards in schools.

I want to affirm again, the absolute commitment of the Coalition parties to freedom of choice in education. It has long been the philosophy of the Liberal and National parties that it is the right of Australian parents and Australian parents alone to choose the education that they want for their children. As a very proud product of a State government selective high school myself, and as a parent of children who have been educated in both the government and the independent sectors, I repeat, again, the absolute commitment of the Government to freedom of choice in education. …

I might also confirm the Government's ongoing commitment to the maintenance of our new approach to the opening up of low fee-paying independent schools. Labor, if re-elected, will destroy that programme and will in effect entrench the very thing it criticises in independent schools, and that is elitism. What on earth can be fair about stopping people who cannot afford to send their children to high fee-paying independent schools the opportunity of establishing ones with low fees. Yet that is exactly what Labor's new schools policy will do. …

In another area, I am proud of what we have done to shun another form of violence, domestic violence. I am particularly proud of the initiatives that the Government has taken in partnership with the business community. To send a message to the men of Australia that they have no respect in visiting violence upon the women and children of this community, that domestic violence is abhorrent, repugnant and unacceptable to all men and women of decency within our community.

I mention those things, my friends, because although economic competence is important and is, without doubt, the major and dominant issue in this election campaign, political parties and governments are also about values and priorities in the non-economic area. Political parties are about expressing what they believe our society should be. And political leaders are about saying what they think our society should be.

My love of Australia is based upon my experience as an Australian. My love of Australia is based upon my innate embrace of a society that judges people according to their decency and their worth and not according to how much money they earn or what school they went to or what class they might think they belong to or what country they were born in or what the colour of their skin may be, or what religion they might profess, or what nationality they might still treasure other than their Australian nationality.

My love of Australia is based upon believing that it is still possible in this country to start with nothing and to work your heart out and to build up a business and to leave something more behind to your children. My love of Australia is based upon the respect we have around the world for a decent, open, tolerant, harmonious community. My love of Australia is based upon our capacity to hang onto those things from our past which we treasure and we regard as important such as these beautiful Australian flags that sit behind me. My love of Australia is also based upon our capacity in the past to embrace fundamental change when Australians know it is in the interests of securing a stronger and better future.

The art of good political leadership, the art of good statecraft, is to preserve those things that are good and continue to benefit society but to reject and turn away from those that are no longer modern and no longer relevant. And that is why we face in this election campaign such a crucial choice in the area of economic reform, particularly taxation. We have outlined, and will continue to do so, the dimension of the choice that we face. It is, above everything else, a question of a choice of what is good for Australia, not what is good for you or for me or for one or other group – it is what is good for Australia.

And I simply say to my fellow Australians, let the decision on 3 October [1998] not be based on fears or concerns or doubts. Rather, let it be the sum of the commitment that all of us have to building a stronger and better Australia so that together we can move confidently into the 21st century.

# Common-sense Australian Values

## "Australian Way" Federation Address
## Queensland Chamber of Commerce and Industry
### 28 January 1999

As Australia was about to enter its second century as an independent nation, the Prime Minister outlined the main domestic goals of his government for the new century. Central to Howard's agenda was strengthening the Australian economy through taxation reform and greater fiscal discipline which would help reduce inflation, interest rates and the budget deficit. The Prime Minister clearly saw a stronger economy as critical to future job creation and employment growth. Far from being an end in itself, however, this burgeoning prosperity would augur well for the country's social stability and quality of life. In addition to giving individuals and families the financial wherewithal, the provision of lasting and fulfilling jobs gave citizens a greater sense of belonging, self-confidence and personal responsibility to contribute to the good of society. In his Government's efforts to bring employment within the reach of more Australians, the Prime Minister lauded the success of the Work for the Dole scheme trialled in 1997 and adopted in 1998. The scheme was significant not only for aiding the transition of the unemployed to work but for reinforcing the principle of "mutual obligation". The notion of free citizens possessing not only rights but also responsibilities was integral to Howard's philosophy.

The success or failure of a nation essentially begins in the homes of its people.

And as we stand on the edge of the new millennium, Australia's fortune lies not so much with parliaments or business, or political parties or money markets, but with individual Australians – young and old, men and women, Australians by birth or choice.

Each one of us is responsible for building our own lives and the life of our nation. All of us are accountable to ourselves, to those around us, and to the future itself.

It has always been so. A century ago, Sir Henry Parkes – that great-hearted champion of federation, declared Australia ready for unity, for the dazzling prize of nationhood because of, in his words, the vigour, the industry, the enterprise, the foresight, and the creative skill of its people.

He knew, as I know now, that self-confidence and self-esteem, that determination and fair play, and success itself, can be the characteristics of a nation only while its citizens possess these virtues and hold dear those values.

This does not mean that governments do not have a role in promoting the values of society. Indeed, they have an important obligation to encapsulate community aspirations, define objectives and to spell out how to reach them.

So it is that in this address I will define the main domestic goals of the Government in 1999, indicate a significant strengthening of the application of the principle of mutual obligation, and announce Commonwealth assistance for a major resource project here in Queensland – a tangible demonstration of our commitment to nation-building as we move into the next century.

The Government has five broad goals in the year ahead:

- We are resolved to pursue policies that are most likely to maintain our remarkable rate of economic growth and strength.
- We are absolutely committed to the implementation in full of our visionary tax plan endorsed by the Australian people at the 1998 election.
- Thirdly, we will not tire in our efforts to further reduce un-

employment which, although now at an eight-year low, remains unacceptably high.

- Fourthly, we will further extend our commitment to the principle of mutual obligation in Australian society.
- Finally, we will work to create an even stronger social coalition to more effectively remedy areas of disadvantage and under privilege.

These goals are not mutually exclusive nor are they the sum total of what the Government wants to do over the next twelve months. Rather, they are a mixture of specific policy commitments and broader social goals which collectively remind us of an important truth of public policy. That is, that economic growth and economic efficiency are never ends in themselves. Rather they are a means by which we can deliver more fulfilling lives for our fellow Australians. ...

In conception and practice, our policies have mirrored the Australian character, Australian priorities, in short – the Australian way.

Our approach has had, at its core, common-sense Australian values – the responsibility to secure the nation's economic foundations; workplace reforms to allow employers and workers to get on with the job; education for our young people to equip them with skills; projects to empower voluntary organisations; and Work for the Dole, to inculcate a work ethic in the young.

We have built upon Australia's position in the world where we occupy a unique intersection of history, geography, culture and economic circumstances. We draw strength from important bonds with all parts of the world – our language, law, cultural and historical ties with Europe, strategic ties with North America and new economic and people-to-people links with our neighbours in this region. ...

### Resolutions for the Millennium

As 1999 begins, we naturally project forward to the new millennium. As always, Australians have a choice. We can resolve to maintain the momentum of recent years and to move forward to improve the lives of individuals and families, the success of business. Or we can take fright and abandon the challenge of further reform.

## *Economic Discipline*

The Government will further strengthen our economy. Guaranteeing our hard won gains – high growth, low inflation and interest rates, falling government debt and unemployment, and rising share ownership – is reason why I will forge ahead with overhauling a tax system which, in its current form, cannot deliver new growth, or encourage new businesses, or provide new jobs. Australians should receive the personal tax cuts they deserve with four out of five taxpayers paying no more than 30 cents in the dollar in income tax.

Workers should not be penalised by punitive tax rates on their incomes and savings, punished for working harder or longer or seeking a promotion. Parents should have greater freedom to choose the caring arrangements for their young children which best suit their needs.

Our tax reform will see pensioners keeping more of their pension for extra income earned and being assured that their hard earned pensions will remain ahead of prices. And provisional tax abolished once and for all.

Our reforms will mean that most small businesses will be able to pay all their taxes once a quarter on just one form. Our exporters can take on the world, bringing wealth back to Australia, without the burden of sales and consumption taxes. And those in the bush will face much lower transport costs through the reduction of 25 cents a litre in the diesel fuel excise for heavy transport.

And, finally, our States and territories will have a secure funding base to provide the roads and bridges, the schools and hospitals, all Australians need.

Failure to pass our plan will keep $10 billion of taxes on business and $4.5 billion of taxes on our exporters – funds which would otherwise be spent on development, marketing, production, sales, jobs and people.

Failure to pass our plan will keep $13 billion of personal income tax on individuals and deny them another $2 billion in family benefits, and will maintain wholesale sales tax and nine other hidden taxes.

In short, failure to pass our plan will mean we have let pass a chance to make things right.

### *Further efforts to reduce unemployment*

As we look ahead, we resolve to continue the fight to further reduce unemployment.

Australia's prosperity, its social stability, the quality of life enjoyed by individuals and families – all these things rely upon building a nation with jobs in abundance. Lasting and fulfilling jobs are at the heart of personal and family security. They also reflect our values of self-esteem and self-confidence and are the means by which we each demonstrate personal responsibility.

I do not claim that this Government, after just under three years in office, has solved the unemployment problem. But we have made significant progress. The unemployment rate has fallen to 7.5 per cent – the lowest jobless rate in eight years. In our time, we have created almost 400,000 jobs, over half of them in small business. And in the year to December, we have created an average of 14,800 new jobs each month.

We have instituted a new Job Network to bring together employers and jobseekers faster, with less cost and less bureaucracy, with a focus on results not process.

Despite the carping criticism of many, the new system is superior to the one it replaced. Let me tell you why. There are now more than four times as many sites to apply for jobs as there were through the Commonwealth Employment Service. And those best qualified to provide services to the unemployed – business, community and charitable organisations such as Drake Australia, The Salvation Army and Mission Australia – are already outperforming the old system.

In December, the Job Network placed 17 600 people in jobs, twice the number placed by the old CES a year earlier. And employers have given a vote of confidence in the new arrangements by listing 34 000 new vacancies with the Job Network in December which is in contrast to only 13 000 listed by the CES in the same month of 1997.

Lower unemployment depends upon strong economic growth, renewed efforts to remove the disincentives which exist in our welfare system and greater labour market flexibility. This greater flexibility should respect the Australian way and the Australian tradition of a social safety net.

A strong job market needs to be flexible and competitive and we have set about building a system based on common interest, not on conflict. With co-operation and common purpose there is less need for regulation, red tape and legalistic rituals. Under the new system some 180 awards have been simplified, and 40 000 Australian Workplace Agreements and 805 non-union agreements covering almost 100 000 employees have been approved.

Consistent with my pledge that no worker would be worse off on an Australian Workplace Agreement compared to their award, we will continue to simplify and enhance the new workplace relations system to secure and promote jobs. And there is much more to do. We will stand by our exemption for small business from unfair dismissal laws to create extra jobs which may number as many as 50 000.

The jobs of 420 000 young Australians on junior wage rates will be protected by retaining age-based youth wages.

We will maximise choice at the workplace by encouraging mediation services as an alternative to arbitration, and by simplifying the approval of agreements. And the interests of individual workers will be promoted over union bosses by introducing secret ballots for protected industrial action and preventing victimisation.

In summary, I resolve to elevate individuals, their choices, their responsibilities above the interests of institutions and pressure groups because that is what Australians want....

## *Creating a strong, social coalition*

Few Australians would deny the proposition that governments alone cannot solve immense social problems. They need the help and understanding of great community organisations, dedicated individuals and the corporate sector.

In reality, we need a social coalition which unites all of those within the nation who seek to address in an effective way poverty and disadvantage – each being encouraged to share responsibility for providing opportunity, each being provided with incentive to offer a fair go to those in need and each being rewarded by playing a greater role in the decision-making process.

I am resolved to provide a modern safety net which encourages responsibility and embraces prevention as much as cure. Traditional State-centred welfare has failed to prevent social problems and has perpetuated dependency rather than re-engagement with work and the community.

This does not mean winding back government assistance for those in need or for those who support them. We will enhance the role of community organisations, not increase the burdens they carry. Every day organisations like the Salvation Army and the Society of St Vincent de Paul display their capacity to enhance the welfare of those in need. Each day they address the very personal impact of social problems in ways that governments simply cannot.

I resolve to build on the initiatives of our first term which, for the first time, involved community organisations in the design and implementation of our Tough on Drugs programme and Youth Homelessness pilot projects.

I resolve to build a stronger social coalition, renewing my call to business both large and small to play their part, to give back to the community from which they profit, to follow the example of many genuine Australian philanthropists, to advise, to donate in cash or kind, to mentor. And I resolve to leave a legacy of this International Year of Older Persons by paying due tribute to older Australians, truly valuing Australia's wealth for their toil.

We have already extended the Seniors' Health Card and the Veterans' Gold Card and provided the farm families assets test concession just as we have recognised the desire of older Australians to be cared for in their own homes through our Staying at Home package. Building on our Staying at Home package announced last year [1998]; and our co-ordinated care trials, I want to provide better health care for older people in their own homes. I also want to enable them to remain active participants in their local communities consistent with the Australian way of a fair go for all.

I have asked Dr Wooldridge [Minister for Health and Ageing] to report to Cabinet on plans to implement these principles. Announcements will be made in the months ahead to help care for older Australians particularly those afflicted with chronic and complex illnesses. Such a goal can only be achieved by involving the health care industry and the medical profession in particular and I look forward to their co-operation.

### *Mutual Obligation*

The dole system that we inherited sent the worst possible message to young Australians. It told them that dropping out of school, out of their communities, escaping personal responsibility, was acceptable and that the taxpayer would foot the bill.

The dole system should be about choice and responsibility – providing young people with the opportunity for training and education but, at the same time, making them fully responsible for their choices and for themselves. This principle underpins our youth allowance which encourages those in receipt of government benefits to finish school and better themselves.

And it holds true for my Government's Work for the Dole scheme. Under the Government's Work for the Dole Scheme 2 000 applications have been received for projects, 410 have commenced and over 18 000 young Australians have benefited from their personal involvement in Work for the Dole.

Young Australians have helped make good damage caused by landslides and flooding after cyclones hit Magnetic Island last January [1998]; specialised gardens have been constructed in Parkes for dementia sufferers; specifically designed boats have been built so that people with disabilities can experience the joy of sailing; historic wooden railway carriages restored to their former beauty; walking tracks completed and other tourism projects undertaken. These have been supplemented by projects to help the frail and aged, the sick, and the disabled, together with projects to help children, other unemployed Australians and the homeless.

Work for the Dole has not only provided young Australians with training and skills, social contact and restored the links with their communities. For so many, it has ignited the work ethic fundamental to sustaining lasting work and broken, forever, the cycle of boredom and despair that was the bane of the young unemployed.

Nearly a third of scheme participants have gone on to fulfilling jobs. During the election campaign, I announced a further 25 per cent expansion of Work for the Dole by requiring all Year 12 school leavers on the full rate of Youth Allowance to join one of the scheme's projects once they have been unemployed for three months. Overall, this means up to 124 000 places will be provided over four years.

Where some would scrap Work for the Dole, I remain passionately committed to extending the principle of asking people to give back something to the community in return for assistance in times of need. Work for the Dole is an important part of our focus on boosting jobs.

Exactly a year ago – in my first Federation Address – I announced a major extension of my Government's mutual obligation initiative. Now that we have the benefit of another year's experience, we propose further improvements.

The first area we are going to change is the obligation to improve literacy and numeracy skills. We know that a school child without basic reading and writing skills will not be able to realise his or her full potential. That is why I commit my Government to requiring unemployed young people who fail basic literacy and numeracy tests to undertake appropriate remedial courses if they are to continue to receive their full dole.

Previously, young people on the dole were able to satisfy their obligation by taking up one of a number of options. But I believe, and most Australians would agree, that reading and writing properly are the most fundamental prerequisites for getting a job.

So, to enhance our mutual obligation policies, this Government will require young people who lack basic literacy and numeracy skills to undertake training in those areas as a condition of receiving their full unemployment benefit. Refusing to learn how to read and write will deny young unemployed the full dole. Further work is being undertaken on improving compliance and extending the coverage of mutual obligation.

## *Conclusion*

As this century nears its conclusion, let us reflect on a nation which has remained true to its spirit. Mistakes have been made, tragedies borne, unspeakable sacrifice endured but, at the end of the century, Australians remain the enterprising, vigorous and creative people of whom Sir Henry Parkes spoke so lovingly.

We retain an echo within us of the yearning for a better life which drove our ancestors to build this country. That spirit was captured very well by the eminent journalist, Sir Henry Gullett,[26] in his description written many years ago. He marvelled at their courage and ability which he ascribed to the fact that all were pioneers, or the children of pioneers, the children of the most restless, adventurous and the most virile individuals.

As Federation fervour ran through the country Gullett also wrote:

> Seldom in the world's history, have a people entered into possession of their heritage under circumstances so auspicious and with an outlook so full of dazzling promise.

When I consider the talent, the energy, the potential amongst us, when I think of how the whole world will turn its focus upon us next year at the change of the millennium, I cannot help but conclude that Gullett's words are even truer today – that seldom in the history of the world will a people enter into possession of the new millennium under circumstances so auspicious and with an outlook so full of dazzling promise.

---

[26] Sir Henry Gullett (1878-1940) served as a Member of the House of Representatives for the Melbourne-based seat of Henty from 1925 to 1940.

# Family Needs and the
# National Policy Agenda

## Address to Menzies Research Centre
## Parliament House, Canberra – 18 April 2006

Shortly after achieving the rare feat of a decade in office, the Prime Minister addressed the Menzies Research Centre to explain how his Government's policies had improved the economic well-being of Australians and their families. From the introduction of the Family Tax Initiative in 1996 to the release of the $19 billion family package in 2004, Howard observed that Australian families now enjoyed greater choice and flexibility to structure their lives than a decade ago. Far from representing "middle-class welfare", the Prime Minister argued that this assistance provided much-needed tax relief for families grappling with the costs of child-rearing, whether they were single income or dual income. In particular, these measures aimed to improve the financial position of low and middle income families. By delivering on necessary tax reform for families to help them realise their hopes and aspirations, the Prime Minister had hoped to fulfil his vision for a government that not only "appreciates the virtues of markets, but also the values of family, community and country".

I am delighted to be back at the Menzies Research Centre, an organisation with a unique place in the Liberal family. It was at the Menzies Research Centre, prior to the 1996 election, where I began a series of speeches setting out the principles, values and policy direction which the Liberal and National Parties would follow in government.

Tonight, I want to revisit the signature commitment which I, on behalf of the Coalition, made to the Australian people more than a decade ago – to put the needs of families at the centre of the national policy agenda. We pledged to restore to Australian families a sense of confidence and optimism about their country's future; to bring within the reach of more families the prospect of good jobs, home ownership and rising living standards; and to open up new avenues of choice for families, especially those on modest incomes. ...

It has always been part of the Liberal tradition to expand the horizons of choice for Australians – in health and education, at work and at home. Liberals instinctively believe that the task of modern government is to enable individuals and families to exercise maximum choice, not to tell them how to structure their lives.

This Government has been especially keen to give families with children greater freedom to choose how they balance work and family responsibilities, including through additional support for those families who desire to have one parent, usually the mother, at home full-time with children in their early years.

Beginning with the Family Tax Initiative in 1996, we have increased total assistance to families by more than $6 billion a year, with the scales tipped strongly in favour of low and middle income families. The maximum rate of assistance for a child under 13 has risen from about $2 420 to $4 200 a year in the last decade.

A New Tax System collapsed 12 family and child-care payments into three, with the benefits of tax reform slanted heavily in favour of families. In 2004, we introduced Australia's largest ever family package, an additional $19 billion to help with the costs of raising children. Withdrawal rates on family payments have been progressively reduced to improve the rewards from working, especially for families where a second earner is in part-time or casual work or where a woman is returning to work after the birth of a child.

With the Family Tax Benefit system, the Government said to Australian families: we recognise your diverse needs and desires; we know that women in particular face difficult decisions about work and family. Most importantly, we believe that governments should accommodate the choices of society, not the other way around.

The numbers suggest a fairly stable pattern among Australian families with dependants. In 19 per cent of cases, both parents work full-time. A higher percentage – 21 per cent of families – relies on a single breadwinner, with one parent caring for children at home. And for some time now, the most common arrangement – today 28 per cent of families – sees one parent (usually the father) working full-time and the other (usually the mother) working part-time.

Diverse families and different arrangements, but the same principle of choice. As well as helping parents negotiate the big decisions about work and family, the Family Tax Benefit (FTB) also offers choice as to how what is, in reality, a targeted tax cut is received.

Language is important here. Those who seek to denigrate what we have done constantly refer to Family Tax Benefits as "middle-class welfare". They are nothing of the kind. They are tax relief for a universal reality – that it costs money to raise children. At a time when there is general dismay at our relatively low fertility rate, what possible public policy justification can there be for affording precisely the same tax treatment to a couple without children on $80 000, compared with a couple with two children on the same income?

A little acknowledged fact is that families can receive the Family Tax Benefits in one of three ways. They can, as most do, choose a fortnightly payment to the principal carer (normally the mother). They can receive a tax rebate on their annual tax return. Or they can have fortnightly Pay As You Go (PAYG) deductions adjusted to take account of the benefit. The fact that most people choose for family budget reasons to take it as a fortnightly payment does not alter its character.

Under the Family Tax Benefit system, according to Treasury analysis, almost 40 per cent of all families this financial year will receive more in cash benefits than they pay in personal income tax. In addition, FTB has meant that working families on lower incomes have experienced greater proportional increases in disposable income than those in higher income groups.

Let me cite three examples of how the Government's policies have helped to improve the financial position of low and middle income families. The real disposable income of a sole parent on 67 per cent of Average Weekly Earnings (ordinary time, for full-time employees) has risen from $34 088 in 1996-97 to an estimated $40 749 in 2006-07. With FTB, their real net tax threshold – the point at which they begin paying tax in net terms, has risen from an annual income of $34 502 in 1996-97 to $44 951 in 2006-07.

A single income couple on average earnings with two children (aged 3 and 8) has seen their real disposable income rise from $38 070 in 1996-97 to an estimated $49 213 in 2006-07. Their real net tax threshold next financial year will also be $44,951, up from $33 931 in 1996-97.

Or take the most common case where one spouse works full-time and the other works part-time. For a dual income couple with two children where one spouse is on average earnings and the other on a third of average earnings, real disposable income has risen from $49 170 in 1996-97 to $61 286. And next financial year, that couple will pay no net tax on the first $47 891 they earn. ...

The Family Tax Benefit system symbolises the great philosophical divide in Australian politics between a Labor Party which thinks government should direct peoples' behaviour and a Coalition which sees its role as letting families make up their own minds.

Whether it is FTB or funding for independent schools or support for private health insurance, Labor's old ideological agenda can never be killed off. So that when it comes to choice: Don't trust them. Don't believe them. Because they do not believe in it themselves.

Now let me turn to a commonly heard complaint about the tax-transfer system – that the Government is engaged in nothing more than a giant "churning" exercise, taking peoples' money with one hand and handing it back to them with the other. Income tax raises revenue according to an individual's capacity to pay, while the family payments system is focused on need, assisting families according to their income and number of dependents. Some so-called churning is the inescapable result of a tax-transfer system where both policy instruments do their respective jobs.

Australia operates what is regarded as the most targeted social security system in the OECD, and probably in the world. Research by Peter Whiteford at the OECD has shown that we also have the lowest churn of any developed country. As the Whiteford research points out, many of the supposed solutions to churning favoured by the Government's critics would likely have adverse distributional consequences for low and middle income households. And because income taxes represent a relatively small component of churning for the bottom 40 per cent of households, they would be unlikely to solve alleged incentive problems.

Again, I do not want to imply that more cannot be done to improve incentives in the tax-transfer system. But critics cannot have it both ways, simultaneously railing about effective marginal tax rates and against middle-class welfare.

Let me make a final point. If the anti-churn advocates get their way, and the Family Tax Benefit system is dismantled in favour of tax cuts for individual taxpayers, the people who will suffer most will be Australian women. One of the distinguishing features of FTB is that it is paid to the principal carer, overwhelmingly the mother. If simply rolled into a reformed income tax system, the bulk of individual tax cuts would go to men, financed by the withdrawal of direct fortnightly payments to women.

What our critics are really advocating is redistribution from women to men.

When this Government came to office, Australia's economy was struggling to create jobs and to raise living standards. Today, it is almost impossible to pick up a broadsheet newspaper without reading a social commentator fretting about the consequences of too much affluence. Faced with a choice, I know my preference. And I think I know what Australian families prefer, too.

But I also know that we would not have survived as a government if we had not worked hard to spread the benefits of prosperity across the community. Our record shows that we have been exactly the government we said we would be, a distinctively Australian synthesis of economic liberalism and modern social conservatism. A government that appreciates the virtues of markets, but also the values of family, community and country.

As I told the Menzies Research Centre in June 1995, I have never seen economic liberalism as an end in itself or a stand-alone political credo. Sound money, responsible budgets and efficient markets are nothing more than the mechanisms to support resilient families, cohesive communities and a stronger Australia.

A country, as Edmund Burke observed, "is not a thing of mere physical locality". Nor is it just individuals in a market place. A country is also connected by a hidden chain of social obligations.

By keeping faith with Australian families – their interests, aspirations, hopes and values – we have kept faith with Australia at its best.

# WorkChoices Reforms

## Sydney – 20 July 2006

In this address to the Australian Chamber of Commerce and Industry, Australia's peak business association, Prime Minister Howard made the case for his Government's recent "WorkChoices" reforms to industrial relations. The name, "WorkChoices", was given to the *Workplace Relations Amendment (Work Choices) Act* 2005, that came into effect on 27 March 2006. The fundamental aim of the new law was to give the nation a uniform industrial relations system to reflect the modern reality that Australia now operated as a national economy.

One of the centrepieces of the *WorkChoices* legislation was exemption of small firms employing fewer than 100 people from unfair dismissal laws. Instead of making it easier for small businesses to sack good staff, the rationale was to give businesses greater flexibility to employ more staff. Whilst the WorkChoices reforms were vigorously opposed by the Labor Party and the trade union movement, Howard believed that they were necessary not only to streamlining the national economy but integral to realising the enduring vision of Menzies "to create a climate in which enterprise will flourish and productivity will increase". Although Howard conceded that Australia had enjoyed a long spell of uninterrupted economic growth, the project of continuing industrial relations reform remained necessary if such future growth was to be sustained.

I want to say a few things about the topic of the day – and I am talking here in the context of small business – and that is the WorkChoices reforms. …

The real test is the impact they have on the Australian economy. Will they make the economy better and stronger in the future, or will they make the Australian economy weaker in the future? Because in the end it is the strength of the economy that determines whether companies make profits and, if companies do not make profits, they cannot employ as many people as they would like. You can have all the regulation in the world, you can have all the protection for employees in the world guaranteed by legislation but, if the economy falls over, people lose their jobs, firms do not make money and retrenchments occur.

We had a very heavily regulated labour market in Australia in the early 1990s and that did not stop us having one million people out of work; it did not stop the unemployment rate going to almost 11 per cent; it did not stop the sense of anguish and despair that many small businesses felt all around Australia and very particularly in parts of Victoria, and South Australia, and Tasmania, which were so heavily hit by the recession of those years.

It all brings us back to the point; it is the impact on the economy of an industrial relations policy that determines whether it is a success or a failure because it is a strong economy that employs people and it is a strong economy that is the guarantor of high real wages and low unemployment.

There is no statistic that I am prouder of than the fact that over the last 10 years, real wages in this country have gone up by 16.8 per cent. Under the previous government, in 13 years, they went up by 1.3 per cent. In other words, the workers have done better out of the Liberal Party than they can ever dream of doing out of the Labor Party. That is a statistic that I am very proud of.

I am also very proud of the WorkChoices legislation. I see it in a very positive light and I ask those in the community who support the Work-Choices legislation to advocate and to prosecute the case of the benefits of these changes. No section of the community will benefit more than the small business community. The abolition of the unfair dismissal laws for firms employing fewer than 100 people represents the culmination of a legitimate campaign by small businesses around Australia since the introduction of the old unfair dismissal laws in 1994.

I can remember, over the years between 1994 and 2006, going to countless gatherings of men and women involved in small business. Whenever I committed the Coalition to the abolition of those unfair dismissal laws for business the response was unambiguous and emphatic. Small business wanted those laws to go. They wanted those laws to go, not to make it easier to get rid of good staff, but to make it easier to employ more good staff, and that fundamentally is the reason why we have changed those laws.

I am fascinated as I look at the three months that have gone by since the new laws were introduced – they were introduced on 27 March 2006 – and I am reminded that the National Secretary of the Australian Workers Union, Bill Shorten, said that the new laws were: "A green light for mass sackings". The Leader of the Opposition [Kim Beazley] said that the laws would make it easy to dismiss 11 million Australians.

Now, it may be only three months since the laws have been introduced, but the field evidence contradicts absolutely the predictions that have been made by Mr Shorten and Mr Beazley. In the three-and-a-half months that have gone by since the laws were introduced employment has actually risen in Australia by more than 100 000 – some mass sackings, some green light! We now have unemployment at 4.9 per cent, which is a 30-year low. Now I am not guaranteeing that it's going to remain at exactly 4.9 per cent; it will bounce around a little. But, fundamentally, there is no evidence that we live in a labour market or we live under a set of laws that are going to bring about or encourage mass sackings.

All of you, as men and women involved in small business, know that we now live in an employees' market like never before. As I go around Australia, what people say to me about employing staff is they cannot get enough good people. They say there are shortages, not only in skilled people, but also with unskilled people, and no employer in his or her right mind, in those circumstances, would envisage letting go of good staff.

The fundamental principle of those changes is that if you provide unreasonable penalties in relation to employment termination, you produce higher and not lower unemployment. That has been the experience of Australia and it has been the experience of countries around the world that have persevered with the sort of rigid labour market polices to which our opponents are committed.

WorkChoices introduces a national uniform industrial relations system. It recognises that we are now a national economy and I best explain this by saying that, when I first started practising law in Sydney in the early 1960s, if you had a client who had a business in New South Wales and he wanted to carry on business in Victoria, he had to go through a process called registering his company in Victoria as a foreign company. Sounds strange, but that – I know it draws laughter from all the people who were too young to go through that experience, but it is true – I can remember doing that on a number of occasions. The registration procedure that you went through was virtually identical to the registration procedure you had to go through if you were going to register the same company in the United Kingdom, to carry on business in the United Kingdom as a foreign company.

Law firms in those days were all city-based, you did not have national law firms, you did not have national accounting firms, the service sector of the Australian economy, which has grown the strongest over the last 30 to 40 years, was very city-centric. You worked for a Sydney law firm, a Sydney accounting firm, you did not work for a national one and that experience was replicated throughout the economy.

I mention that semi-personal anecdote to make a point that we have become, in so many ways, a national economy, the likes of which we would not have dreamt of 30 or 40 years ago. Thus we need a national set of laws, of national uniformity to respond to those national circumstances.

But, overwhelmingly, the reason why we need these new laws is really the point that was touched on in the introduction: the competition race in which we are involved is unending. Because we live in a globalised world economy, we can never take for granted that our place in that economy is assured. We can never guarantee that the position we now have, we retain. It might have been possible in a different period when we lived behind a high protective tariff wall, we had a fixed exchange rate and we had certain natural endowments and national advantages that other countries did not have. But all those things are gone.

Overnight our comparative competitive position can be challenged and can be altered. Each government that gives up on the cause of reform is a government that has no plans for the future, and I know that in any big reform there are challenges. But I believe in these workplace reforms because they will be good for the future of the Australian economy. Something that is good for the future of the Australian economy means more jobs and higher wages for Australian employees. That is the fundamental essence of our commitment to these new laws.

I therefore regard the commitment of my political opponents at a federal level to rollback these laws as a reversion to the politics of the 1960s and 1970s. To go back to a labour market which would be dominated by the trade union movement, to go back to a labour market based upon the principle that no man or woman has enough gumption to negotiate a contract in his or her own interests if they want to do so, to go back to a labour market where you would throw out potentially up to one million Australian Workplace Agreements, because that is the number we are likely to have at the time of the next Federal election. Australian Workplace Agreements in industries such as the mining industry, which is so important to the wealth that we are generating, which is fuelling the strength of our economy at the present time, is to turn your back on Australia's economic future.

There was a time when I thought we had a consensus in this country on the agreed goals of economic reform and the economic future of Australia. We certainly do not have any agreement in relation to Work-Choices.

So I assert the positive benefits of this change. I do not see the debate on WorkChoices in the context of responding to criticisms made by our opponents, although we do that on the merits and on the detail.

I am for these laws because they will improve the Australian economy. They will give small business the flexibility to take on more staff. They will give us a uniform national system. They will give to both employers and employees, subject to proper guarantees and protections, greater flexibility and simplicity in concluding their own workplace arrangements. Just as other countries that have freed their labour markets have enjoyed the benefits, so will Australia.

This country is prosperous, it has been greatly endowed by providence with natural resources beyond the comprehension of most and we can only convert our natural advantages to our benefit if we have the right economic settings. Just as this Government is prepared to seriously examine an issue such as nuclear power, because a proper exploitation of our energy resources is important to our future, so it is prepared to embark upon further economic reform. Good success and good economic management in the future belongs to countries and to governments of countries which are prepared to push ahead with reform.

It will be easy for me to say, "Well, look how terrific the economy is. We have got low unemployment, we have a terrific Budget surplus, we have just cut taxation, everybody thinks Australia is a wonderful country, it is booming. I do not need to do anymore. I can rest on my laurels, I can put aside any further difficult and challenging decisions".

Once a prime minister or any political leader gets to that stage, he or she should give the game away, he or she should recognise that the zest for economic reform and economic change has gone.

Well, I want to tell you that the Government I lead remains energetic, it remains committed, it remains enthusiastic about further reform to further strengthen the Australian economy. I know and you know that the prosperity we now have is the product of the economic reforms of earlier years.

You and I equally know that the prosperity of future generations will be the product of the reforms that this generation is courageous enough to carry out. That is why we are committed to WorkChoices. That is why we believe it will be great for small business and that is why I am delighted to talk to you tonight.

# Climate Change

## Sydney – 13 November 2006

With the issue of climate change gaining greater political traction during Howard's fourth term in office (2004-07), the Prime Minister addressed the Business Council of Australia to clarify his position on the matter. Dispelling claims that he was somehow a "sceptic" because of his Government's decision not to ratify the 1997 Kyoto Protocol, Howard accepted that the weight of scientific evidence pointed to the adverse effects of greenhouse gas emissions on the environment and the climate. Accordingly, he voiced in-principle support for proactive measures by the world's major emitters to deal with this problem.

The Prime Minister was not convinced that the Kyoto Protocol, which had come into force the previous year, would be conducive to Australia's future economic growth. Noting that the Kyoto agreement had been "largely fashioned to accommodate the environmental goals and positions of European countries", Howard maintained it did not afford sufficient consideration of countries like Australia whose economies depended heavily on resource industries such as coal, gas and uranium. As the alternative to a climate agreement that compromised the advantages Australia enjoyed from its abundance of natural resources, Howard called for a new, revised treaty to address the greenhouse gas challenge effectively in a way conducive to Australia's economic interests.

I want to thank the Business Council for again giving me the opportunity of addressing its annual dinner, to share some thoughts with you about the state of the economy, the business outlook, and the important ongoing relationship between the Government and the major business organisations of this country, and, in particular, the Business Council. ...

I do want to say something about the related issues of climate change and energy security. And I very deliberately link the two of them because you cannot think of the reaction of relevant countries to climate change without understanding the importance to them of energy security. Some of the heightened concern about climate change issues in recent months, indeed, in recent years, are very directly related to energy security.

We need to understand some fundamentals about the two of them, China and India. Put bluntly, there is no way that a country is going to embrace climate change measures or responses to the growth of greenhouse gas emissions, which in any way imperils its energy security. This is particularly so of countries such as China and India, which are for the first time in four or five hundred years reclaiming their position in the world economy, enjoying extraordinarily rapid economic growth which is very largely fuelled and supported and facilitated by cheap suppliers of energy from countries such as Australia, but also from their own and from other sources.

To expect a country like China to embrace change in relation to the climate, which in some way imperils its energy security, just at a time when it is beginning to enjoy the fruits of remarkable rates of economic growth, is to expect the unachievable and the unrealistic.

I think it is important to keep the challenge of climate change in perspective. I share your President's view that it is happening and, although I have been accused, and continue to be accused, of being somewhat of a sceptic on the issue, the truth is I am not that sceptical. The weight of scientific evidence suggests that there are significant and damaging growths in the levels of greenhouse gas emissions. Therefore, unless we lay the foundation over the years immediately ahead of us to deal with the problem, future generations will face significant penalties and will have cause to criticise our failure to do something substantial in response.

The debate is about the intensity and the pace of the damage being done by climate change. There will continue to be very intense debate about that. We have made it very clear that we will not ratify the Kyoto agreement. We took that decision some years ago because we feared that ratifying that agreement in the form in which it then and still largely exists could have damaged the comparative advantage this country enjoyed as a result of our abundance of fossil fuels and the importance of that abundance to Australia's export and general performance. Nothing has happened since to alter that fact. In the meantime, however, we have committed ourselves to achieve the target of 108 that was given to us at the Kyoto meeting in 1997 and we are on track to achieve that outcome within the time stipulated.

It is very obvious, both from what Michael Chaney[27] said, and from what others have said in recent weeks, that we do need to find, call it what you may, a new Kyoto. We do need, as a world community, to try and find a new global solution and that global solution must include all the major emitters. And we have to understand some of the fundamentals that drove the original Kyoto.

The original Kyoto was largely fashioned, I do not say this critically, I hope I say it objectively, to accommodate the environmental goals and position of European countries. It was not built with sufficient regard to the position of a country such as Australia, a highly developed country which was a net exporter of energy and, therefore, I think the formation of AP6,[28] which includes, in aggregate, almost 50 per cent of the world's emitters, also close to 50 per cent of the world's population and also close to 50 per cent of the world's GDP, that particular grouping can provide an extremely sure foundation for development of a new international covenant or new international understanding on this issue.

It is imperative from our point of view that, as we look at such issues as an emissions trading system, that we fashion here in Australia, and see fashioned globally, a trading system that protects the natural advantages this country has. This country does have enormous natural advan-

[27] Michael Chaney is a Perth-based businessman who served as chairman of Woodside Petroleum Ltd.
[28] The Asia-Pacific Partnership on Clean Development and Climate (AP6) was formed in July 2005.

tages in our resource industries, not only coal and gas but, importantly, uranium as well.

Let me say that – something I have said on a number of occasions in recent weeks – there is no one single solution to the global challenge. We need to maintain the profitability that our great abundance of fossil fuels has given us; we need to accelerate development of clean coal technologies, and the like that were identified two-and-a-half years ago in the Energy White Paper. We need to recognise that as a purifier, but not as a contributor to base power load generation, renewables, such as solar and wind can make a valuable contribution.

We also need, particularly as we develop clean coal technologies with the inevitable consequences they have for pricing, to examine and keep on the table the nuclear option. It is some years off but, in a couple of weeks, Dr Ziggy Switkowski's[29] committee will report and that report, will, I hope, make available, in a very objective fashion, the analysis of nuclear power, both in terms of safety, availability, supply and the economics of it in the whole climate change equation.

I have indicated in the past that I do not intend to preside over policy changes in this area that are going to rob Australia of her competitive advantage in the industries that are so important to us, I repeat that commitment. I welcome the contribution that the Business Council has made, and many other people in the business community have made, to tackling this issue. Many of you will know that over the past few weeks the Government has reiterated its broad approach. Later this week, I will meet some significant business figures, some of them are in the room, who are involved in the resource sector to discuss aspects of the Government's response to the climate change challenge.

The Government will establish a joint government-business task group to examine in some detail the form that an emissions trading system, both here in Australia and globally, might take in the years ahead. I think it is important to involve the business community in an analysis of this issue because decisions taken by the Government in this area

---

[29] Zygmunt Edward "Ziggy" Switkowski (1948 - ) is a Polish Australian business executive and nuclear physicist.

will have lasting ramifications for Australia's business community. We all recognise that we have to examine in the time ahead how we might devise an emissions trading system which properly cares for and accommodates the legitimate interests, and therefore maintains, the competitive advantage that this country enjoys in the industries that are familiar to you.

We do not want a new Kyoto that damages Australia. We need a new Kyoto that includes Australia, but includes Australia on a basis which is appropriate to our interests and our needs. So I indicate to you tonight that we will be establishing, in discussion with the Business Council of Australia and other business groups and individual business leaders, a joint government-business task group. This will examine, against the background of our clearly identified national interests and priorities, what form an emissions trading system, both here in Australia and globally, might take. One that will make a lasting contribution to a response to the greenhouse gas challenge but in a way that does not disproportionately or unfairly damage the Australian economy and the industries which have been so enormously important to the generation of our wealth and the development of our living standards over the last 10 or 20 years. …

# V

# Working Together in a Social Coalition

## Social Welfare and Social Policy

# Reform, Innovation and Renewal in Service Delivery

## Canberra – 24 September 1997

A centrepiece of the Howard Government's overhaul of Australia's social security system was establishment of a new streamlined agency, Centrelink. Originally established as an agency within the Department of Social Security, Centrelink became the peak government body for social security services in September 1997. In this address to launch Centrelink, the Prime Minister explained that the new body would consolidate many of the services the Government presently provided to students, pensioners, families and unemployed people in one streamlined outlet. In so doing, it would provide the Australian public with more efficient services and a "human face". Centrelink offices would be established in more than 400 locations throughout the country. The streamlining of Australia's social security system was designed to enhance government efficiency and reduce the cost of welfare provision whilst providing needy Australians with a better and more personalised service.

Thank you very much Senator Newman [Minister for Social Security]. To Senator Grant Tambling, the Parliamentary Secretary; to my other parliamentary colleagues; Ministers; to Mr Marrett, the Chairman of the Board; to Ms Vardon, the Chief Executive Officer; and, most particularly, to the 25 000 to 30 000 employees of Centrelink who are participating in this video hook-up.

This is certainly a very important day. It is a day to tell the Australian community that the process of reform and innovation and renewal is very much alive in the service delivery area of the Commonwealth

Government and Commonwealth agencies. In administrative terms, this is probably the biggest single reform undertaken in the area of service delivery during the past 50 years. And it is a very special tribute to the ministerial leadership of my colleagues, Jocelyn Newman and Amanda Vanstone, and a particular tribute also to the heads of their departments.

I do want to take this opportunity in talking about the administrative significance of Centrelink and its launch. I want to take this opportunity on behalf of the Government as Prime Minister to thank all of those people who work in the public service.

Mine is a proudly private enterprise government. But that does not gainsay the fact that we regard a strong public sector providing necessary services for people as an integral part of modern government and as something that delivers necessary support to those in the community who need it. ...

The consolidation in Centrelink of so many of the services of the government that interact with people will provide, of course, a more human face. It will provide a more efficient service. It will lead to far less public dissatisfaction. Very importantly, it will also give a new sense of career and a new sense of career opportunity to the thousands of people who work for Centrelink, because Centrelink is carving out a new horizon and a completely different horizon. It is a demonstration that there is an Australian way, a unique Australian way, of delivering service support to those in the community who deserve and need our help and our assistance.

It will reach millions of people. It will touch millions of families. It will help the too many unemployed within our community. It will bring a modern understanding all over the country to the need for public services to relate in, not only a sympathetic way, but also a responsible way towards those in the community who are getting government assistance.

I have often spoken in the last few months of the principle of mutual obligation. That is a principle which says that it is the obligation of a decent, civil society to provide a social security safety-net and underpinning for those in the community who need help. I never want the Australian tradition of providing that safety net impaired or withdrawn.

We have a solemn obligation to help those in our community who are deserving of help. Equally, we have a right, as a responsible community, to ask of those who are receiving help, where it is reasonable to do so, that they do something in return for that assistance and something that is commensurate with the help and their own circumstances.

That is the principle of mutual obligation and it is the principle that underlies our approach to Work for the Dole. It is the principle that underlines the determination, the responsible and sensitive determination with which the minister, Senator Newman, in particular, has pursued the eradication to the maximum extent possible of fraud and abuse within the social security system. It is only a minority of people who undertake that. We owe it to the millions of honest Australian citizens who do not try and abuse or rort the system to ensure that, in all the manifestations of government, those who would seek to do so are properly pursued in accordance with the due processes of the law.

These services of Centrelink will provide new opportunities, more efficient services and more hope, not only for individuals, but also for families and for a whole range of those people. I understand that Centrelink will provide services and payments to over 7.8 million Australians, including 1.6 million pensioners, almost two million families receiving family allowance and 800 000 unemployed people. There will be over 400 locations across the country. ...

Reform and renewal and innovation are not only confined to the private sector of the Australian economy. If we are to realise the true potential of Australia, as we move into the 21st century, we must constantly look to ways of not only improving the efficiency with which the private sector of our economy operates but also the efficiency and the compassion with which services to the less fortunate, in particular, in our community operate.

We need, as far as possible, to take away the notion of dependency from the delivery of services. We need to develop a balance between compassion and responsibility. We need to deliver services in an efficient and friendly manner but, nonetheless, with an eye to our overall obligations to the taxpayers of Australia who pay for the services and the support which is delivered to others within the community. ...

I am very excited and very proud to be the head of the Government which has been responsible for such a major public sector reform, and one that will have a lasting impact on the morale of those who work in this area. We are talking about a very large number of people whose work is very greatly valued and it will also have a very significant effect on the way in which services are delivered.

So, I wish Centrelink well. I thank and congratulate all who work within it for their efforts of the last 12 months. I wish them great career prospects and plenty of encouragement in the years ahead. I particularly thank the Chairman of the Board and the Chief Executive Officer.

I want therefore to declare Centrelink officially opened and to launch the national campaign to inform the Australian public about the benefits of this important and innovative reform.

# Practical, Warm-Hearted
# Christian Charity

## Sydney – 1 May 2001

As one of Australia's oldest continuing charities, the Catholic Society of St Vincent de Paul invited the Prime Minister to launch their 2001 Winter Appeal. Since coming to office in 1996, Howard was determined to carve out a new government approach to social welfare. A key part of his Government's approach to social welfare was assembling what he called "a social coalition" of bodies to help the disadvantaged. Comprised of government agencies, churches, charities, voluntary associations and businesses of all sizes, this social coalition would find practical ways to assist the needy and less fortunate in the community.

In addition to rendering practical relief and assistance at the coalface, Howard foreshadowed that charities such as St Vincent de Paul could be involved in policy formation to provide governments with direct advice about how they could better handle the challenges of social welfare. With the Prime Minister according a greater role to charities in the social welfare sector, however, he emphasised that this was not about the Government abrogating its responsibilities to care for the disadvantaged but about the Government constructively partnering with non-government organisations to deliver better services. As part of this social coalition, the Prime Minister envisaged an active role for businesses as well as charities. Accordingly, he was keen to foster a culture of philanthropy in Australia where the corporate sector would play its part in helping the disadvantaged.

I am very pleased to have the opportunity to involve myself in the launch of this Winter Appeal by the Society of St Vincent de Paul. First and foremost, it gives me an opportunity to publicly honour the great work of the Society in helping the disadvantaged, not only in Australia, but around the world.

The Society is one of a number of great institutions which have been in existence for a long time who have been based upon a desire to help our fellow countrymen and women who have either fallen upon hard times, or through other combinations or circumstances, are in need of help. It is a reality that no matter how generically wealthy any community may be, no matter how much we may be able to boast of economic growth and, from time to time, dazzle ourselves with statistics about national economic performance, there are always a group of people within our community who have missed out – a group of people who are deserving and understanding of dignified support, of sensitive treatment, and of what I am sure all of us would describe as practical warm-hearted Christian charity. The Society has been in the forefront of welfare organisations in Australia and it has built up a great reputation, a deserved reputation, for helping the disadvantaged within our community.

In the time that I have been Prime Minister, I have spoken a great deal about the importance of trying to build within the Australian community a social coalition to tackle social and welfare issues. It is important when talking about a social coalition to understand that that is not some kind of euphemism or some kind of excuse for the Government reducing its role or retreating in any way from its responsibilities.

There will always be a fundamental and important role for governments to provide income support, to draw upon the general fund of taxpayers to help the needy and the less fortunate in our community. That responsibility can never be abandoned, it should never be abandoned, and it can never be negotiated away.

But there are, I believe, approaches which better combine the capacities of the Government, philanthropic individuals, the welfare sector, and the business community. The social coalition is really about each of

203

those groups getting together and doing what they can best do in order to help the disadvantaged within our society.

Governments are good at writing cheques. Governments are good at drawing upon tax-payers' money to provide pensions, unemployment benefits and forms of welfare support. Governments are not always good at the coal face, and that is where organisations such as your Society come in. The human compassion dispensed by the Society of St Vincent de Paul, by the Salvation Army, the Wesley Mission, by Anglicare, and I can go on to name all the great welfare organisations of Australia. That kind of human compassion is irreplaceable and unmatchable and can only be provided by warm-hearted members of organisations such as your own Society.

But your organisations can do more than provide relief and human compassion at the coal face of disadvantage. Drawing on your experience, you can also provide policy advice. You can be involved in reshaping and remaking the policy approaches that governments adopt in relation to welfare problems. One of the things that we also have endeavoured to do is to draw upon the policy expertise of the welfare organisations of Australia.

Most of you will be aware of the McClure Report, taking its name from Patrick McClure,[30] the executive director of Mission Australia, another great welfare organisation. That report has given the Government a blueprint for welfare reform, and that will be a focus in the budget to be delivered on the 22 May. It will not be, as I mentioned earlier, any kind of platform or excuse for the Government to reduce its role; rather for the Government more energetically involving itself in the process of welfare reform.

We have endeavoured to involve organisations such as your own in building a new approach, a better approach, in relation to delivery of welfare assistance. But there is a role also for the corporate sector of Australia. I frequently call on the corporate sector to give and support those in need. My call is not so much that business should give more,

---

[30] Patrick McClure (1949 - ) served as CEO of Mission Australia from 1997 to 2006 and was a key adviser of the Howard Government on welfare reform.

but that more businesses should give. There are some very spectacular examples, and you would know many of them, of great generosity on the part of wealthy people in Australia. The point is that not all people who are able to give do give. And I hope that the spirit of corporate philanthropy, which I am pleased to say is focusing more prominently in the thoughts and in the attitudes and in the minds of many business leaders in Australia, I hope that spreads even more widely. And the growth of partnerships between companies and welfare organisations in providing relief and help for the disadvantaged has been a very welcome feature of the whole welfare scene in Australia over the past few years.

Your Society deals right where it occurs. Yours is an organisation which daily comes into contact with human suffering and human misery. You bring to the relief of those in need a sense of compassion, of Christian understanding, a spiritual commitment which is the basis on which the Society was formed, taking its guide from that great injunction in St Matthew's gospel. It is an organisation that I very warmly support. I admire, I appreciate, the battles that it has fought over the years in the name and in the interest of the disadvantaged within the Australian community.

I hope that this Winter Appeal is a great success. I announce that the Commonwealth Government will itself contribute $100 000 to the Winter Appeal. I know that you will provide warmth and comfort to many Australians in need of that assistance. I renew the commitment I have made on many occasions that the Government seeks to work in a constructive manner, in as bipartisan a spirit as possible in the political atmosphere, with organisations such as your Society to provide help and hope and sustenance and inspiration to those within the Australian community who are less fortunate than we. I declare the appeal open. I wish it a great success. I commend it to generous Australians. I hope it provides a real vehicle for relief of distress and suffering within the Australian community.

# A Stronger More Cohesive Society

## Canberra – 6 August 2001

Shortly after the release of the 2001 McClure Report, the commissioned Report chaired by Mission Australia Chief Patrick McClure, the Prime Minister outlined the approach of his Government to social welfare in an address to the National Conference of Mission Australia.

A key recommendation the Prime Minister took from the McClure Report was that every Australian of working age should be encouraged and supported to participate in society. Accordingly, his Government's plans to reform Australia's social welfare system were framed around the principle that the best form of welfare was a paid job. To increase the workforce participation of Australians from disadvantaged backgrounds, the Howard Government launched its $1.7 billion "Australians Working Together" package to aid the transition of unemployed people from welfare to work. Embracing a vision to build stronger families and communities, the strategy was to give more Australian people job opportunities. The Government's overarching welfare reform agenda was to combat not only unemployment but also drug abuse, suicide and homelessness.

This forum provides an appropriate opportunity to recognise the role that your organisation has played, together with the individual City Missions over nearly 140 years, to assist individuals in need and to strengthen our community. In the words of its own mission statement, Mission Australia exists "to spread the love of God and meet human need". The City Mission movement began in July 1862 when a public meeting resolved to establish a Sydney City Mission based on the London City Mission. The relatively recent emergence of Mission Australia after a process of amalgamations and new formations has spread the movement's work to over 450 services, drawing upon the efforts of 3 000 staff and over one thousand volunteers.

In establishing the Sydney City Mission in 1862, Benjamin Short was not only working to meet human need but was also demonstrating that strong, fair and cohesive communities rely upon successful partnerships between individuals, business, government and the community, each contributing their own unique resources and expertise to tackle disadvantage at its source.

This is the notion of a social coalition that has guided much of the Government's thinking about the implementation of good social policy. It was soon after the last election that I addressed the Australian Council of Social Services (ACOSS) national congress about the values and principles that would underpin our second term social policy agenda. It is now appropriate, almost three years on, to reflect upon that speech, assess our progress and draw instruction for the future.

In my ACOSS address, I said that a legitimate role for government is, in a very strategic way, to protect the dignity of the individual so as to strengthen families and communities. Strengthening families and communities has been the focus of much of the Government's energy in its second term, while maintaining steadfast support for a strong social security safety net.

We have sought to harness the ambitions of parents to make a better life for themselves and their children, the energy and sensitivity of community organisations to those in need as well as the drive and innovation of business, both large and small, to produce real results. Working together in a social coalition, partnerships of these different groups are able to respond to entrenched social problems in new and flexible ways that embrace prevention as much as cure.

## Strong Economic Foundations

A prime role of any government is to secure the nation's economic foundations without which acceptable living standards are impossible to achieve. Far from being mutually exclusive, a government's social and economic goals should support each other. Just as without a strong economy, a cohesive community is that much harder to achieve, so too, responsible individuals, caring families and robust communities are fundamental to building a strong economy.

In the task of responsible economic management the Government has made considerable progress. High rates of economic growth have led to the creation of more than 800,000 jobs since March 1996, and reduced the rate of unemployment from well over eight per cent to under seven per cent today. ...

### *Strengthening our Modern Social Safety Net*

One of the benefits of good economic management is the capacity for sustainable strengthening of the social safety net. There has been much debate over recent years concerning the Government's changes to the Australian taxation system. Once again this is not a forum to go into a detailed analysis of those changes, except to the make the point that one of the fundamental virtues of a broad-based indirect tax such as the Goods and Services Tax is that it gives to any government, the wherewithal to fund, in growing proportion over time, the responsibilities it has to provide services to the community.

All of the GST is appropriated to the States. It means in the years ahead there is a built-in growth tax for those States to provide for the ongoing bread and butter services which are the responsibilities of States under our constitutional arrangements. In a very direct sense, a Goods and Services Tax provides a guarantee of the capacity of a compassionate community to care for those who need help years into the future. Without a Goods and Services Tax, governments would have to look to other areas of revenue raising that would be both less efficient, less palatable and therefore likely to be less available for the provision of those services which are so important.

Implementation of the New Tax System has also provided an important opportunity to review and improve our support for families and others in need. The New Tax System provided an extra $2.4 billion a year in additional assistance to over two million families including increases in family assistance and child care benefits…

## *New Directions in Social Policy: Building the Social Coalition*

As I indicated in my ACOSS speech, maintaining and strengthening the social safety net is not enough to meet modern social challenges. Our unique contribution in government has been to build the capacity of the social coalition to provide effective help to communities, families and people in need, and to provide more opportunities.

Our efforts in this second term of government have centred upon applying the important principles underpinning the social coalition in several new frontiers of policy. Principles include:

- all partners in the social coalition contributing to policy formulation;
- engagement of community organisations to deliver services relevant to local needs;
- focus on early intervention and prevention; and
- encouragement of participation rather than passive dependence.

I have said on numerous occasions that business has a key role to play at both a national and local level to strengthen communities. In my ACOSS speech,[31] for example, I said that my goal is to cultivate a greater philanthropic tradition in Australia. That is why I established the Prime Minister's Community Business Partnership two years ago to raise the profile of corporate social responsibility. Members of the Prime Minister's Community Business Partnership have helped develop a suite of new taxation measures designed to encourage greater corporate and personal philanthropy.

Key measures have included new concessions to promote gifts in kind, including gifts to environmental and heritage organisations and

---

[31] John Howard was referring here to his first speech to ACOSS entitled "Fair Australia", delivered on 13 October 1995. This was one of three "Headland Speeches" Howard gave whilst still Leader of the Opposition.

the removal of capital gains tax penalties applying to bequests. We have also established a new type of private charitable fund providing families and individuals with greater freedom to set up their own trusts for philanthropic purposes.

It is appropriate here to acknowledge the contribution of Patrick McClure, a member of the Prime Minister's Community Business Partnership tax working group, to these specific initiatives. I look forward to working with this group on further such initiatives in a third term Coalition Government.

There are many other instances in our approach to social policy where we have used the social coalition to draw on the expertise of different sectors to not only implement but design our response to specific social problems.

Our approaches to tackling the unemployment problem provide good examples. The success of the Job Network, over the government-run monopoly it replaced, in putting jobseekers in work is, to a large extent, a function of better incentives and the mission that many Job Network providers possess to satisfy human need. According to the OECD, the Job Network and associated programmes have been at least as effective as former programmes in helping participants find work at about half the net cost to taxpayers.

Similarly, the key to the success of Work for the Dole has been the way it has involved charitable and community organisations to complete important local projects. Added to this are the improvements to the self-esteem and work ethic of the young unemployed that are encouraged by Work for the Dole.

A study into the scheme in 2000 found that 30 per cent of participants were no longer on unemployment benefits three months after leaving the programme. The same study found that the prospects of getting off the dole were 76 per cent higher for those who had participated in Work for the Dole compared to similar job seekers who had not been part of the scheme.

I would like to acknowledge the role that Mission Australia continues to play in countless Job Network outlets and Work for the Dole projects across the country. …

A more recent social coalition initiative is our $240 million Stronger Families and Communities Strategy, launched last year [2000]. The Strategy develops practical projects at a local level to identify and encourage potential community leaders, build up the skills of volunteers, and help communities promote their own "can do" spirit, objectives very much in harmony with the theme of this Conference. It also aims to help families with young children, given the crucial importance of the early childhood years.

We have already committed funds to many practical projects, such as Jumpstart, a Queensland Police Citizens Youth Welfare Association initiative to help address the training needs of young unemployed people in Brisbane who did not complete high school.

The work we are doing with the National Advisory Council on Suicide Prevention to develop the National Suicide Prevention Strategy is also an example of the social coalition in action. We have committed $48 million over five years to this initiative and funds are now being rolled out. In October 2000 I announced the first round of projects to be funded including an extra $100 000 each year to the youth counselling service, Kids Help Line, to allow the service to take an additional 15 400 calls a year.

This being National Homeless Persons' Week, we have an opportunity to take stock of what we, as a community, are doing to address homelessness. It is also a time to recognise and commend those organisations and individuals, including Mission Australia and its staff, who do so much every day to tackle this difficult issue and support those who find themselves in this situation. Tackling homelessness has been a high priority for my Government. In my ACOSS speech, I mentioned our Youth Homelessness early intervention pilots as an early example of the Coalition Government's approach to social policy.

The report of the Advisory Committee on Homelessness, released yesterday by Senator Amanda Vanstone, the Minister for Family and Community Services, indicated areas requiring further attention. Of course, this must be seen in the context of more spending on crisis and support services than ever before, including over $800 million for five years on the Supported Accommodation Assistance Programme. More recently, we have announced extra support through the Australians Working Together package to help vulnerable groups, such as those who are homeless, to get the help they need.

## *Welfare Reform*

The Reference Group on Welfare Reform, established by the Government in September 1999 and chaired by Patrick McClure, was a further demonstration of our commitment to use the social coalition to review major areas of policy. Patrick has made a tremendous contribution to the development of Australia's welfare reform agenda. He brought a wealth of practical experience and compassion to the work of the Reference Group.

The notion that every Australian of working age should be encouraged and supported to participate in society was central to the recommendations of the report of the Reference Group. For many people, the most desirable kind of participation is an economic one. It is participation in paid work that so often provides independence, builds self-esteem and self-reliance. Without jobs, many people can lose hope as well as self-esteem and feel alienated from society. Children growing up in jobless families are at greater risk of ending up jobless themselves.

The $1.7 billion Australians Working Together package announced in the 2000 Budget was the first step in the reform process charted in the McClure Report. The package is a clear demonstration of the Government's commitment to striking a fair balance between providing help and requiring participation.

The package was also a significant investment in Australia's social infrastructure – an investment that will deliver returns to taxpayers over the years in the forms of less joblessness and less welfare dependence.

Australians Working Together expanded the support and assistance available for all to participate, including $324 million for unemployed people, $251 million for parents, $177 million for people with disabilities and $83 million for Indigenous Australians. The package also took an important first step towards addressing the financial disincentives against taking up paid work through the $506 million Working Credit initiative.

The McClure Report recognised that together with economic participation, social participation is also important. This is because social participation brings many of the same benefits. It builds self-esteem and self-reliance, promotes mental and physical health and well-being, builds social cohesion and helps to foster sense of community. A large number of people receiving income support already make a significant social contribution through parenting and caring, voluntary work and community work. Our approach supports and values these contributions.

We also recognise that community participation can also help people in the transition to paid jobs by building and maintaining skills, self-esteem and social networks. To ensure that people can participate to their full capacity, Australians Working Together included significant additional spending on support for people who experience severe barriers to participation. For example, we are spending $140 million on Centrelink Personal Advisers and $154 million on a Personal Support Programme.

### Next Steps in Welfare Reform

Australians Working Together was the first step in a longer process of welfare reform. We will continue to work with the Welfare Reform Consultative Forum to develop a strong medium-to-longer term agenda, consistent with the McClure Report.

We are committed to taking further steps to move Australia's excessively complex income support systems towards the McClure ideal of a single benefits system. The McClure model of a layered single benefit structure, including a basic payment, and supplements to assist with participation costs and provide participation rewards, will guide initiatives further. This approach is already in evidence with the training supplement announced in the recent budget.

We are also committed to taking further steps to reducing the in-built disincentives of the present systems to move from welfare to paid work, the so-called poverty traps. Significant progress in this direction was made in the Government's tax reform package which reduced marginal tax rates and reduced withdrawal rates of family benefits. The Working Credit measure announced in the budget was a further step. The following principles will underpin all future work:

- our commitment to making up front investments that will deliver returns to taxpayers later on as people move from welfare dependence to economic and social participation;

- our commitment to working in consultation with the community, through the Consultative Forum; and

- our undertaking that nobody's benefit will be cut as a result of changes in the benefit system.

Building social partnerships and community capacity was a high priority of the McClure Report and will be a high priority of a third term Coalition Government. We want to motivate business to work in more effective partnership with their surrounding communities through better workplace policies and practices – policies that give people more choice of when and how to work throughout their working lives.

The Prime Minister's Community Business Partnership is uniquely placed to take this initiative forward, given its representation from the business and community services fields. Funds have already been allocated to support this activity in the Australians Working Together package.

The problem of regional unemployment also warrants further examination including a strategy to improve employment services in regional areas and, through community capacity building, building on the results of our Stronger Families and Communities Strategy.

Welfare reform, like tax reform, is something that most of us have known for years is necessary. As with tax reform, the Government has shown that it is willing to make decisions that are both strong and fair. With welfare reform, we have established a comprehensive inquiry, built

214

a robust mechanism to consult with the community, and spent months on the painstaking policy work before the budget. These credentials equip us well for the work to be carried out in a third term.

## *Conclusion*

In my National Press Club Address last week,[32] I identified a number of other issues that will be important priorities for a third term Coalition Government. I spoke of the challenge of Australia's ageing population, planning for the health and aged care needs of the future and encouraging greater self-reliance through higher savings and retirement income planning. I also spoke of the need to help parents to balance their work and family responsibilities.

Our efforts to continue building the social coalition provide a strong linkage between each of these priorities and welfare reform. The idea of the social coalition has proven remarkably fruitful in our time in office. It has enabled us to advance new frontiers of policy but there is considerably more to be done.

Since I made my ACOSS address almost three years ago, the Government has worked hard to encourage greater personal responsibility and to use the social coalition to address some of the key social challenges such as combatting unemployment, drug abuse, suicide and homelessness as well as building stronger families and communities.

I believe that we should not stand back and merely accept these problems simply as facts of modern life. Supporting self-reliance through participation as well as early intervention and prevention offers new hope to build a stronger, more cohesive Australian community and to work to ensure that no individual is left behind.

---

[32] John Howard is referring here to the address he gave at the National Press Club in Canberra on 1 August 2001.

# Building Self-Esteem and Self-Confidence
## Melbourne – 25 October 2001

In this address to Australia's peak welfare advocacy body, the Australian Council of Social Services
(ACOSS), the Prime Minister, John Howard, reaffirmed
the guiding principles behind his Government's approach to social welfare reform. Touching again on the
findings of the McClure Report, he emphasised that the
aspirations of building a social coalition, providing early
intervention in individual cases, and increasing the self-
reliance of needy individuals were central to his reform
agenda.

Regarding the social participation of disadvantaged
Australians as a significant antidote to poverty and welfare dependency, the Prime Minister appreciated that
Australians engaged in paid employment, family responsibilities and community work benefited not only fi-
nancially but enjoyed higher levels of self-esteem, self-
reliance, mental health and physical well-being, which,
in turn, augured well for greater social cohesion and a
richer community life. Affirming that a government's social and economic goals were always mutually reinforcing, he observed that while a healthy society needed a
strong economy, a cohesive society of responsible individuals, caring families and robust communities was
fundamental to economic growth and prosperity. For
the nation's welfare system to remain sustainable over
the long term, Australia needed both firm economic and
social foundations.

I was not only delighted but, indeed, determined to keep my commitment to address this annual conference of ACOSS because I have valued
the contact I have had with your organisation in the time that I have been

216

Prime Minister. This is a marvellous opportunity for me, and I hope you, too, derive some benefit from that contact as well to report on the social policy approach of the Government over the last three years. It is also an opportunity for me to canvass some of the detail of the Government's third term agenda of welfare reform. And I do so during a day here in Melbourne in which I will not only be canvassing the Government's third term agenda in relation to social policy, but also in the important area of health policy.

Our plans for welfare reform will provide for further strengthening of the social security safety net and dramatically improve the incentives for Australians in welfare to achieve the transition which we all support to employment that is both paid and satisfying. …My Government's social policy record is built on a set of shared Australian values of:

- opportunity and choice;
- a fair go for all;
- increasing self-reliance;
- working in partnership; and
- mutual obligation.

In advancing these values, we realise that governments cannot do it all and cannot do it alone. We need to draw on the strengths that businesses, communities, families and individuals bring to our shared society.

That is why in my 1998 address to the ACOSS, nearly three years ago, I committed the Government to working more closely with all of the partners in what I called then, and still call, the social coalition. This is a coalition of governments, community, businesses, families and individuals working together to address the challenges we face and to build opportunities for us all.

It draws on the perspectives, the experience, the expertise of the organisations and individuals all represented here today who, every day, are exposed to the causes and consequences of the problems we face as a society, and who have an important role in helping to find the solutions.

The Government has a critical role to play in the social coalition, ensuring that the Australian economy is strong enough to generate opportunities and choices for all Australians. We are very proud of our record of economic management. It has delivered strong economic growth, even in times of marked regional economic downturn. More than 830 000 new jobs have been created since March 1996. The unemployment rate, although I would like it to be lower, has fallen significantly.

Real wages have grown strongly, by more than 9 per cent under my Government, compared with growth of just 2.3 per cent between 1983 and 1996. Inflation has been more than halved under this Government and yesterday's Consumer Price Index figure was right in line with the Government's predictions at the time the new tax system was introduced…. Australia's strong economy has already enabled us to strengthen the social safety-net that ensures that Australians get a fair go. …

Public health insurance membership has increased by around three million since the rebate was introduced. Private hospitals have experienced increased growth in utilisation and in the benefits paid. We are also moving to fix the gap and, as I said in answer to that question that public hospital funding to States will increase 28 per cent in real terms over the five years of the current Australian Health Care Agreements.

The social coalition, early intervention and increasing self-reliance have also been central to our approach to welfare reform. Our welfare reform agenda was informed by the recommendations of the Reference Group on Welfare Reform chaired by Mission Australia's Patrick McClure.

It affirms the principle that every Australian of working age should be encouraged and supported to participate socially and economically wherever possible. This is because economic participation promotes independence, the ability to make choices and to take up opportunities. It builds self-esteem and it builds confidence. By contrast, unemployment can have a devastating effect on self-esteem, leaving people dispirited and socially alienated.

The $1.7 billion Australians Working Together package, announced in the 2001-2002 Budget, initiates the process of welfare reform recommended by the McClure Report. ...The package represents a careful balance between requiring participation and providing the assistance and the incentives needed for people to help themselves.

We believe that it is not only necessary but it is also fair in proper circumstances to require people to participate. And once they have begun, most people recognise the benefits of participation. Australians Working Together expands the support and assistance available to encourage participation:

- $324 million for unemployed people, including 16,500 extra Work for the Dole places and 30,000 Job Search Training places.
- $251 for parents returning to work, including more after-school child care places and a new Transition to Work Programme.
- $177 million for people with disabilities, including 28,300 new employment assistance and rehabilitation places.
- $83 million for Indigenous Australians, including help for 10,000 CDEP participants to get a job through Indigenous Employment Centres.

It will also take an important step towards fixing financial disincentives to taking up paid work through creating the $506 million Working Credit initiative.

All of these spending initiatives are committed to by the Government and they apparently represent some of the spending priorities of the Coalition which have been roundly criticised as profligate and unnecessary by the Labor Party during the course of this election campaign.

Social participation is also important because it builds self-esteem and self-reliance. It promotes mental and physical health and well-being; it builds social cohesion and a sense of community.

A large number of people receiving income support already make a significant social contribution through parenting and caring, voluntary work and community work. Our approach greatly values and respects these contributions.

Community participation also facilitates the transition to paid work by building and maintaining skills, self-esteem and social networks.

Our welfare reform agenda recognises that some people may find participation difficult, because of a lack of opportunity or skills, or because of difficult personal circumstances. To ensure people can participate as fully as possible, Australians Working Together provides significant support for those people facing barriers to participation. For example, we are spending $140 million over four years on Centrelink Personal Advisers, and $154 million on the Personal Support Programme which will help people facing severe or multiple personal problems such as homelessness, drug or alcohol addiction, mental illness or domestic violence.

We want to build people's self-esteem, both to improve their personal circumstances and to build capacity in our community.

Building self-reliance is an increasingly important aspect of our approach to practical reconciliation. We want to help Indigenous Australians with practical measures that build the capacity for self-reliance.

The 2001-02 Budget includes new spending of more than $327 million over the next four years to build on the Government's approach to reducing Indigenous disadvantage through practical reconciliation. Our programmes are helping Indigenous Australians break the welfare dependency cycle by providing effective training, creating jobs and encouraging sustainable economic development in Indigenous communities. ...

I recently emphasised the Government's commitment to:

- Involving all partners in the social coalition in the policy formulation process.
- Enabling community organisations to deliver services relevant to local needs.
- Focusing on early intervention and prevention; and
- Encouraging participation rather than passive dependence.

Participation will remain the underlying principle of our welfare reform agenda.

220

Implementation of the $1.7 billion Australians Working Together Package will be a major priority for a third term Coalition Government. ...We also want to remove disincentives to people moving from welfare dependence to paid work.

The Working Credit initiative is a valuable step in this direction. Advances were also made through reductions in marginal tax rates and reduced withdrawal rates for family benefits which were a principal feature of the Tax Reform package. ...

Welfare reform is about strengthening our society by supporting and encouraging people to identify and make the most of opportunities. We are committed to helping all Australians share in this country's prosperity and future. No one should be left behind, least of all because they lack the skills, the support or the opportunities to participate in our community's social and economic life.

As I think we all know, children and young people are best guided and nurtured in their transition to adulthood by strong families supported by strong communities. Balancing the demands of family and the workplace in modern Australian society is an increasingly important and challenging issue. We need, amongst other things, to cater for the realities of an environment where around 50 per cent of school aged children have two working parents or a sole custodial parent who works. ...

I have tried to give an account to you and through you to the Australian people of what we have tried to do in this very important area. I conclude by reminding those of you who were present when I delivered a speech to the ACOSS Congress in October 1995, when I was still the Leader of the Opposition, and I gave a number of commitments on behalf of my party which would be binding on it if I were to win the election of March 1996.

The central commitment that we made was that we would preserve and protect the social security safety-net and I believe with all my heart that we have done that. We have not always done everything you have wanted. We have often done some things that you have not wanted and you have not agreed with but we have preserved and protected the social security safety-net. We have added to it, we have broadened it and we have introduced a number of improvements and a number of initiatives. Can I say that has been made possible because we believe in social justice, we believe in a fair Australian society.

We also believe in an Australian society where people can aspire to achieve and to better themselves, but we also believe that you can only deliver a fair and just society if you have a strongly growing economy. The foundation of the capacity of any government, whether it is Liberal or Labor, to deliver better social welfare benefits in the years ahead, together with more funding for health and more funding for education, is a sound and growing economy with well-constructed taxation and industrial policies. Unless you have that, you do not have the capacity to aspire to deliver the kind of decent balanced society that I know all of us, whatever our politics or our backgrounds, really believe in.

Ladies and gentlemen, I wish you well in the work you do for the less privileged in the Australian community. It is work that the Government respects. It is work that your fellow Australians respect and I appreciate very much the opportunity you have provided to me this morning to outline some of the Government's plans for the next three years.

# All about Choice

## Parliament House, Sydney – 1 June 2007

> The public debate about how governments could best support women to balance work and family responsibilities remained topical throughout the Howard years. With an increasing proportion of women combining careers with family responsibilities, the Howard Government understood that this would have far-reaching implications for its policy approach to social welfare and taxation.
>
> Whilst Howard had a deep personal admiration for individual women who chose to be a full-time parent at home with young children, he appreciated that his Government needed also to cater for the women with children who chose to work part-time or full-time. To this end, his Government's Family Tax Benefit was designed to provide benefits to both stay-at-home mothers and working mothers, thereby making the choice for all women easier. In keeping with Liberal thought, he did not believe it was the function of government to prescribe how parents organise the care of their children. Government's role was, instead, to empower parents freely to choose the work and care arrangements best suited to their family needs and circumstances.

This is but the latest of the occasions that I have had the opportunity of opening the Federal Women's Committee conference at the beginning of our Federal Council meeting.

The philosophy of our Party about the role of women or, indeed, the role of men, in society has been all about choice. And the Party has for many, many years recognised the central role of women both in the organisation and, increasingly, in the Federal Parliament. We have never embraced the patronising approach of quotas; we have never reserved particular seats or places on a Senate ticket for women. We have sought over the years through the logical process of the Party organisation making rational decisions to see women emerge in increasing numbers and that has been the case.

It happens to be the Liberal Party and the Coalition in government that has produced a Cabinet with the largest number of women in Australia's history; it happens to be the Liberal Party that has produced the longest serving female Cabinet Minister in Australia's history and, of course, Senator Helen Coonan is for the first time a member of the Leadership Group of a party in government.

These are facts; they are indisputable; they are incontrovertible but they do not connote a belief by the Liberal Party that there are quintessentially women's issues. All issues are of concern to women. There are some issues in politics where women bring special perspectives that we men recognise and respect. But, fundamentally, the view of a woman on defence and foreign affairs is as important as the view of a woman on child-care or health policy and, equally, might I say, the view of a man on the responsibilities and challenges of raising children is as relevant and as responsible as the views of a woman.

Having stated those markers, as it were, to define where I am coming from, can I thank all the female members of the Liberal Party for their outstanding support and loyally towards me and to my parliamentary colleagues and the contribution over the years that they have made to the strength and the vitality of the Liberal Party organisation.

I have a great story to tell about the way in which the opportunities for both men and women throughout Australia have been enhanced over the last 11 years. One of the things that warms me as much as anything has been the extraordinary growth in the number of women starting their small businesses. Of the small businesses that are opened each year, growing numbers, now somewhere between 30 to 40 per cent, of small businesses in Australia are now opened by women and it connotes an expanding role and expanding set of opportunities for women in our society.

Women have shared very, very dramatically in the explosion in employment over the last year. Average weekly earnings for women have increased by six per cent in the last year to March. The number of new female jobs increased by 134 000 or 2.9 per cent in the last year to April; the same exactly as the increase in the number of jobs for men. And the changes and improvements to Family Tax Benefits have been of enormous benefit for both men and women. It is a society where there are expanding opportunities and expanding choices available to women.

All of the policies that have defined my approach to the responsibilities of men and women towards their children, and mothers and fathers towards their children, have been defined by the philosophy of choice. The decision to be a full-time parent at home when your children are young is a noble choice exercised freely by, overwhelmingly, but not always by women and a choice that should be totally respected. But equally it is not the role of the Government to tell parents how to organise the care of their children. It is the role of the Government as far as possible to make the exercise of all of the choices men and women would want possible, and that is what we have done with our Family Tax Benefit policies. It is infinitely easier now for a low and middle-income family to have a parent at home than used to be the case if that is their choice.

Equally, the changes we have made to Family Tax Benefits, the easing of the taper in relation to the withdrawal of welfare benefits in the operation of the tax system and, indeed, the most recent tax changes announced by the Treasurer, Peter Costello, which will come into operation on 1 July 2001, will be of particular benefit for women in the workforce. The great bulk of women in the workforce with dependent children who work part-time, and the proportion that benefit from those tax changes, where the point at which the 30 per cent tax rate comes into operation, is increased from $25 000 to $30 000. It will deliver in proportionate terms far greater benefits to women with dependent children in the workforce than to men with dependent children in the workforce. This is because the great bulk of women with dependent children who are in the workforce are in fact working part-time and it is an aspect of those tax changes that will become more apparent after they come into operation. ...

I thank you again, very warmly, for your contribution to our great cause. I salute the contribution of the women within my Parliamentary Party and pre-selections for the Senate have yielded a growing number of them in recent months. They will add to the ranks of those who are already there.

# VI

## Members of the Great Australian Family

### Immigration, Citizenship and Indigenous Affairs

# The Chinese Contribution to Australia
## Generous, Immense and Impressive

### Sydney – 21 February 1997

The Prime Minister, in this address to the Chinese Australian Forum, paid tribute to the rich contribution Australians of Chinese descent had made to the life of the nation. He spoke from personal experience as the Member for Bennelong, an electorate with one of the highest proportions of Australians from a Chinese background.

He observed that the association of Chinese people with Australia had been a long one but not always a happy one. Resolved to put right many of the past prejudices and injustices suffered by these Australians, the Prime Minister affirmed their right to dignity, tolerance, respect and membership of the broader Australian family.

Declaring racism and bigotry to have no part in the "true Australian spirit", Howard reflected that Australia was a more vibrant, cosmopolitan, global and outward-looking society than that of several generations ago. Howard believed that Australia was ultimately a better country for this cultural enrichment. At a stage of his prime ministership where Howard was perceived by many of his detractors to be "soft" on racism and anti-immigration sentiment, Howard seized this opportunity to articulate clearly his appreciation and admiration for one of Australia's oldest immigrant communities with roots stemming back to the mid-1800s.

I decided a couple of months ago that I would like an occasion associated with the Chinese New Year to address a large gathering of Australians, including the goodly number of Australians of Chinese descent.

The occasion of the Chinese New Year offers the opportunity to do a number of things. First and most important, on behalf of the Government of Australia and on behalf, therefore, of all of the people of Australia, it is an opportunity to honour the enormous contribution that Australians of Chinese descent have made to the building of the modern Australia. The association of Chinese people with Australia is a very long association. There have been occasions in the past when it has not been a happy association. But to most Australians, the contribution of Chinese people has been generous, it has been immense, it has been impressive and it is very much part of the miracle which is modern Australia.

Chinese people have brought to this country industry, integrity, a respect for and commitment to the importance of the family in Australian society, a flair for entrepreneurial expertise, professional skills, entertainment skills, recreational skills. Indeed, in every walk of Australian life in the 1990s, we find Australians of Chinese descent or a Chinese background and the particular association of Chinese Australians with the city of Sydney is very well known indeed.

Sydney is a different city from what it was when I was born here in 1939 and grew up here through the 1940s and 50s. I did not know many Chinese boys at Earlwood Primary School in the late 1940s; I did know one at Canterbury Boys High School in the early 1950s. My children, by contrast, as they have gone to primary school at Greenwich Public School and, later, to private school on the lower north shore, have known many, and that is just a function of the changing character, the diversifying character, of modern Australia.

The other reason that I wanted to come here tonight was to take the opportunity to honour the Chinese New Year and to say something about the fundamentals that bind all of us together as Australians. It is certainly true that there is no country in the world which has a finer appreciation of the values of freedom and openness and tolerance than does Australia.

Australia has its flaws, Australia has its blemishes, Australia has had its failures in the past. But if you compare this country with the other nations of the world, there are many things about it which entitle us to boast of – tolerance and openness and warm heartedness and of decency. There are some within our ranks who harbour prejudice and bigotry and who do display intolerance whether it is on ethnic or racial grounds or other grounds. I want to say that for my part, and for the part of my Government, that that is no part of the true Australian spirit. Any manifestation of racism in our ranks is repugnant to everything for which Australia has always stood. It ought to be denounced, it ought to be identified and it ought to be guarded against.

The other side of the equation is the remarkable tolerance and the remarkable receptivity and generosity that this country has displayed towards so many, especially over the last 30 or 40 years. It remains the case that in the late 1970s, on a per capita basis, Australia took more refugees from war-torn Indo-China than any nation in the world, a very special demonstration of the contribution and the generosity of the Australian community towards an area of very particular need. It is necessary that we debate issues of sensitivity, issues such as immigration, issues such as the character of Australia, what contributes to the modern Australian personality and the modern Australian character. We recognise in the course of that debate that the composition of the Australian population has changed a great deal over the last 30 or 40 years.

We are a more diverse, we are a more vibrant, we are a more cosmopolitan, we are more global and we are a more internationalised society than what we were several generations ago. One of the many contributions that Australians of Asian, especially Chinese, descent make to modern Australia are the links that they provide with the countries often of their birth and certainly of their family association. I have lost count of the number of Australians of Chinese descent who over the last couple of years have provided me with valuable insight into the culture and the politics and the attitude of countries within our region.

Within a few weeks I will be visiting the People's Republic of China. It will be the first visit that I have paid to the country as Prime Minister. The relationship between Australia and China is very important to my

Government. I recognise that of the Chinese Australians here, not all of you have come from the People's Republic. Many of you, perhaps a majority of you, have not. And I know there is a variety of views about the People's Republic of China as there are a variety of views about a whole lot of other issues.

But nothing can gainsay the fact that the association between this country and the People's Republic is an important one. Our values on many political issues are different. Australia is an open democracy, the People's Republic is not. But we have very close and important economic and other ties, and it is the responsibility of any Australian government, be it a Liberal government or a Labor government, to look always to Australia's national interest.

Australia's national interest lies in fostering the economic, the cultural and other links that now exist between Australia and not only China but the Chinese diasporas in other parts of the world.

So it is with those things in mind, and a determination to build further a pragmatic common sense relationship based on mutual respect, and on a recognition of the importance of welcoming China into the family of nations in the Asia-Pacific region, that I will visit Beijing and Shanghai during Easter.

I spoke earlier of many of the contributions that Chinese Australians had made to our country. It is impossible to think of the Australian economy, particularly the small business sector, without thinking of the contribution of so many entrepreneurs of Chinese and of Asian descent in this country. The lively way in which so many members of the Chinese Australian community have contributed to the building of the modern Australian economy is very widely recognised, it is very warmly appreciated. We would not be the people we are, we would not be the success we are, we would not be the increasingly respected community that we are becoming amongst the economies of the world, had it not been for the contribution of so many of those members of the Chinese Australian community. ...

On behalf of that modern Australia, I want to say to all members of the

Chinese community in Australia: you are an integral part of Australian society. You are welcomed; you are honoured; you are respected; your right to dignity, to security, to peace and to tolerance and respect is something which is part and parcel of what I regard as a civilised and acceptable Australia in the 1990s.

It is part and parcel of Australian democracy to have vigorous exchanges and vigorous debate. Some of it on occasions is not the most intelligent of exchanges that one could be engaged in. But it is never part of civilised or acceptable or robust debate to think of people in terms of the colour of their skin, or except perhaps, in a humorous and entirely fun-loving way, their country of origin.

Australians are, I believe, a tolerant people. They are a fundamentally very decent people, the most decent in the world, and I think the great majority of Australians hold very dear that most cherished ideal of the Australian ethos is the ethos of the fair go. I want to say to all of you that a fair go for all is as much a part of the Australian ethos now as it has ever been.

To all of you, have a very happy Year of the Ox. I hope all of you have the occasion during the year to have peace and prosperity and personal happiness and personal success. And once again, on behalf of the wider Australian community, and on behalf of my Government, can I say a word of very warm thanks and deep appreciation for the contribution that you have made to our country and how much a pleasure it is for me to celebrate with you our joint great good fortune and that is to celebrate the miracle together of being Australians.

# Rotary – "Service above Self"

## North Sydney – 7 March 1997

With the ethic of volunteerism representing not only a tenet of Liberal thought but a core Australian value, the Prime Minister was keen to affirm the voluntary endeavours of community service organisations such as Rotary. While not a member of Rotary himself, the Rotary Club of Australia had conferred John Howard with a special Award in March 1997 in recognition of his public service. In responding, the Prime Minister lauded the contribution of Rotary to enriching the social fabric of the nation over several generations. Founded in 1905 by the Chicago-born lawyer and philanthropist, Paul Harris, the organisation bore "service above self" as its motto and guiding ethos. With its projects of community self-help and charitable relief, Rotary was seen as giving tangible expression to the principle of mutual obligation where citizens would contribute to the community that had helped and supported them. As with his philosophy of social welfare, the Prime Minister saw this ethic of mutual obligation as integral to Australian citizenship. For Howard, the self-giving ideals of Rotary were thus key to what it meant to be a good Australian citizen.

I am very touched by this Award. Those symbolic gestures in life are always in a sense more rewarding and have a lot more meaning than more material gestures.

I am not a Rotarian, although I have attended many Rotary functions in my life. I feel as though I know and understand Rotary extremely well. I take the opportunity as Prime Minister to acknowledge the tremendous contribution that Rotary makes towards building a better Australia and building a happier, more cooperative world.

We would never be able to keep Australia going without the help of literally hundreds of thousands, if not millions of Australians who volunteer their time and their energy and their effort to doing those things that no government, whatever its attitude may be, no government can ever do. Australia has a tremendous tradition of volunteerism. Being a volunteer and getting out and helping people in an unsung, very selfless fashion has always been an important characteristic of being an Australian.

We are very good at it, and, although, as you all know, the Rotary movement started in the United States, the natural appeal of Rotary to Australians was very understandable. This has been evident in the way in which so many Australians joined Rotary, and through the years have cooperated in the local efforts of Rotary, have involved themselves in the international exchanges, the encouragement to community involvement and community self-help, and the building of an understanding of what good citizenship is all about.

The nurturing of the notion that our society is really a lot about mutual obligations. We have mutual obligations each to the other. We have rights but we also have responsibilities. As a society we also have an obligation to look after those within our midst who are less fortunate than we are and, from time to time, we have a right to say to people who are assisted that it is part of the mutual obligation of being a member of the Australian community that something is done in return for the effort that is extended to help them.

Rotary has been very much part of this and, in the process, hundreds of thousands of Australians have found a great deal of personal satisfaction in involving themselves in the affairs of Rotary, in raising funds to help needy causes and, very importantly, promoting international understanding.

I was reflecting, as I drove here tonight from Gladesville, just how many people, how many young people I know, including members of my extended family who have been the recipients of those great international student-Rotary exchanges. One of the great ways in which young people have learned about other countries and the understanding that is so important, particularly in a world where communications and the globalisation of the world economy has demolished and removed the differences that used to exist.

So, in many ways, Rotary is owed a great debt of gratitude by the Australian community, and I want, on behalf of the Government, to express my personal gratitude to all of those Rotarians in Australia who, over the years, have done so much to build and nurture the spirit of Rotary and have made such a magnificent contribution to improving understanding here in Australia, and for making it possible between peoples and between nations.

# Openness and Tolerance

## Perth – 24 July 1998

Having earlier praised the contribution of Chinese immigrants to enriching Australian society, the Prime Minister's theme in this address to the Chinese Chamber of Commerce Golden Jubilee Coffee Shop Forum in Perth was how immigration, in general, had changed Australia for the better. Hailing the success with which Australia was able to absorb immigrants from some 150 nationalities, Howard regarded this as one of the nation's greatest achievements.

While acknowledging the scope for legitimate public debate about Australia's approach to immigration, he maintained that current immigration policy should be guided by a number of principles. The first was to recognise the potential for future immigrants to make a positive contribution to Australia by enriching the cultural tapestry and making the country more outward-focused; and, second, the principle of "non-discrimination" where any consideration of race or nationality in the selection of immigrants would be disregarded. A third principle was that of "mutual obligation". For its part, the host-nation had an obligation to be warm, welcoming and accepting of newcomers joining Australia; immigrants, in return, had an obligation to embrace the major values of their new homeland.

I am especially delighted to have the opportunity on this visit to Western Australia to address the Chinese Chamber of Commerce. It is a timely occasion to say a few things that are important to relations between Australia and Australia's neighbours in the Asia Pacific region. It is also an opportunity for me to say something about the values that bind all of us together as Australians, irrespective of our racial or ethnic background...

Australia has a very long record of openness and tolerance towards people who have come to our shores from all around the world. In the years that immediately followed the Second World War, the doors of Australia were thrown open wide to hundreds of thousands, indeed millions, from different parts of Europe. But for a long time the doors were not thrown open to people from Asia. And it was the prime ministership of Harold Holt who had led a Coalition Government in 1966 to abandon, formally, what was known as the White Australia Policy. From then on, progressively, Australia adopted and embraced a non-discriminatory immigration policy.

The level of immigration and the composition of the migrant intake to Australia will always be a matter of legitimate debate. There are strongly held views on both sides of the argument as to whether Australia would benefit from, in present or immediately foreseeable circumstances, a significant increase in the migrant intake. That is a debate that should be encouraged.

The Government that I lead has made a number of decisions since it came to power, which it believes have been in the national interest to alter the intake with a greater emphasis on skilled migration and a slightly lower emphasis on family reunion. And we have also, because of our assessment of economic circumstances, induced a reduction in the overall intake. There are those in the community who will disagree with that. There are those in the community who will argue that it ought to go further and that is a matter of legitimate political debate in Australia.

So far as I am concerned, and so far as the Government is concerned, we bring to that debate a number of very important principles. The first of those principles is that over the decades, particularly since the Second World War, migration has made an enormous contribution to Australia. It has helped to change Australia for the better, not for the worse. It has helped to make Australia a more outward looking, more welcoming, and more interesting country. Perhaps the most valuable thing that I have observed over the years is the way in which we have been able to absorb into Australia people from something like 150 different countries with a remarkable degree of harmony. That has been one of the great Australian achievements. I cannot think of a country in the world that has done it more successfully. Nor can I think of a country in the world that has been able to do it and, in the process, preserve a core set of Australian values that maintain a long continuity of values connecting us now in the last years of the twentieth century, with the early beginnings of the Australian federation almost 100 years ago. As a government, we bring to that debate our view that immigration has been an enormous plus for Australia, and for Australia's development.

Another principle or another value that we bring to the debate about immigration in Australia is that immigration in this country should be based firmly and absolutely on the principle of non-discrimination. In other words, we will not choose people according to their race, their ethnic or national origin. We do not prefer somebody because he or she is of a particular ethnic background against somebody else who is of another ethnic background. I do want to make it very clear that the Government is firmly and resolutely opposed to any change in the non-discriminatory character of our immigration policy. It remains an important cornerstone, a core value, of the approach that we bring to immigration. We believe that Australia's links to the various parts of the word have been enormously enhanced by the way in which we have been able to absorb people from different parts of the world.

We are proud of our record of tolerance. But, like all things that we hold dear, like all values that are central to our being as a nation, the principle of tolerance and openness is not something that can be taken for granted. There are some in our community who would seek to foster division based on race and ethnic background. It is the obligation of all of us, whatever our political beliefs, to hold firm against those attitudes. I believe they are minority attitudes. I believe they are attitudes that are held in contempt by the overwhelming majority of the Australian community. They are certainly attitudes that are held in contempt by the members of the Government I have the privilege of leading.

I have often spoken, ladies and gentlemen, within the context of other policies of the Government, I have often spoken of the principle of mutual obligation. We have a policy in relation to Work for the Dole, which speaks for the principle of mutual obligation, that we as a civilised, decent society have a belief that people who, through no fault of their own, are not able to get work, should be supported by the community, subject to certain principles and certain tests. But we say that in return for that support, those people should be willing to put something back into the community if it is reasonable of us to ask them to do so. That principle expressed through the policy of Work for the Dole has been quite well received within the Australian community.

I often see the interaction between people who come to settle within Australia as being, in another way, the working out of that principle of mutual obligation. We who live in Australia have an obligation of welcome, of acceptance, of decency, of harmonious treatment and of tolerant understanding, of people who come to our country. In return, those who come have an obligation to embrace, along with all other Australians, whether they were born here or have come from another nation, the values that bind us together as Australians irrespective of ethnic background.

I have had occasion, in other circumstances, to remark that the things that unite us as Australians are infinitely greater and more enduring than the things that divide us or put us apart. Those things that unite us as Australians are things of which we should frequently remind ourselves. They are things and values to which Chinese Australians, along with Australians of other ethnic origins, have made an enormous contribution.

They are the principles of tolerance and of fairness; a striding towards an essentially classless, egalitarian society; a belief in individual effort and individual liberty; as well as a respect for the right of every Australian to treasure, to practise, and to mark his or her own cultural heritage consistent with their membership of the broader Australian community....

There is no place within modern Australia for any semblance of racism or any semblance of intolerance based on racial difference. There is no place within our community for those who would argue that race or ethnic background should be a determining factor in the way in which people are treated or the way in which people are entitled to exercise their rights under the law.

I believe very strongly in a united Australian nation in which all people are equally accountable under the same set of laws and from which all Australians, irrespective of their background, are entitled to an equal dispensation of justice. ...

We spend an enormous amount of time in this country navel-gazing about what kind of society we are. It seems that, on some occasions, we engage in a form of public fretting about what it really means to be an Australian. It always strikes me as unnecessary and rather odd and unproductive. National identity, in so many ways, is instinctive. It is something that belongs to the emotions rather than to the formal description.

You do not write down what it means to be an Australian. You feel what it means to be an Australian. You do not indulge in some kind of intellectual exercise in trying to enumerate Australian qualities and Australian values. You practise them. And we are practising one great Australian value here tonight with such an enormously diverse audience, in terms of ethnic and racial background, yet we are bound together by something that is far greater than that diversity and that difference and that is a common love and a common commitment to our nation.

Ladies and gentlemen, I congratulate the Chinese Chamber of Commerce. I congratulate the Golden Jubilee Coffee Shop Forum on having made such a great contribution to the city of Perth, to the understanding and the harmony that exists between people of different backgrounds within the Australian community.

# Diversity – Source of Great National Strength

## Brisbane – 20 November 1998

Continuing to highlight the success story of Australian immigration, the Prime Minister, addressing the National Conference of the Federation of Ethnic Communities Council, said that the arrival of an immigrant on Australian shores represented not simply an end in itself, but the beginning of a new journey towards Australian citizenship. With Australia representing a nation of immigrants, Howard emphasised that an overseas-born Australian, of whatever nationality, was as worthy a citizen as a native-born Australian. Far from representing a land mass simply inhabited by tribes of disparate nationalities, however, Australia had drawn its people from all corners of the Earth to evolve into a new, national community in its own right, bearing its own distinctive character, ethos and values forged by shared experiences. While most Australian citizens had hailed from a diversity of countries, races and cultures, it was eminently possible for them to be united by a set of core Australian values that included classic liberal-democratic principles, the notion of a "fair go", and what Howard termed "practical mateship". In essence, Australia as a nation was able to enjoy "unity in diversity", whereby citizens were free to cherish their own culture and heritage at the same time as embracing widely-shared Australian values.

The next three years does provide all of us with tremendous opportunities to celebrate and showcase the Australian achievement. Our achievement as a nation of immigrants will be central to our national celebrations during that time. 1999 will mark the 50th anniversary of Australian citizenship, and the year will provide the chance to reaffirm the value of Australian citizenship and its role as a unifying force in our culturally diverse Australian community.

The Olympic Games in the year 2000 will be an opportunity to show-case our success as a harmonious and united nation with a commitment to shared values, excellence and respect for each individual. And, most importantly, the Centenary of Federation in 2001 will allow us to reflect on the Australian achievement and how far we have come as a nation and what our aspirations are for the new century.

Above all, in observing these things and celebrating these events, we must celebrate the values and principles that have made us such a cohesive nation. We are a society united in the belief that each of us should have the same opportunity to reach our full potential and share in what this great country has to offer. Our society is underpinned by those uniquely Australian concepts of a fair go and practical mateship, integral features of our community and national identity. Ours is a resilient and optimistic community that has extended the gift of welcome to people from every corner of the world. Whether Australian by birth or by choice, we join as one people strengthened by a diversity of experience and cultural background. But, above all, we share a strong set of values.

We honour the importance of family life where the hopes of our children can be realised and where our elderly can be given the respect that they have earned and deserved. We dedicate ourselves to the principles of free enterprise, to the fruits of working hard and taking risks. We revere our democratic national institutions and respond to calls for personal responsibility and the provision of practical help for the less fortunate. We are ambitious for Australia to succeed into the next century and for all of us to share in that prosperity. These enduring values hold important messages for all of us.

First and foremost, we are all Australians, and no Australian need feel foreign in their own land. No-one is better or worse than any other. There exists no qualification by birth or race, wealth or heritage, which limits a person's pride in this nation or the stake they hold within it.

We all belong to Australia and we all have an equal right to regard it as our home, with all the sanctuary that a home provides. There is no place within our community for those who would traffic, for whatever purpose, in division based on a person's religion, their place of birth, the colour of their skin or their ethnic makeup. There is no place in Australia for any semblance of racial or ethnic intolerance.

In October 1996 the Commonwealth Parliament passed a resolution that contained a simple, direct and unambiguous statement of certain values and principles including the commitment to maintaining a non-discriminatory immigration policy and the denunciation of racial intolerance.

What I never want to see, and I know no person in this audience wants to see, is an Australia where people of a particular racial background feel unwelcome. That would be a denial of everything that our country stands for. We have welcomed people from all around the world and all deserve to be treated equally and with an equal share of decency and civility. That is one of our common bonds as Australians.

My answer to all of those who feel threatened by our immigration programme is that they need not feel that way. I do not call them racist. I genuinely believe, however, that there are some who seek to prey upon community fears to encourage a sense of hostility towards people of particular racial backgrounds.

This is something that we should all oppose very strongly and I believe we should be reassured by the message sent by the Australian mainstream at the election that we are in essence a great-hearted people and small-minded policies will never hold sway over us. One of the great virtues of being Australian as we come to the close of the century is that we occupy a unique intersection of history, geography, culture and economic circumstance. Australia is a projection of Western civilisation in this part of the world. We have deep and enduring links with Britain and the other nations of Europe and we share much of their great legal, cultural and democratic political inheritance.

We have profound links with North America and we have shared many experiences with the United States in both war and peace. We are geographically located in the Asia-Pacific region, and we have within the Australian community a vibrant community of people of Asian descent who add to the strength and the vitality and the tolerance and the great cross-section of modern Australia. This unique intersection means that we can draw strength from our diversity and our understanding of the region. We have an opportunity to use these unique characteristics in an effective way to achieve what no other country can.

Having just come from a meeting of APEC [Asia-Pacific Economic Cooperation] in Kuala Lumpur, and that is an organisation that brings together leaders of all of the Pacific nations, and therefore a great cross-section of that enormous community, it was a reminder to me of just what a special intersection of those circumstances of history, geography and culture and other things that Australia really occupies. We do have insights and understandings because of that particular background. The diversity of that background gives us an opportunity to project a view which is superior and more enlightened and more comprehending of what is needed in that part of the world than that possessed by any other country.

It is because of that combined background, our European associations, our long association with the nations of North America, our location in the Asia-Pacific region and our understanding of the people-to-people contact that that location gives us all of those things combined in a very special way to give Australia a capacity to influence events that no other country can possibly possess. Our diversity is a source of great national strength. Particularly since the Second World War, migration has made an enormous contribution to Australia's economy, Australia's society and Australia's culture.

There is not an example anywhere else in the world of the successful absorption of such a diverse group of new citizens. Multiculturalism involves the principle of mutual obligation. Within the framework of an overriding commitment to Australia, it respects the right of each individual to celebrate his or her particular cultural identity in an atmosphere of tolerance, understanding and mutual self-respect.

As a Liberal Party Prime Minister of Australia I am proud to be the recipient of the Liberal Party heritage of compassion and common sense behind our immigration programme. In the post-Second World War years, both sides of politics pursued policies which brought millions of migrants to Australia and greatly strengthened Australia. Liberals, in particular, are grateful that it was the Liberal Party of Australia that did away with the White Australian Policy. It was under the Fraser Government that Australia realised its full humanitarian obligation by taking, on a per capita basis, a larger number of refugees from war-torn Indo-China than any other country in the world.

This tradition, which has given Australia a level of tolerance and harmony without parallel, lives on today in our own immigration programme which seeks to strike a proper balance between compassion and the national interest. When the Coalition came to power in 1996, we set about making changes to the programme to restore confidence in it.

Any sovereign country has the right to determine how it will dispense its compassion and determine the level, from time to time, of its migration programme. In our view, our predecessors failed to assert control over the programme in the national interest and overtly politicised aspects of immigration and multicultural policies. That is why we have now fine-tuned programme levels in accordance with Australia's economic situation. It is why we altered the skill composition and selection criteria to better reflect future development requirements. That is why we have not exempted this area from fiscal consolidation and why we have cracked down on illegal immigrants and over-stayers.

During our second term, we aim to build on our achievements to ensure that the immigration programme continues to be managed with integrity and compassion so that it enjoys the confidence of the entire Australian community.

We will continue to run the programme in the national interest. This means balancing economic and non-economic components of the programme and ensuring an appropriate dispersal of our migrant intake. We will examine the recommendations of a Commonwealth-State working party which is due to report next year [1999] on options to increase the number of skilled migrants in regional areas.

It is important that the immigration programme be managed in an open and publicly accountable manner and that migrants are selected on an objective case-by-case assessment of applications against clear legal criteria. To maintain community confidence in our programme, we will curb the number of applicants who seek to abuse the review process by reintroducing legislation in the Senate to restrict access to judicial review in all but exceptional circumstances.

We will also reintroduce legislation, which was delayed in the Senate, to streamline the two-tier review process of non-refugee visa decisions to a single review by the Migration Review Tribunal. We will also continue to balance the humanitarian, family and economic components of our immigration programme. The skilled proportion of the migration programme increased from 32 per cent to 52 per cent in the last financial year [1997-1998]. Skills in short supply in Australia will continue to be the principal determinant of skilled migrant entry. Employer nomination, where migrants are guaranteed employment, will be accorded a higher priority for skilled entry. Minimum thresholds will be established to remove anomalies in the current points test and we will introduce factors more relevant to gaining employment in Australia.

During the election campaign, I committed the Coalition, if re-elected, to consult community groups, academics and others on settlement and multicultural policies and to engage all sections of the community in the settlement process. The goal of our settlement programme is to allow our newest arrivals to participate fully in our community. Over the next term of office we will maintain the role of community organisations in providing settlement services, support for migrant resource centres, the community settlement services scheme and funding for the Adult Migrant English Programme.

We will tender out the AMEP Research Centre and ensure that the eligibility criteria for programmes are sufficiently liberal and flexible to achieve more lasting benefits for non-English speaking migrants. We will maintain funding to English language and literacy training and education. We will also provide better access to the translating and interpreting service as well as put the operation of the service on a commercial basis.

Australia is one of the oldest democracies in the world and democratic principles are deeply etched in our national character. It is that very democratic tradition, so much part of the Australian way, which has allowed the cultural diversity produced by our immigration programme to flourish so successfully. In 1997, the Government established a new National Multicultural Advisory Council, chaired by Neville Roach,[33] to recommend policies and an implementation framework to ensure that cultural diversity remains a unifying influence. The Council's report is expected shortly. As you are aware, after appropriate consultation and research we launched the first stage of the "Living in Harmony" campaign to promote community harmony and the enormous benefits of cultural diversity within Australian society....

Let me conclude with a couple of general things. I have every confidence as we head towards a new Australian century that we can become even stronger and more united. I take a profoundly optimistic and positive view about the character of Australian society. I believe that the things that unite us as Australians will always be more powerful and more enduring than those things that divide us. Our nation has been immensely enriched through the successive waves of immigration over the years that have brought new people from every corner of the world. We have succeeded better than any other nation on Earth in recognising that we are a community of many parts and many origins. We do have a level of tolerance and understanding that is the envy of most nations. We are essentially a united people, but we respect the different cultural heritage of those within our community and we recognise and support their right to celebrate their own particular culture and their own heritage in a completely tolerant and open fashion.

We are a nation like others, not without our blemishes. We have within our ranks those who are intolerant, and those who would seek to exploit differences based on race for their own particular purposes. As a

---

[33] Neville Roach is an Indian Australian businessman who chaired the Multicultural Advisory Committee from 1996 to 1999.

community, we face the challenge of achieving an effective and widely accepted reconciliation between the Indigenous people of this country and the rest of the Australian community. I particularly welcome the presence here today of Gatjil[34] and Evelyn[35] in that context. But it is important that we approach these issues in a spirit of both optimism and hope.

The Australian achievement, and I believe it is a glorious one, is quite special, it is unique. There is an Australian way, there is an Australian character and all have made a contribution to it. And whether you were born in this country or your parents and grandparents were born in this country, or whether this is your country of choice, it is equally our own and we all have a right to share in its benefits and we all have a right to enjoy both its tolerance, its respect and its protection. I have great confidence that the twenty-first century holds enormous prospects for Australia. I have a great belief that the unique intersection of which I spoke gives a capacity to leave a mark, not only on this part of the world, but on the world generally, which would be denied to any other community.

I thank the Federation of Ethnic Communities Council for inviting me here. We will continue to have, as a Government, and at a political level as two Coalition parties, a constructive ongoing dialogue with your organisation. We will agree on some things, we will disagree on others. You will like some of the things we do; you will dislike some of the other things we will do. That is in the nature of public office and public life. But I come on behalf of the Government in goodwill, with a positive attitude to all of the organisations and all the different groups that are represented here.

---

[34] Gatjil Djerrkura (1949-2004) was an Aboriginal leader and Indigenous spokesman who chaired the Aboriginal and Torres Strait Islander Commission (ATSIC) from 1996 to 2000.
[35] Evelyn Scott is an Indigenous Australian social activist and educator who chaired the National Council for Aboriginal Reconciliation in the late 1990s.

# Pursuing Practical Reconciliation

## Canberra – 13 December 2000

On Indigenous issues, Prime Minister Howard brought a distinctive policy approach which differed from that of his Labor predecessors in two important respects. First, Howard believed that the best way of helping Indigenous Australians was to include them within the mainstream of the Australian community and ensure, to the greatest extent possible, that they could share in the bounty of Australia's prosperity. It was for this reason that Howard rejected calls for a treaty between Indigenous and non-Indigenous Australians as it would serve only to entrench rather than heal existing divisions between the two peoples.

The second feature of his approach was that efforts towards Indigenous reconciliation needed to move beyond the merely symbolic to practical, tangible measures to improve the day-to-day lives of Indigenous Australians. Acknowledging reconciliation as an "unstoppable force", the Prime Minister used this address to give voice to both of these objectives. Identifying with the historical sufferings of Indigenous Australians at the hands of injustice, the Prime Minister nonetheless did not desire this to breed a culture of dependency and victimhood. To do so would hamper the rightful contribution of Indigenous Australians to the life of the nation. While citing some improvements to Indigenous well-being, Howard acknowledged that there was much further work to be done. Symbolic gestures of reconciliation were welcome, but would only have real meaning and effect if accompanied by perceptible improvements to Indigenous health, education and living standards.

Ladies and gentlemen, first may I acknowledge that I speak to you on the traditional lands of the Eora people.

This is an important day. The Menzies Lecture Series has traditionally been an opportunity for Liberal leaders to speak on issues of national significance and to present our Party's perspective on matters fundamental to the well-being of this nation.

Today is no different and I would like to thank Andrew Robb and his team for arranging today's event – an opportunity to properly put into context the Government's approach to policies affecting Indigenous Australians and how we may best move forward together towards a shared and prosperous future.

I am also pleased that this lecture series will later include contributions by Joseph Elu[36] and Leon Davis.[37] Both are prominent and highly respected Australians and will be able to offer useful insights into the views held within their respective constituencies.

This address comes just a few days after the Government received the final report of the Council for Aboriginal Reconciliation and the announcement of our support for a new body, Reconciliation Australia, through seed funding and ongoing tax deductibility.

We have also committed to construct a site within the Parliamentary Triangle to be known as "Reconciliation Place" to honour the importance of reconciliation in the nation's life and to recognise the shared journey between the different peoples of the Australian nation. It will also include a memorial and depiction of the removal of children from their families as part of the very difficult and traumatic experience of the Indigenous people of this community.

I would like to acknowledge the dignified and inspiring leadership of Dr Evelyn Scott and the fine work of the Council in general in promoting the cause of reconciliation throughout Australian society.

In just a few weeks, we begin celebrating the Centenary of our Fed-

---

[36] Joseph Elu is an Indigenous Australian leader and businessman who would later chair the Torres Strait Regional Authority.

[37] Leon Davis is an Australian businessman who held top posts in Rio Tinto and was, subsequently, Chairman, Westpac Banking Corporation.

eration. It will be a time when Australians will look back on past accomplishments but, of equal importance, consider the type of nation and the type of people they wish to be in years to come.

I regard Australia's social cohesion, born out of a distinctive form of egalitarianism, as the crowning achievement of the Australian experience during the last one hundred years.

Yet we can never feel satisfied, nor can we feel complete, until that cohesion is extended throughout all sections of the community and, specifically, until Indigenous Australians enjoy the same opportunities and the same plentiful lives as any other Australian.

This is significant because, as we approach the end of 2000, there can be no doubt that the mood of the Australian community is overwhelmingly in favour of reconciliation. Over the last twelve months in particular, it has become an unstoppable force and I believe the nation has been enriched and is a better, more united nation as a consequence.

In May 2000, Australians witnessed Corroboree 2000, an historic event involving every political leader – Federal, State and territory – in which a commitment to address ongoing Indigenous disadvantage was made. And, importantly, a commitment to recognise the special status Aboriginals and Torres Strait Islanders are entitled to feel as Australia's first peoples.

On the same weekend, the walk across Sydney's Harbour Bridge gave an opportunity, the first of many, for Australians to demonstrate their strong support for the process of reconciliation.

There can be little doubt that the Olympics was a momentous and positive event for Australia and Australians and many people saw the Games as making a major contribution to furthering reconciliation.

Others felt their very success demonstrated that our nation was far more reconciled than had been previously allowed for. If true reconciliation is manifest by a sense of pride and unity shared by all Australians – Indigenous and others – then the Games proved beyond doubt that Australians have travelled a great distance towards this goal.

There can be nothing more crucial than preserving and nurturing this mood of public support if we are to complete the journey towards reconciliation.

For this reason, it is important to focus on building on the gains made over past years. I am reminded that the Council of Reconciliation's Corroboree 2000 vision acknowledged that there are many paths to reconciliation. That is true.

On issues as complex and difficult as the call for some form of legal treaty or formal national apology beyond expressions of personal sorrow and regret, people of genuine goodwill can and will legitimately hold different points of view.

It is important to acknowledge that reconciliation is, as I have said, now an unstoppable force. Rather than a disproportionate focus on what is the preferred path, our collective priority must be to strengthen support for the ongoing process and, most importantly, improve the lives of Indigenous Australians.

Whatever differences, of emphasis and direction, may be apparent in any meaningful discussion of Indigenous issues, there are many more areas on which we can all agree. I believe that, within the Australian community, a great level of goodwill exists towards the Indigenous people of our nation and a determination is apparent to honour in a sensitive and understanding way, the special place that they will always occupy in the life of this nation.

The respect owed to them now and into the future does not mean we are reluctant to acknowledge past injustices. Indigenous Australians have suffered enormously in the past and, as a defined group, continue to do so. No one can, nor should attempt to, deny the devastating impact the introduction of Western culture has had upon their civilisation.

I have said many times, there can be no doubt that the treatment of Aboriginal and Torres Strait Islander peoples in earlier times represents the most blemished chapter in our history. Most Australians accept that.

It remains true that basic living standards – from employment to health, from education to mortality rates – remain unacceptable.

It is true, as was noted recently, that past policies designed to assist have often failed to recognise the significance of Indigenous culture and resulted in the further marginalisation of Aboriginal and Torres Strait Islander people from the social, cultural and economic development of mainstream Australian society. This led to a culture of dependency and victimhood, which condemned many Indigenous Australians to lives of poverty and further devalued their culture in the eyes of their fellow Australians.

The inconsistencies between Indigenous and non-Indigenous approaches remain at the root of much of the current difficulty. It is captured in what Noel Pearson recently described as the gaps:

> Between immediate sharing and individual accumulation, between loyalty to kin and impartiality to all, between individual autonomy and the authoritarian practices of the school and industrial workplace, between individual advancement and remaining at one with the community, between exploiting land and living with it.

We are determined to design policy and structure administrative arrangements to address these very real issues and ensure standards in education and employment, health and housing improve to a significant degree.

The Council of Aboriginal Reconciliation's vision seeks an Australia which not only promotes mutual respect but provides "justice and equity for all". Who would not agree? Yet the fulfilment of these two principles is inextricably bound to improving the day-to-day realities of life for Indigenous Australians.

For this reason, our focus has been, and will be, on addressing the needs of today's Indigenous Australians. This is a living, active community, not a generation from the past. These are people who can be found, not in the pages of history books, but in our cities, in our towns and in remote corners of our country. Among them are Australians whose children are sick, whose lives are empty, and whose prospects are dim. Among them are Australians who need our help.

Symbolic expressions of support are important. However, they are given real meaning when backed with improvements in living standards. That is why we place a great degree of emphasis on practical reconciliation.

A measure of the genuineness of the Government's commitment to practical reconciliation is that the $2.3 billion now annually spent on Indigenous-specific programmes is, in real terms, a record for any government – Coalition or Labor.

I have looked at the level of progress made over the past 20 years and, while no one denies that as a nation we need to do better than we have in the past, there are examples of real achievement in the Aboriginal and Torres Strait Islander communities.

I do not agree with those that say that the community has little to show for what is now some 30 years of effort. This criticism, that nothing is getting better, is common to both extremes of the debate – those who would abolish all such special programmes, and to those who say that nothing less than a legally enforceable treaty and special constitutional rights will "solve the problem".

Neither view is correct, nor is the underlying premise that things have not been improving. There is in fact indisputable evidence of long-term improvement in many Aboriginal socio-economic indicators. For example, the proportion of Indigenous Australians who own their own home has increased from one in four to one in three since the 1970s. The proportion of Indigenous students completing high school has quadrupled over the same period. The infant mortality rate has been cut from up to twenty times the non-Aboriginal rate to four times the national average today.

Aboriginal enrolments in higher education increased by 60 percent in the 1990s.

At least 15 per cent of the continent is now Aboriginal owned or controlled.

And the Aboriginal imprisonment rate relative to that of non-Aboriginals has been trending down (and over the past three years on average per capita deaths in prison custody for Aboriginals have been lower than for non-Aboriginals).

It is particularly encouraging that improvement is occurring through harnessing the talents, the resources and the enthusiasm of those within governments, within business, within community organisations and, most importantly, within Indigenous communities themselves.

Whether you call it a social coalition or simply pulling together, it has particular relevance to Indigenous issues. For instance, the Army has been working alongside community members in some of the most needy Aboriginal communities in Australia, developing and building important infrastructure. In Bulla, a remote community in the Northern Territory, ten new dwellings were built, a reticulated sewerage and septic system constructed and the community airstrip refurbished.

The success of such projects is not only measured by infrastructure improvements. In each community, the Army has been able to deliver additional services such as primary health, dental and veterinary care as well as providing training opportunities for local community members ranging from health, hygiene and home management to trade and construction skills.

We have seen Australians within communities such as Moree decide they are simply not willing to allow division and disharmony to affect the day-to-day lives of their citizens and the future which awaits their children. Moree's Aboriginal Employment Strategy, managed and operated by Indigenous Australians and centred around the magnificent cotton growing industry of that region, works with both prospective employers and Aboriginals to find employment opportunities within mainstream sectors, retail, manufacturing and on farms.

Towns like Moree are proving the critical correlation which exists between employment and the restoration of fractured community leadership and cohesion.

For this reason, it is especially pleasing that some 34 major Australian corporations have given a commitment to the Government to generate more job opportunities for Indigenous Australians. The Commonwealth is funding a scheme to train one hundred trainees at the Century Mine project. Western Mining is set to employ a similar number of young Aboriginals on its mine sites in Western Australia.

These types of initiatives are important to the reconciliation process. Yet true reconciliation can never be said to have occurred until Indigenous Australians enjoy standards of opportunity and treatment the equal of their countrymen and women.

There are distinct and disturbing problems to be confronted if this equality is to be realised and I am heartened by the increasingly candid and open discussion of these complex issues by a number of courageous Indigenous leaders.

This Government is guided in its policy deliberations by core Australian values. And the principle of equity and a fair go, at the heart of the Australian character, is also at the heart of practical reconciliation programmes.

It is a matter of basic Australian fairness and, indeed, basic Australian pragmatism, to seek to redress disadvantage, and poor education, to tackle systemic ill-health and joblessness, to combat tragic levels of domestic violence and substance abuse. But causing and sustaining many of these problems is the loss of dignity and specifically the loss of self-reliance by individuals and their communities. And the promotion of this last virtue is a key goal of this Government.

We are gaining new understanding of the links between economic and social engagement. The McClure Report ranks paid employment as a major source of self-esteem. Without it, people become disengaged from – or fail to develop – employment, family and community networks. Material poverty is compounded by poverty of purpose. And, as the report makes clear, this often leads to physical and psychological ill-health, to life opportunities being reduced both for parents and their children.

Indigenous leaders are saying the same thing. Evelyn Scott regards welfare dependency as "almost totally destroying Aboriginal culture". Peter Yu asserts that communities are being "crushed with the weight of the welfare economy".

And Noel Pearson argues persuasively that "the scale and nature of Indigenous problems changed dramatically after passive welfare become the economic foundation of their communities". He contends that "there is a causal connection between the change in their economy and their social relationships" and that it is "passive welfare combined with substance abuse that threatens to disrupt traditional values", values which had previously mandated reciprocity and responsibility.

My point is this. Through policy initiatives that will flow from perceptive investigations such as the McClure Report, we can develop new and better ways to empower individuals and promote self-reliance throughout their communities. New and better ways to help all Australians, Indigenous and non-Indigenous.

As I said earlier, this Government is committed to maintaining and strengthening broad-based support for reconciliation and for proper respect to be shown towards Australia's first peoples – the respect so evident in past months.

True reconciliation is, in our view, to be best found within practical means to improve the well-being and happiness of Indigenous Australians and raising standards to levels enjoyed and expected by all of us.

There have been very real resources applied to this end – a 50 per cent increase in spending on Aboriginal health since we won office; a national Indigenous literacy and numeracy strategy; housing programmes which account for 20 per cent of estimated total Commonwealth spending on public and community housing, and, in the 2000-01 budget, funding of a further 1 500 places in ATSIC's Community Development Employment Projects scheme.

In short, a targeting on the basics, with almost three-quarters of the Commonwealth's $2.3 billion Indigenous-specific budget directly applied to the priority areas of housing, health, education and employment – things that can change lives.

That being said, we all know, it is not simply a matter of spending more money. We need to ensure funds are spent wisely and applied to those most in need. We need to work with communities and individuals with local knowledge and a real understanding of how we can best make a difference.

The Round Table hosted in October 2000 showed a commitment to cooperative effort. In the years ahead, this type of approach will loom large in how we identify problem areas and address them. For instance, Senator Newman[38] and Senator Herron[39] announced on that occasion that $20 million would be earmarked under the Stronger Families and Communities Strategy to help strengthen Indigenous communities, build self-reliance and rebuild self-respect.

The Roundtable, comprising respected Indigenous community leaders, has been asked to advise the Government on how best to use these funds.

The COAG meeting in November 2000 committed the Federal Government and all of the States and territories to collectively pursue new approaches – to invest in community leadership, to deliver practical measures that support families, children and young people, to tackle the symptoms of community dysfunction such as substance abuse and violence, and to forge greater links between the business sector and Indigenous communities.

We have come a long way in recent years. In many ways, we are the envy of the world – rich in resources, rich in opportunity, united in our values and united in the hopes we hold for the future.

The way forward towards true reconciliation is surely to build upon this unity and the many areas of common agreement. In this, as in other important national endeavours, the things that unite us are far stronger than those that divide us.

By working together, by sharing endeavour, and by sharing goals, I have no doubt we can all ultimately share success.

---

[38] Jocelyn Newman served as a Liberal Senator for Tasmania from 1986 to 2012 and as Minister for Family and Community Services from 1998 to 2001.

[39] John Herron served as a Liberal Senator for Queensland from 1990 to 2002 and as Minister for Aboriginal and Torres Strait Islander Affairs from 1996 to 2001.

# Joining the Australian National Family

## Canberra – 26 January 2007

Addressing an Australia Day Citizenship Ceremony after nearly eleven years as Prime Minister, John Howard reaffirmed many of the core values underpinning modern Australian citizenship. Acknowledging that it would prove difficult for Australians to arrive at full consensus on a fixed and immutable set of national values, he nonetheless considered that there were principles which most Australians, of any ethnic background, would regard as integral to their national identity. These included such traditions as the rule of law, the independence of the judiciary, a free press, the equality of men and women, a "fair go", equality of opportunity for all and the notion that a person's standing was determined by their character and not their class, race or creed. While urging new Australian citizens to embrace Australian values, he assured them that their new national family would always recognise their affection for their culture and country of origin.

Can I start by thanking and acknowledging the Ngunnawal people and that wonderful dance presentation. It was, as always, very inspiring, very enjoyable and really struck a wonderful note for the commencement of this citizenship ceremony.

It is great to be here at Regatta Point again and I start by saying to our more than 100 applicants, nominees, candidates for Australian Citizenship, how very deeply honoured we are that you have chosen Australia to be your national family for the rest of your life because becoming a citizen is joining the national family.

As always the people who are becoming citizens today are drawn from the four corners of the Earth, and that is how we like it to be, that is how it has been for a very long time and that is how it will be for years and years into the future.

You may be drawn from the four corners of the Earth but you are united by a common love of this country of ours and you are united by a common commitment to its traditions, its values, its triumphs as well as an acknowledgement of its failures, its successes as well as its mistakes. We have had over the last few months quite a debate about what is loosely called Australian values, and I think it would be rather odd if I did not say something very briefly about that issue on this Australia Day in 2007.

As is rightfully the tradition of a great democracy, there is no one absolutely immovable, unalterable, set in stone set of values. People will have different views about what are the values of this country. But I do think there are some things that most of us hold very dear and hold to be the essence of what it is to be an Australian. We all embrace and hold very strongly to the fact that this is a great democracy. Australia is one of only a handful of countries, you could count them on the fingers of your two hands, that remained continuously democratic through the entirety of the 20th century, and that was a remarkable achievement.

It was one of the countries that earlier in time gave full voting rights to women, although it lagged sadly in some parts of the country – I stress some – in giving voting rights to the first Australians, the Indigenous people. We are a nation that holds very strongly to the rule of law, the independence of the judiciary. We believe very strongly in a free press. There are some of us on occasions who feel a little uncomfortable about certain ways in which that freedom is expressed, but we would not have it otherwise because it is fundamental to our democratic way of life.

We believe very passionately in the equality of men and women. It is something that Australia strives very hard to practise and it is something that Australia believes in very strongly. Many of us express this in different ways but we do believe in the notion of the fair go, the idea of equality of opportunity. We believe very deeply that a person's worth is determined by their character and by the effort they put in to being a good citizen, not according to their social class, or their background, or their religion, or their race, or their colour or their creed.

Most of us have a fundamental pride in what Australia has achieved. We can debate our history, as we should, but fundamentally the verdict of history is that Australia has been a remarkable success and we have built in this country a great nation, an outward-looking nation, a very generous nation and a nation that holds tenaciously to the view that we should play our part as a good international citizen.

Finally, most Australians think it is very important that we embrace as our common method of communication with each other, a single language, and that is the English language, because citizenship and interaction with each other is impossible unless we can effectively communicate with one another.

I say all of those things in acknowledging that the people who will become Australian citizens today come from a diversity of backgrounds. I say to all of you that in asking you, as we all do, and knowing that you willingly accept the responsibility to do so, to become part of the Australian family, we do not ask you to forget your homeland. We recognise that from now until the day you die you will have a special place in your heart for the country in which you were born. That is only human, it is only natural and it would be mean-spirited of your new country to expect you ever to lose a particular affection and a special place in your heart for the country in which you were born.

In that spirit I welcome all of you to the great Australian family. It is a wonderful nation, it is the greatest on the Earth, we think we are pretty good and we are. We have made our share of mistakes, we have not always treated some of our citizens as well as we should have, and I think particularly of the earlier treatment of the Indigenous people of Australia, but we are in every sense of the word a generous people and we are so very grateful that you have decided to become part of our great Australian family.

# "Their Spirit Still Shines"

## Old Parliament House, Canberra – 27 May 2007

On 27 May 1967, more than 90 per cent of Australians voted "Yes" in a referendum to include Indigenous Australians in the Census and to give the Commonwealth power to make laws for Indigenous Australians. Four decades later, the Prime Minister, John Howard, observed that Australians had "said in a loud and collective voice that Indigenous Australians deserved a fair go" and "should not be second-class citizens in their own country". After paying tribute to the trailblazers of this historic reform, Howard reminded his audience that, while it was a milestone to celebrate, there was no cause for the nation to be smug and complacent about the continuing disadvantage of Indigenous Australians. On the contrary, it was a sobering reminder that much needed to be done to elevate the dignity and well-being of Australia's first people. Returning to his vision of "practical reconciliation", the Prime Minister told his audience that reconciliation needed to be a "bottom-up", grassroots movement of ordinary citizens and organisations resolved to advance Indigenous welfare. Genuine reconciliation was not the responsibility of government alone, but also of Indigenous leaders, elders, families, schools and voluntary organisations to realise the success of Aboriginal and Torres Strait Islander Australians. Like the 1967 referendum, the success of reconciliation would be contingent on the goodwill of the Australian people.

May I pay tribute to the Ngunnawal people, the traditional owners of the land on which we gather, and thank Matilda House for her customary warm and enthusiastic welcome. And Joyce[40], can I say, you have stolen the show. My fellow Australians, and I acknowledge particularly the Minister for Indigenous Affairs, Mal Brough, the Leader of the Opposition, Kevin Rudd, and to Jackie Huggins and Mark Leibler, who have done such outstanding work in being the co-chairmen of Reconciliation Australia in organising this event.

Today Australia remembers one of the finest and fairest days in our history. The 1967 referendum has carried its own mythology down the years, portrayed variously as extending citizenship rights or the right to vote to Indigenous Australians. The truth, as we know, is a little more prosaic. Aboriginal Australians were to be counted in the Census and the Commonwealth was given formal power to make laws for Indigenous Australians. To discount the power of myth is, however, to miss the larger meaning of this historic moment 40 years ago. Myth-making has always been part of how a country becomes a nation, and if it spurs a nation on to a better one, well, so much the better.

On 27 May 1967, Australians said in a loud and collective voice that Indigenous Australians deserved a fair go; that the first Australians should not be second-class citizens in their own country. This was the most resoundingly successful referendum ever in Australia. We recall today the bipartisan spirit in which it was carried. More importantly, we remember this as a campaign of grassroots democracy, a peoples' campaign in which Indigenous and other Australians worked side by side.

Today, our nation honours the patriots who pricked our national conscience 40 years ago. We particularly honour those here from the Federal Council for the Advancement of Aborigines and Torres Strait Islanders, as well as friends and colleagues who have since passed on. We pay tribute to all who took up the cause; gathering signatures, raising awareness, persuading politicians and challenging prejudice.

The 1967 referendum was a landmark in the shaping of Indigenous identity. It also helped bring many remarkable individuals like Charlie Perkins and Faith Bandler to national prominence. In a way, Neville

---

[40] Joyce Clague is an Australian political activist and Bundjalung elder who was influential in instigating the 1967 Constitutional Referendum.

Bonner's public life began that day. Legend has it that my dear old departed friend was helping a Liberal distribute how-to-vote cards, advocating a Yes vote, when a Labor man told him he should be handing out ALP material, also advocating a Yes vote. Never one to be pigeon-holed, Neville promptly joined the Liberal Party.

The last thing that a Charlie Perkins, a Faith Bandler or a Neville Bonner would want is for today to be just a national pat on the back. Too many of the hopes expressed so resoundingly and genuinely 40 years ago remain unrealised. As Prime Minister I am very conscious of that.

This is a moment to reflect on the wider meaning of what Australians were trying to say in 1967, including about Indigenous rights. I recognise the importance of rights to Indigenous aspiration. I recognise the special status of Aboriginal and Torres Strait Islanders as our first peoples with 60 000 years of history, the starting point for our nation's history which every Australian child should learn. I recognise, too, the spiritual importance of connectedness to country and of Indigenous languages. And with others I celebrate the way Indigenous culture is now so central to Australia's cultural expression to the world.

But in recognising all this, I come back to what I think the Australian people were trying to get at 40 years ago. The right of an Aboriginal Australian to live on remote communal land and to speak an Indigenous language is no right at all if it is accompanied by grinding poverty, overcrowding, poor health, community violence and alienation from mainstream Australian society. Reconciliation has little meaning in a narrative of separateness from that society. We have spent a lot of time these past decades analysing the causes of Indigenous failure. In a way, that has been part of the problem. We should have spent more time thinking long and hard about the causes of Indigenous success.

This single question: what does Indigenous success look like must be our starting point. It is at the heart of what we as a Government are trying to achieve in areas like housing, health, employment, business development and education. Part of our collective frustration is that there is so much common ground on what Indigenous success looks like.

We can all agree, I think, that it means a healthy child born into a loving family. It means a young boy or girl at school and ready to learn. It means a safe community. It means a young man or woman discovering a sense of self in a culture of responsibility, enriched by his or her Indigenous heritage. It means Indigenous Australians enjoying the same opportunities as other Australians. It must never mean reconciling ourselves to lower expectations for 30 or 20 or 10 per cent of Indigenous people.

This vision can only be realised in a culture of shared responsibility. Sometimes this will demand more from government; more listening, more responsiveness on the ground and, where it can make a difference, more resources. And I simply note that real spending on Indigenous-specific programmes has increased by 42 per cent since this Government came to office, and will reach a record $3.5 billion in the coming financial year.

But for Indigenous success to shine through sometimes, frankly, it demands less from government and more from Indigenous civil society; from the little platoons between the individual and the state. Like the family, the school community, the elders, the voluntary sector and Indigenous leadership. Only then will we be able genuinely to marry the best of government intentions and resources with the wisdom of local knowledge.

I come from a political tradition that values such knowledge; that values independence and personal responsibility, as well as freedom, equality and civic duty. It is here that the spirit of 1967 carries so many lessons for Australians today. As Jackie Huggins has said, the movement for change in 1967 did not start just because a government wanted it to. It started because enough of the Australian people wanted it.

Under the umbrella of Reconciliation Australia, this same spirit is inspiring more and more of our people and companies to the cause of Reconciliation; a very Australian, bottom-up, do it yourself Reconciliation. Not in a way that absolves government of its responsibilities. But in a positive way that affirms this as a cause that begins with people

# VII

## "Ours to Tend,
## Ours to Cherish"

### Australian National Identity

# A Story of Sacrifice and Suffering, of Constancy and Compassion

## Hellfire Pass, Thailand – 25 April 1998

To honour the thousands of Australian men and women who had perished as Prisoners of War during the Second World War, the Prime Minister attended an Anzac Day commemoration ceremony to open a new museum dedicated to their memory at Hell Fire Pass, Thailand. Forming part of the notorious Burma Railway built by the forced labour of Australian and allied POW's, Hellfire Pass was noted for its brutal conditions and heavy loss of life. In construction of the railway, the Australians and their allied comrades suffered from torture, starvation, exhaustion, dysentery and cholera. Moved by their deeds of fortitude, courage and selflessness in the face of tremendous adversity, the Prime Minister delivered this poignant and poetic address to pay homage to their service and sacrifice. To John Howard, these heroes of Hellfire Pass epitomized Australia's Anzac spirit. Their example had served to inspire and enrich the Australian character.

As we gather here to face the dawn,

We honour those who faced the night.

Not a night of rest, nor dreams,

Not a night of shared laughter or the warmth of homefire.

But a monstrous corruption of nature,

An eclipse of humanity itself.

And yet, when we look at the night sky,

The wonder we feel is surely for the stars, not the black veil behind them.

So, too, our wonder is for these men, whose sparks of courage shine bright through the distance of time.

Their story of sacrifice and suffering, of constancy and compassion, illuminates the very essence of the Anzac spirit. For, of all our heroes, they were armed with human virtue alone and their victory was over the darkest recesses of the human heart.

To a superb tradition of self-discipline under fire was added selfless-ness and ingenuity. To a heritage of wild, reckless bravery was added cold calculated valour sustained for years.

To the world, proof was given that tyranny, in the end, has no power over the courage and decency of ordinary men and women.

It is an example to which we all aspire, as relevant in peace as in war, to our future as to our past.

And on this sacred day, at this most sacred place, we honour all Aus-tralian service men and women who gave or offered their lives in war.

We pay tribute to our veterans, unique Australians who have known the blessings and hardship of both conflict and peace.

On this day, we give grateful thanks to friends and allies who shared our danger, and we add our pledge that their loyalty will neither be for-gotten nor unreturned.

On this day, we enrich ourselves for, it has been said, a nation reveals itself not only by the men it produces but by the men it honours, the men it remembers.

On this day most of all, we mourn the fallen, long years of love and talent lost, of potential unrealised, of generations unborn.

We would have them know of our firm and steadfast belief that they rest not in shades of darkness but bask in the brightness of an Australian sun.

We would have them know that we will remember them.

# "We the People"
## Preamble to the Constitution
### Canberra – 11 August 1999

During the Constitutional Convention in 1998 at which the future prospect of an Australian republic was debated, the delegates who had assembled at Old Parliament House in the first two weeks of February 1998 arrived at a consensus about the need for a new preamble to the Constitution.

Shortly after re-election of the Government in October 1998, the Prime Minister spoke about recognition of Australia's Indigenous people in a new preamble. With the public still yet to vote on the matter of an Australian republic, the Prime Minister in February 1999 suggested that the new preamble be "republic-neutral". After seeking joint-party support for a new preamble, John Howard announced that he would prepare this preface to the Constitution in consultation with the poet, Les Murray. Releasing the first draft on 23 March 1999, the Prime Minister described it as one produced "in cooperation with a great wordsmith". In light of public comment about its content and wording, the text was revised and a second draft released on 11 August. The Parliament agreed to a referendum on the revised preamble simultaneously with that on an Australian republic. The vote was held on 6 November 1999. The proposed preamble did not succeed at the ballot box, but it nonetheless stands as an eloquent exposition of the heritage, ideals and aspirations of the nation as it entered its second century.

With hope in God, the Commonwealth of Australia is constituted as a democracy with a federal system of government to serve the common good.

We the Australian people commit ourselves to this Constitution:

proud that our national unity has been forged by Australians from many ancestries;

never forgetting the sacrifices of all who defended our country and our liberty in time of war;

upholding freedom, tolerance, individual dignity and the rule of law;

honouring Aborigines and Torres Strait Islanders, the nation's first people, for their deep kinship with their lands and for their ancient and continuing cultures which enrich the life of our country;

recognising the nation building contribution of generations of immigrants;

mindful of our responsibility to protect our unique natural environment;

supportive of achievement as well as equality of opportunity for all;

and valuing independence as dearly as the national spirit which binds us together in both adversity and success.

# Australian Democracy is a Vigorous Thing

## Faulconbridge, NSW – 7 April 2000

In the Blue Mountains town of Faulconbridge, 77 km west of Sydney, there lies a stately corridor of oak trees in a public park near the grave of Sir Henry Parkes (1815-1896). Following in the footsteps of each of his predecessors as prime minister, John Howard was invited to plant the newest addition to the "Corridor of Oaks". The Prime Minister paid tribute to Parkes as the "Father of Federation" and pioneer of modern Australian democracy. Together with his twenty-four predecessors, Howard saw himself as standing on the shoulders of a giant, whose legacy was best honoured by contributing to the contemporary health and vitality of Australian democracy. As eminent testimony to Parkes's enduring vision, Howard proudly cited the fact that Australia was one of only a handful of nations that had remained continuously democratic in a turbulent century racked by war, revolution and the rise and fall of several tyrannies. Australia's durability as a democracy filled Howard with confidence that Australia could become an even greater nation in the twenty-first century.

I am here to continue a very long tradition of Australian prime ministers on both sides of politics. That is to plant an Oak tree, to join my 24 predecessors (or their descendants) who have done so. I look at these trees, this Corridor of Oaks, and I find that the great bulk of them, indeed, planted the trees in person. And I feel very humble and very honoured to join my 24 predecessors in this very simple but very symbolic ceremony.

In the process, we honour one of Australia's most significant political figures, Sir Henry Parkes, who did more than any other person to bring about the federation of the then Australian colonies in 1901 and to build the Commonwealth of Australia, the centenary of which we will celebrate together next year.

Sir Henry Parkes left his mark not only in this local community, because the name of the town of Faulconbridge was taken from his mother's maiden name, with Faulconbridge House built in the 19th century, but he left his mark on the State of NSW, and he left his mark on the Commonwealth of Australia.

So, in many ways, this ceremony, which brings together the people of the local community, is a local ceremony, reminding you of a great son of the Blue Mountains. It is also a simple, national ceremony, which allows the community to mark in a quiet and dignified, but effective, way, the contribution of 25 people who have held the most privileged office that anybody could possibly aspire to, and that is the office of Prime Minister of Australia.

I will not talk about the contribution of different people to that office, other than to acknowledge the contribution of each, in their own different way, whatever their political perspectives were. As I look at the list, I see people with whom I have had profound agreement, such as Sir Robert Menzies, others with whom I have had some disagreement on occasions over the years. But we have, all of us, been united in a commitment and a dedication to the service of our country, to the service of the legal and community ideals in which we believe.

One of those great community ideals, and one of the great cornerstones of Australian democracy, is the right of individuals to express their views on whatever subject in a lawful and, on occasions, vigorous fashion.

Australian democracy is a vigorous thing, Australian democracy is bound up with the vigorous exchange of views. But, in the end, we have always resolved our differences in a peaceful, harmonious way. Whatever political differences we may have, there are one or two things that have shone through the experience of Australian democracy. We are a most tolerant, cohesive society; we are a society that has welcomed people from different parts of the world. Despite the protestations of some, we are a society which is free of racial intolerance and hatred.

We are a society which is a proud example to the rest of the world and we have demonstrated, in recent times, our capacity to stand up for the principles of liberty and independence. We have in that sense been an example to the rest of the world.

I want, in being here today, to thank my colleague and friend, Kerry Bartlett, the Member for Macquarie. I take the opportunity of warmly thanking him for the articulate, energetic representation he brings to this very diverse electorate in the National Parliament. I can assure all of you who are here, all of his constituents, that he is doing a magnificent job representing you in the National Parliament.

I want to mark this occasion by an exhortation to all Australians to understand and revere the history of this country. It is a history that has not been without blemish. It is a history of a country which has built a mighty, impressive, powerful and widely admired democracy as we have entered the 21st century. Australia is one of fewer than 10 nations that remained continuously democratic throughout the entire 20th century.

It is a country whose history is rich; it is a country with a history of which we can be proud, whilst recognising that we made mistakes, and allowed injustices and unfair treatment. But if you look at the great balance sheet of Australian history, it is an achievement of which all of us can be immensely proud. As we come to celebrate the Centenary of the Commonwealth of Australia, it is an opportunity to reflect on that history, it is an opportunity to thank people like Sir Henry Parkes who made such a contribution to the building of modern Australia. It is an opportunity to resolve, to work together to build an even greater nation in the 21st century.

# ANZAC

## Ours to Guard, Ours to Cherish, Ours to Live
## Gallipoli, Turkey – 25 April 2000

Having both a father and grandfather who saw active duty in the Great War, the significance of ANZAC Day for John Howard was deeply personal as well as national. As a boy growing up in Sydney's Earlwood during the 1940s and 1950s, the Prime Minister had received first-hand accounts of his father's wartime experience on the Western Front which imbued him with a profound appreciation of the service and sacrifice of Australia's ANZACs.

In April 2000, Howard travelled to Turkey to deliver the address at the Anzac Day dawn service. In contrast to his immediate predecessor, the Prime Minister appreciated the centrality of the ANZAC legend to Australia's national ethos and character. For Howard, the ANZACs did not simply represent the hapless recruits to an ill-conceived plan by British war strategists to invade a far-off land, but Australian patriots who displayed exemplary comradeship, bravery and valour in the face of overwhelming odds.

In this address, he memorably described the story of ANZAC as "ours to guard, ours to cherish, ours to live", as future generations of Australians strove to emulate the example set by their valiant forebears on the cliffs of the Dardanelles.

To this ancient land, the passing of 85 years must seem but an instant in time. A mere moment in its journey towards forever. But to us it is the distance of human life. Thus we come to this place at this hour, on this day, to observe not only a dawn but a dusk. For dusk has all but fallen on that great-hearted generation of Australians who fought here. The shadows gather on a time and a world in which our nation's spirit was born. Soon the story of ANZAC which forever joins the people of Australia and New Zealand will pass gently from memory into history. Soon the fire struck here will be ours to tend. Soon its record once written on pages wet with tears will be ours alone to guard, ours to cherish, ours to live.

It is a remarkable legacy. Only now from the sheltered safety of our time can we comprehend what was dared and done here. Only now from the vantage point secured for us by others' lives can we see the scale and the scope of their achievement. For those young Australians, as wild and free as the land they loved, left us a creed to which we can all aspire in the gentle years of peace as surely as in the hard and hungry years of war.

The inheritance we claim today is not a fallen sword, nor have we come to extol a warrior's code. The respect of gallant foes and the high regard of comrades is the praise that soldiers seek. It is not for us to give. Let them rest, far from thoughts of battle.

Instead we come to claim from them a heritage of personal courage and initiative. Of daring and determination in the face of overwhelming odds. A heritage that requires of each of us a conscious decision to do what is right regardless of the resistance we meet or the fears we hold.

We come to seek the inspiration of stories of compassion and comfort given to others in their time of need. Knowing that there are opportunities in our own lives to ease the burden of those suffering adversity and hardship. We come to draw upon their stirring example of unity and common purpose. To believe that, whatever our differing circumstances, we are all companions with each of our countrymen and women, and together we travel a single path. We come to join with those that rest here in a shared love of our nation, bathed in sunlight and so blessed with bounty. We come to stand on soil rich with the lives of our kin and vow that what they began, we will finish.

For they fought to build a nation which would stand proud and respected amongst the free people of the world. A nation where ordinary men and women would live long lives of happiness and fulfilment. A country where children would grow nourished by the land's harvest, and by the love of their parents. A country where prosperity and opportunity are derived not by birth, but by endeavour. A people made independent, united and free for all time. And in the attainment of these ideals, in the keeping of a decent and responsible Australia, in every year of peace between the nations of the world, we will build for all those who have served and suffered in war, a monument upon which evening will never fall.

# Australians
## Competitive, Resourceful and Talented
### Sir Donald Bradman Oration
### Melbourne – 17 August 2001

Famously described by former Australian cricket captain, Mark Taylor, as a "cricket tragic", John Howard has had a lifelong love of the game which remained his great interest outside of politics. At the age of nine, he recalled his father taking him to the Sydney Cricket Ground on 28 February 1949 to see Don Bradman play for the last time at that ground in the Kippax-Oldfield Testimonial. Howard recalled that "it was the only occasion on which I saw the great man play". As a teenager, Howard listened avidly to cricket commentator Johnny Moyes, devoured books about cricket and played competition cricket for both Earlwood Methodist Church and Canterbury Boys High School in the school's 2nd XI. As Prime Minister, Howard did much to personify Australian affection for the game with frequent attendances at Test matches and visits to the commentary box.

For Howard, the universal appeal of cricket in Australia was such that it invariably transcended considerations of ethnicity, class and party-politics. In this paean to Australia's greatest cricketer, Howard lauded Sir Donald Bradman (1908-2001) not only for his cricketing prowess but also for his personal integrity and character that had inspired a nation in depression, war and peace. In a rapidly changing world, Howard believed that the best way for Australia to honour the Bradman legacy was to nurture the game of cricket by preserving

its best traditions whilst embracing new methods and
approaches to ensure its enduring appeal.

It is a special honour to have been invited by the Australian Cricket
Board to deliver the inaugural Sir Donald Bradman Oration.

I have no doubt that the Oration will become an important occasion
– an opportunity to honour Sir Donald's continuing example to us all, to
reflect upon his remarkable achievements and to extol the qualities of a
game so indelibly a part of Australian life.

I saw Sir Donald Bradman play but once.

As a ten-year-old boy I sat on the now banished Hill of the Sydney
Cricket Ground to see him score 53 runs in just 65 minutes in a testimonial match for two former State captains, Alan Kippax and Bert Oldfield,
in front of a crowd of over 41 000 people. It was his last match on that
famous ground.

As other "cricket tragics" in the audience will know, some matches
remain with you forever. That was certainly one. Another was an opportunity in 1997 to take time out from official duties and watch Australia
battle England at Lords in the Second Test. The first day was ruined by
rain. The second day was ruined for England by Glenn McGrath as he
headed towards 8 for 38 in one of the finest displays of fast bowling I
have ever seen.

Rumour has it that I am not the first Prime Minister to take an interest
in cricket.

Sixty years before me, Sir Robert Menzies, not yet then Prime Minister, was determined to see Don Bradman's Australians in action against
England. In organising a ministerial visit to Britain he sent word ahead
in the hope that those arranging the meetings would have a full list of
cricketing fixtures at hand and that Menzies may offer himself, in spite
of physical improbabilities, as the team's mascot.

I can report that Menzies saw much more of the English summer of
cricket than I did. In fact, he contrived to see something of most of the
matches in which Australia played.

Faced with some criticism of my own visit to Lords, perhaps I could have repeated a statement of Menzies before he departed for England sixty years earlier, "We are all disposed to look kindly at each other in regard to cricket. Many might be indifferent at it. None were indifferent to it."

Prime ministerial passion for cricket is utterly bipartisan. Bob Hawke also loves the game. To his great credit, after becoming prime minister in 1983, he revived the practice of a Prime Minister's XI match against the touring side which had fallen into disuse when Sir Robert Menzies departed the scene in 1966. That event continues to this day and is stronger and better than ever.

Likewise, Ben Chifley on arriving in the United Kingdom for an official visit during Australia's famous tour in 1948 is said to have immediately quizzed his English greeter with, "who won the toss"?

So I have not been the first Prime Minister of Australia to have recognised Sir Donald Bradman as a unique Australian, a man representing many of the values, and much of the character of his countrymen. Even now, in another century, in a world scarcely recognisable to that in which he played, the name Bradman resonates with meaning, talent, determination, commitment, fair play, honour.

What, then, does this say about Bradman and what does it say about Australians that Bradman was so elevated to the honoured status that he now occupies in the national psyche?

It could be said that that his place was assured by his unparalleled record at the crease and certainly no exponent of the game has neared his achievement. After all, here was a man who had scored his first Test century at the age of 20, who had scored a triple Test century at the age of 21 (including 309 runs in one day alone), whose record of scoring three double centuries in one Test series remains unequalled to this day and who easily maintains the record of 12 Test double centuries.

Indeed, Bradman's ability to accumulate runs was relentless and, in his famous Test average of 99.94, there is the sobering comparison that the next highest average of a long-serving Australian is that of Greg Chappell with a still outstanding 53.86 runs.

Bradman's domination of the record books can be seen in the simple, yet irrefutable fact that no other batsman of any longevity has averaged above 65 in the history of international Test matches and that the Bradman average is at least 50 per cent above all of them.

I was reminded recently of the often told story of the journalist who asked Sir Donald what he thought he would average if he was playing today with the professionalism of modern players and their approach to fitness and so on.

"Oh, about 50 I suppose," Sir Donald was supposed to have said.

"Do you really think cricketers have improved that much?" said the journalist.

To which Bradman replied, "you have to remember, I'm over 90".

Some might claim that Sir Donald Bradman's enduring legend found form at a time when Australia was in desperate need of a hero.

It is true that some of Bradman's best cricket was played during the depths of Australia's worst depression and it helped lift the spirits of the nation. It held us together when the squalid sentence of mass unemployment risked splitting apart the social fabric of the nation.

The sheer volume of the unemployed who quite simply had nothing else to do with their time swelled the cricketing crowds who witnessed the young Bradman play during his early career.

And his message of hope carried throughout the country by the powerful new medium, radio, which could not only reach, but inspire vast numbers of the population.

He reminded Australians that they were capable of great things in their own right, that at a time when confidence ebbed away from their collective soul, they were competitive, resourceful and talented people. They were well and truly separate from England, comprised a sovereign nation, and displayed an egalitarian individualism that was uniquely Australian.

Bradman and his team-mates during those difficult years, helped nurture and reinforce the national spirit borne out of a generation's sacrifice during the War.

Sir Donald's capacity to sustain his countrymen during their dark, desperate days is undoubted. But it is not a past generation of Australians alone who have found cause to be inspired by his profound example. In every decade since the 1930s Australians have come to celebrate the Bradman record.

And so, in my view, it is not his record alone, not just the times in which he played, but also the quality of the man himself, which has elevated Sir Donald Bradman in the eyes of many to the status as the greatest living Australian.

In his book, *The Art of Cricket*, first published in 1958, Sir Donald Bradman cast his own pen over what he saw as the many qualities fostered by cricket. But, in doing so, he revealed his own virtues.

Foremost amongst others, he said, was the development of character. He wrote, "I have no doubt that it moulds in an individual the right type of character better than any other sport. If that can be substantiated no other recommendation is required because character must surely be one of the greatest assets any nation, through its citizens, can possess."

Nor was he in any doubt that the imprint of cricket on the life of an individual would be indelible. "Common clay must go through the heat and fire of the furnace to become porcelain," he said. "But once through the furnace it can never be clay again. In the same way a man's character must remain permanently enriched by his experiences at cricket."

Bradman understood how important it was to acknowledge defeat, the umpire's adverse decision and a hundred other things with a smile.

I can only concur. There is no more easy task in the world than humbly coping with victory, but it is our response to defeat that reveals a person's moral fibre, together with their ability to learn and move on with honour.

Sir Donald also spoke about the more physical ways in which cricket helped to sharpen the mind and how the game helped to develop the ability to think, to reason out a problem, and to act quickly.

"Then there is the moral as well as physical courage," as Bradman put it, "of facing up to hard training, to bowl fast for hours under a hot sun on a flint hard pitch, to feel the agony of seeing dropped catches nullify your best work".

He noted that "the margin between defeat and victory can be so small it may even depend upon the sportsmanship of an individual. Such acts of sportsmanship are the very essence of this great game."

Sir Donald also reflected upon the qualities of leadership that were necessary in the game. "A good captain must be a fighter; confident but not arrogant, firm but not obstinate, able to take criticism without letting it unduly disturb him, for he is sure to get it, and unfairly too."

"I don't know any game which entails such a severe and prolonged strain on the skipper, but, like the master of a ship, he must exercise control and accept the responsibility."

These are lessons for all who aspire to the mantle of leadership, whether the captaincy of a cricket team or elsewhere.

These are Bradman's lessons, it is his living legacy.

So how shall we use them? What future lies ahead for the game of cricket?

Firstly, we must make certain that Australia's one truly national sport remains at the very centre of our lives.

Our lifestyle, unique and the envy of the world, has always been defined by an abundance of light and space and our climate and our geography would seem to guarantee the summer will always belong to cricket.

Certainly, there can be no doubt of cricket's continuing popularity. It is a remarkable tribute to the game that it can still hold the passion of so many people during a Test match played over a period of five days in the fast moving "just in time" world in which we all now live.

Proof of this was the attendance at last summer's Test matches against India – support for the third Test when the series had already been decided was extraordinary.

But it would be foolhardy to become complacent about the sport we love so much. It has survived so well throughout the decades because of its willingness to retain what is good about the past and relevant for the future, whilst embracing new ideas, techniques and approaches.

Cricket has been able to deliver what we often seek in other aspects of our lives. We feel instinctive ties to certain traditions and the enthusiasms of past generations but we also want to enjoy them in a way that's relevant, contemporary and successful in our own times.

Steve Waugh typifies this spirit. His skill and mental toughness has played a huge part in the current strength of Australian cricket at an international level. Yet he has a well-known affection for the traditions of the game, typified by his idea that the first Test team to play in the year 2000 use the style of caps worn exactly a century before. …

Ladies and Gentlemen, in conclusion, history has shown us we have every reason to be confident about the future of cricket, not just in this country, but throughout the great fraternity of cricketing nations around the globe.

Future generations of young Australians, learning to love this game in their local schools and clubs, as we did, will ensure its survival and success.

With well-founded optimism about the game's future, I share in Bradman's hope that cricket expand even further. For, as Sir Donald once said,

> there are no tariff barriers, licences, restrictions, or any other obstacle in the way of exporting this game which can bring such benefit and pleasure to a whole nation. May cricket continue to flourish and spread its wings. The world can only be the richer for it.

With the example of Sir Donald as our inspiration – not just in cricket but in life – we can make this dream, or any dream, come true.

# One Hundred Years
# of the Australian Spirit

## Sydney – 1 January 2001

The anniversary of Australia's Federation is generally not a cause for the display of patriotism characteristic of Anzac Day, nor an occasion for public introspection about Australia's national identity typical of recent Australia Days. The centenary of this constitutional milestone in 2001, however, was regarded by the Prime Minister and his Government as worthy of recognition and national celebration. In this address at Sydney's Centennial Park, where Australia was inaugurated exactly a century earlier, the Prime Minister reflected that the Federation of the six former colonies on 1 January 1901 represented simply the beginning of a long list of accomplishments that would mark Australia's first century as an independent nation. Far from simply marking an anniversary, the Centenary of Federation was an occasion to celebrate what successive Australians had achieved in terms of forging an egalitarian, harmonious and prosperous country rich in talent, enterprise and future promise.

The story that we have just followed and we will resume in a moment has been more than a story about constitutional formation, more than a story about the coming together of six colonies, important though that was and successful though that was. It has been more than the story of inspiring political leadership one hundred years ago. Most importantly, it has been the story of one hundred years of the Australian spirit. It has been the story of how, over a century, the spirit of Australia and the spirit of the Australian people in so many ways in the right time when required has come to the fore to give to this nation of ours a reputation around the world that is so well deserved.

It is a spirit that saw so many hundreds of thousands of Australians go forth to defend their country, and the freedoms that we value so dearly, in two world wars. It is the spirit of a people that pull together in times of adversity. It is the spirit of a people that can call forth the volunteer efforts of tens of thousands of Australians not only in adversity but also in times of great national celebration such as the Olympic Games. It is the spirit of a people that has produced the most fiercely competitive sporting nation on Earth. It is the spirit of a people which, population-wise, has produced well above its weight, some of the most outstanding medical scientists in the world. It is the spirit of a people that has produced men like [Sir Frank] Macfarlane Burnet, and Victor Chang. It is the spirit of a people that has produced great artists. But, very importantly, my fellow Australians, it is the spirit of a people that has produced a level of social cohesion and national unity that is, indeed, the envy of the world.

On this day, of all days, it is important for all of us as Australians to acknowledge the reality that those things that unite us as Australians and bring us together as part of the great Australian nation are always more important, they are always more enduring, and they are always more emphatic than the things that divide us.

We are a people that have found the great genius to select those things from our heritage which are of enduring value, yet to reject those things of our heritage which will hold us back. We embraced from the British the great principles of the rule of law and parliamentary democracy, but we rejected from the British and other Europeans, notions of class-consciousness. The great egalitarian spirit of this country, which has meant so much to us over the years, and will mean so much to us in the years ahead, is very much a gift of this soil, it is a gift of the air we breath together, it is a gift of the land that we share together.

One of the other great aspects of the spirit of Australia, my friends, is the way in which this nation has been able to absorb, from more than 140 countries around the world, a great variety of people. We have come together, particularly since World War II, to build a nation of great diversity yet nonetheless a nation that honours the long-standing traditions of the Australian community.

Thus, as we celebrate one hundred years, our centenary as a nation, this beautiful evening here in Sydney, I say to all of you, my fellow Australians, we all have great reasons for deep pride. We owe a debt of gratitude to those who formed Australia. We owe a great debt of gratitude to those who fought to defend it. We owe a great debt of gratitude to all of those who have gone before us.

We have every reason to feel pride, we have every reason to feel a great sense of hope and optimism about the future. We are a nation that has achieved its ambitions. But like all nations, we must set ourselves further ambitions and strive to achieve further goals in the years ahead.

We celebrate a great one hundred years. We face the future with tremendous faith that, under God, we can achieve so much more for our people and build upon the great inheritance and the great legacy of the years that have gone before us.

My friends, one of the great characteristics of Australia has been the way in which we have taken people from so many parts of the world, and have seen them contribute so vitally to the building of the great Australian nation. The next segment of this programme will be very much about the story of the journey of people from different parts of the world that have contributed so much to the building of the modern Australian nation.

# ANZAC
## Eternal Place in the Australian Soul
### Gallipoli, Turkey – 25 April 2005

Five years after the first occasion when he addressed the Anzac Dawn Service at Gallipoli, the Prime Minister returned to pay his respects to the fallen. In *Lazarus Rising*, Howard recalled he would always remember Anzac Day 2005 in Gallipoli, where he was "greeted with spontaneous warmth at that service by thousands of my fellow countrymen and women". The sea of thousands of young Australians draped in the national flag on the shores of Gallipoli was something that evidently warmed the Prime Minister's heart. To him it provided welcome assurance that Anzac was not something owned solely by the government or the elites of society, but by ordinary, every-day Australians from all walks of life. Appreciating this enduring appeal of Anzac, the Prime Minister spoke to the audience of how the departure of the original Anzacs spelt not the death of a legend but its rebirth in the souls of today's men and women who served the nation with courage and self-sacrifice in both war and peace. This was because the memory of Anzac had lodged itself in the Australian psyche with successive generations inspired by the noble deeds of those first Anzacs.

Ninety years ago, as dawn began to break, the first sons of a young nation assailed these shores. These young Australians, with their New Zealand comrades, had come to do their bit in a maelstrom not of their making.

Over eight impossible months, they forged a legend whose grip on us grows tighter with each passing year. In the hills, ridges and gullies above us the ANZACS fought, died, dug in and hung on. Here they won a compelling place in the Australian story. Today, we remember the 50 000 Australians who served in the Gallipoli campaign and the more than 26 000 who fell or were wounded here. We remember, too, the sons of New Zealand who died and suffered. Let us not forget the sons of Britain, France, India, Newfoundland and, of course Turkey, who died in their countless thousands on this peninsula.

Gallipoli began our involvement in a cataclysm that would cut down the youth not only of Australia but of many countries across the world. Nearly two-thirds of the 330 000 Australians who served abroad in the Great War would become casualties. Sixty thousand would never see Australia again. We remember today a century of Australian sacrifice, the more than 100 000 Australians who have died in war and for peace in our name. From Villers-Bretonneux to Tobruk, Kokoda to Long Tan, and Afghanistan.

Those who fought here in places like Quinn's Post, Pope's Hill and the Nek changed forever the way we saw our world and ourselves. They bequeathed Australia with a lasting sense of national identity. They sharpened our democratic temper and our questioning eye towards authority. We used to say that the ranks of the original ANZACs were thinning with each passing year. They are all gone now. Now what swells with each ANZAC season is a hunger for their stories. Now we remember them not as old soldiers but as young Australians, often from the same suburbs, streets, districts and towns that we come from. Just as many of you have come here today with your brothers and your mates, so it was 90 years ago that the young of Australia surged forward to enlist along with their brothers and their mates.

We imagine young men swimming amidst death and danger, anything to escape the heat, the fatigue, the flies and the lice. We think especially this morning of the families broken here and in other foreign fields. James and Janet Hallahan of Western Australia sent four sons to the Great War. Three never came home. One of them, Wally, survived Gallipoli and the Western Front only to be killed in the final exchanges of November 1918.

History helps us to remember, but the spirit of Anzac is greater than a debt to past deeds. It lives on in the valour and the sacrifice of young men and women that ennoble Australia in our time, in scrub in the Solomons, in the villages of Timor, in the deserts of Iraq and the coast of Nias. It lives on through a nation's easy familiarity, through Australians looking out for each other, through courage and compassion in the face of adversity.

And so we dedicate ourselves at this hour, at this place, not just to the memory of Anzac but to its eternal place in the Australian soul. Soon we go to Lone Pine where the names of almost half of our Gallipoli casualties are recorded. One of them buried there is Noel Edwards of Bendigo, who took part in that charge against Turkish trenches.

Before heading into "No Man's Land", Noel shared a meal with his two mates, Gil Dyett and Curly Symons. Gil was severely wounded in the attack; Curly was to win a Victoria Cross; Noel fell at the place the Turks called the Ridge of Blood. After the war, Noel's mother, Harriett, penned some words that evoke the painful loss of life's promise that echo down the ages and remind us why we are here:

> How shall I miss him – when from overseas The Anzacs come 'mid shouts of victory; when eager voices answering smiles awake, and hands press hands for old remembrance sake. Full many a face will wear a mask of joy, with heartstrings aching for the absent boy.

In our time, and for all time, we will remember them.

# Australia's History
## Setting the Record Straight

### Sir Paul Hasluck Foundation Inaugural Lecture
### The University of Western Australia
### 27 September 2012

With public debate raging about the merits of the new National Curriculum introduced by the Gillard Labor Government in 2012, John Howard believed it was timely to reflect on how the critically important discipline of history is taught in the school curriculum. In this lecture, given in Winthrop Hall at the University of Western Australia in honour of the Australian historian, Cabinet minister and Governor-General, Sir Paul Hasluck (1905-1993), and in the presence of several members of his family, the former Prime Minister told his audience that the nation's success story needed to be told in the history curriculum for Australian students.

Howard lamented that the draft history curriculum released by the Commonwealth Government did not afford sufficient emphasis to the British inheritance and Judeo-Christian tradition in the formation of modern Australia. Essentially he saw the curriculum as suffering from a lack of self-belief in Western civilisation because of its efforts to appease the grievances of the cultural left about the past failings of Western nations such as Australia. While he acknowledged that Australia's history was by no means perfect, particularly with respect to the nation's poor treatment of its first peoples, he emphasised that "the story of Australia was an overwhelming positive one".

Accordingly, he concluded that through instruction in

history, Australia needed to appreciate the influences
that had made the nation not only great but also attractive to the many newcomers it had welcomed.

It is a great honour to deliver the inaugural Sir Paul Hasluck Lecture.
The University of Western Australia is where Sir Paul studied, and later
taught history, the great passion of his life. ...

Those who fail to learn history, Winston Churchill famously said,
are doomed to repeat it. But history, if taught well, can point us not
just to the mistakes we should never repeat but also to the successes
that we should build on. As Prime Minister I often spoke of the Australian achievement as a way of describing the epic success which has
been the Australian nation. I did not coin that term; it was the description proposed by the Fraser Government in the early 1980s for the then
forthcoming Bicentenary celebrations in 1988. The Hawke Government
dropped it, which I thought a pity as it was a neat, but expressive, way
of describing our national success story.

There are many components of the Australian achievement. Unlike so
many other countries, we were able to create a functioning democratic political system without ever resorting to violence or conflict. We were one
of the first countries in the world to provide full voting rights to women.
We introduced the secret ballot, known for a time around the world as the
Australian ballot, one of the most important features of true democracy.
We were one of the first countries to abolish property tests for voting,
and introduce the one man, one vote principle. Well before the rest of the
world, Victoria introduced salaries for members of parliament to ensure
that poorer men could afford to give up their jobs to stand for office.

Of course, along the way, we got things wrong. It took us far too
long to recognise the special place of Indigenous people in the history
and culture of this country. In common with the rest of the world, it
took us far too long to extinguish racial prejudice from our immigration policies. In common with the rest of the world, it took us far too
long to recognise that men and women were capable of making an equal
contribution to society. But I do not think we should ever let honest
acknowledgment of this country's past mistakes obscure its remarkable

achievements. The story of Australia is an overwhelmingly positive one. One component of the Australian achievement which has always stood out has been our capacity in numerous areas of human endeavour and public policy to achieve a sense of balance, which, in many cases, is absent in other countries.

Despite what any self-appointed cultural dieticians tell you, Australia is part of Western civilisation. We speak the English language; so many of our institutions are inherited from Britain; and we share all of the advantages and identity of Western civilisation. The Western liberal tradition continues to infuse our public life. We have been quite clever with our legacy. In building our egalitarian society, we took the good bits – we took the rule of law; we took the parliamentary system; we took the freedom of the press; we took an essentially civil approach to political differences and political discourse – but we rejected class distinction and needless barriers to social mobility. The fundamental freedoms of Australia are protected by our robust parliamentary system, a highly ethical judiciary and a free and vigorous press, all of which are part of the Western liberal tradition. …

The draft history curriculum released by the Commonwealth Government will be implemented in most States by the latter half of 2013. It sets out a framework for what students will learn through to Year 10 and must be taught in what will now be a compulsory subject. Also outlined is the curriculum for those who choose history in Years 11 and 12.

It is good that history will become a compulsory subject to Year 10. It is also good that there will be more emphasis on Indigenous history which must include a frank but objective assessment of past mistakes. Asian history will be more prominent, and no one can argue with that. …

Beyond those praiseworthy features there is much about the curriculum that I find unbalanced, lacking in priorities and, in some cases, quite bizarre. The curriculum does not properly reflect the undoubted fact that Australia is part of Western civilisation; in the process it further marginalises the historic influence of the Judeo-Christian ethic in shaping Australian society and virtually purges British history from any meaningful role.

The teaching of history is meant to explain what happened, why and what lessons can be learned from the past. The structure of this curriculum will not facilitate this occurring. The laudable goals of enhancing the teaching of Indigenous and Asian history could have been fully achieved by the curriculum's authors without relegating or virtually eliminating the study of influences vital to a proper understanding of who we are as a people and where we came from.

It is a fact that modern Australia is a product of Western civilisation; the Judeo-Christian influence is a reality and the British inheritance self-evident. We cannot properly understand our nation's history without fully recognising that this is the case. The curriculum's treatment of human rights is ultra-legalistic, as if they were first discovered by those who wrote the United Nations Charter in 1945. The recommended study of political thought and movements, more generally as well as with application to Australia, is slanted to the progressive left view of the world – with the most egregious example being the perpetuation of the leftist myth that it was Gough Whitlam and not Harold Holt who brought down the White Australia Policy.

Beyond a study of the two World Wars, momentous events of the past 100 years such as the rise and fall of Soviet communism and the economic globalisation of recent decades, which has lifted hundreds of millions from poverty, are treated in a piecemeal fashion and not given the prominence their importance commands. That our Western heritage appears to be so conspicuously absent from the history curriculum reflects a growing retreat from self-belief in Western civilisation. It is as if the West must always play the villain simply because it has tended to enjoy more power and economic success than other parts of the world since 1500.

If it is thought that I exaggerate, have a look at the curriculum for Years 10 to 12 dealing with the 20th century. Students are invited to choose a study of one nation from each of two lists. Incredibly, Australia and the United States are in list one along with Germany and the Soviet Union – and this is for the period 1905 to 1945. The rationale for grouping Australia and the United States with Germany and Russia is that they were "Western nations beset by crises and that shared the following historical experiences; involvement in World War I, challenges to their democracies from ideologies such as Fascism and Nazism." Such a grouping justifies the description of bizarre. Neither Australia nor the United States faced any internal threat from Nazism or Fascism during that time. Self-evidently, those ideologies would only have affected Australia if Germany had been victorious in World War II. Also, when in that period did Russia, apart from the interregnum of the Provisional Government under Alexander Kerensky – which lasted from February to October 1917 – enjoy anything approaching democracy? Did not the revolution take Russia from the absolutism of the Tsars to the dictatorship of the Soviets?

The purging of British history from the curriculum is particularly blameworthy. The influence of British institutions on Australia is a fact, not nostalgia. Magna Carta, parliamentary democracy, the language we speak – which, need I remind you, is now the lingua franca of Asia – much of the literature we imbibe, a free and irreverent media, our relatively civil system of political discourse, the rule of law and trial by jury. Indeed, some of the sports we play, these are all owed in one form or another to the British. How these institutions developed, and the individual and community struggles involved, is our history as much as it is British history. We cannot know the modern Australia well without having a proper understanding of the British story. How can young Australians ever be expected to understand how fragile and hard won the rule of law is without knowing a little about the English Civil War?

Noel Pearson enjoys wide respect as a forthright, articulate Aboriginal leader. One of his great strengths is that he speaks of Aboriginal issues in the broader Australian context. He once had something to say to me about the British influence on Australia. In a long, impassioned and thoughtful letter, written to me as Prime Minister in 2007, subsequently published, he said that Aboriginal Australia and the British inheritance were the two great formative influences on our nation. For him, both were critically important to what he saw as a fully reconciled Australia.

The curriculum dwells heavily on human rights, but in a fashion which suggests that the source of human rights is to be found in the United Nations Charter, the Declaration of Human Rights and various legislative enactments both in Australia and around the world. These are important legal codifications of human rights but are anything but the full story. They represent no guarantee that human rights will be observed. History, including quite recent history, is replete with examples of fine sounding words, even in constitutions, being swept aside, and human rights trampled upon, if the domestic as well international political will, as well as the capacity to protect them, is absent. The proper human rights story cannot be told without a context which traces the evolution of the concept of individual liberty from early times, dealing with practices such as slavery, and how it ended, as well the most horrific instances of human rights violations such as the Holocaust. After all, the most basic of all rights is the right to live.

I have always respected the secular tradition in Australia, but this tradition is in no way in conflict with a full and objective understanding of the extent to which the Judeo-Christian ethic has moulded our society. Indeed, Christianity has often reinforced and inspired many of our most important secular ideas and values, including freedom of speech and freedom of association. The curriculum does not reflect this. There is some irony here. The more zealous secularists in our midst justify pressure to exclude, progressively, the Christian religion from the public space by invoking the mantra of the separation of Church and State, in seeming ignorance that the very foundation of that important principle is to be found in the injunction of Christ in the Gospel according to St Matthew when he said "render therefore unto Caesar the things which are Caesar's and unto God, the things that are God's".

Another illustration of the bizarre is to be found in the Year 10 curriculum which is the final part of the compulsory course. In it, students are required to do what is called an in-depth study of one of three aspects of globalisation from 1945 to today: the options are popular culture, environmental movements or mass migration movements. Now I looked at that, and I read it several times, and I thought to myself: since 1945, what has been the most significant element of globalisation that

296

has really affected the world and Australia? Surely it has to be economic globalisation? Surely it is the fact that the spread, through market forces and more open trade, of economic growth to countries like China, India and other nations in our region, has helped liberate literally hundreds of millions from poverty? It is a process that is set to continue transforming the global balance of power and remains the key to eradicating poverty in places like Africa. It is also why the future of our country is so closely intertwined with that of China and the North Asian region. ...

The curriculum is repeatedly unbalanced in the choice of subjects which have an obvious political context. It is impossible, adequately, to teach any country's history without touching on political issues. That is only proper. But it is imperative that balance and objectivity are scrupulously observed. One can have no objection to the progressive left view being reflected in the curriculum provided it is balanced with other views.

This is not the case with this curriculum. For instance, in Year 9, students are given the option of learning about the "progressive ideas and movements" of the 19th century. The ideas which feature are socialism, imperialism, nationalism, egalitarianism, Darwinism, capitalism and Chartism. Not one mention of conservatism. Not one mention of liberalism, which is extraordinary given that the Western liberal tradition is pervasive both in Australia and similar countries. In the same context, students will study the reasons why one key idea emerged and/or developed a following. Naturally, the example suggested in the curriculum is the influence of the industrial revolution on socialism. Where is the counter balancing example?

In Years 11/12 one of the electives is workers' rights. Students will learn about the Tolpuddle Martyrs, the influence of Chartism as well Engels and Marx. The International Labour Organisation (ILO) will be studied, so will the International Federation of Trade Unions and their methods to advance workers' rights. Once again, where is the balance? Where is the elective inviting a detailed study of free enterprise, including the central role of private property ownership? Surely that should be included in any balanced study of our social history.

In areas such as this, the assumption of the curriculum is that wealth will always be there and scant regard need be paid to its generation. Students can learn about the Harvester judgment, the introduction of pensions, and workers' rights, and there can be no objection to that, but where, for example, is the reference to the decisive rejection in the late 1940s of attempts to nationalise Australia's banking system. If success-ful those moves would have fundamentally altered the direction of the post-World War II Australian economy. And as for the role of small busi-ness in the history of the Australian economy – not a mention.

Its coverage of modern Chinese political history inexplicably stops at 1976, two years before Deng Xiaoping introduced liberal economic reforms that would dramatically transform China's economy, although some reference is made elsewhere to China's contemporary economic performance; once again, however, the context is wrong.

I am sure it will astonish you all to know that students will not be required to do a detailed study of the mainstream history of Australia between 1750 and 1918. Let me explain why. The study of Australian history is first introduced into the curriculum in Year 6 but, understand-ably, it is of a generalised kind, and does not contain any of the so-called "depth studies", which are introduced in later years. The curriculum re-turns to Australian history in Year 9, under the heading of Making a Bet-ter World (1750 – 1914). Yet, incredibly, students will not be required to study Australian history in depth for that period because such a study is offered only as an alternative to an in-depth study of an Asian country. It is not compulsory.

So, under this curriculum, Australian school students will not be re-quired to learn, in detail, about the formation of the Commonwealth of Australia through the Federation of the colonies in 1901, without ques-tion the most important event in our national history. Need I say more?

Choices have to be made in any curriculum and it is impossible to satisfy everybody, but my fear is that, if this curriculum remains un-amended, young Australians of the future will be denied a proper knowl-edge of our nation's history. If something is to be done about this cur-riculum then only State governments and, in particular, their Education ministers can do it. We have so much to be proud of. The common sense and balance we have achieved in so many important areas is a product of who we are and where we have come from. Let us never forget those influences, and those values that have contributed to the nation that so many are desperate to come to. We must have got a lot right and I just hope we are smart enough to defend what we have got right and where it came from.

# VIII

## Australia and the World

### No Need to Choose between Geography and History

# Strengthening the Australia-Indonesia Relationship

## Jakarta, Indonesia – 16 September 1996

Shortly before his election victory in March 1996, John Howard told an audience at the National Press Club that Indonesia would be the first country he planned to visit as prime minister. On his visit to Indonesia in September 1996, the Prime Minister held talks with President Suharto where there was evidently goodwill on both sides for a strong Australia-Indonesia relationship. Despite speculation that Howard would retreat from closer relations with Indonesia and the Asia-Pacific more generally, the Prime Minister assured his Indonesian hosts that Australia's relationship with its nearest neighbour enjoyed firm bi-partisan support. Observing that more Indonesians and Australians than ever before were learning about each other's country, the Prime Minister expressed his confidence that the existing links in education, trade, security and defence would strengthen between the two neighbours. He concluded that while Indonesia and Australia were two very different countries, they each stood to benefit from a close and cooperative partnership of mutual interests.

Mr President,

I wish first to thank you for your hospitality. I am very pleased to be back in Indonesia, on this occasion for the first time as head of a new Australian Government. ...

I particularly welcome this first opportunity for me personally to reaffirm to you, Mr President, my commitment and the commitment of my Government as a whole to Australia's relationship with Indonesia. This relationship is of the very greatest significance to Australia and brings substantial benefits to our region as a whole.

That our relationship has become far richer and so diverse reflects the natural complementarity of our national interests. But it also reflects the work that governments in both countries have put into nurturing it. I would like to thank you, Mr President, for the evident interest and care you have taken in it.

I also acknowledge the contribution made by our predecessors in government in Australia. The relationship with Indonesia enjoys bipartisan support from both sides of politics in Australia and this has a long history.

Indonesia had the support of Australia in its move towards independence after the war under a Labor government. It was a Liberal-Country Party government which welcomed the stability brought by the New Order government in the second half of the 1960s and, in those early days, helped in establishing the international financial arrangements to support Indonesia's development. In more recent years, the Fraser, Hawke and Keating governments all played their part in strengthening the relationship.

The stability and unity of Indonesia and its economic growth under the New Order, so much of which is due to your personal leadership, Mr President, have been a feature of our economic and strategic landscape for 30 years and of great benefit to Australia and the region. Our relationship now has many dimensions. Our bilateral economic links are flourishing. A decade ago, trade between us was worth less than $1 billion. In 1995-96 it was worth $ 4.2 billion. That was 30 per cent higher than the year before. Our investment links are also expanding rapidly.

In part, this reflects the transformation of the Indonesian economy which has increased in size over five times since 1966. The dividend of wise policy choices by Indonesia is evident in the economy's growth and attractiveness to foreign investors.

I am pleased to say that Australia is deeply involved in this transformation. We are one of Indonesia's ten largest investors. Over 300

Australian companies have a presence here. We are your fifth largest source of imports.

This is a good start to making the most of the great potential of our economic relationship. But we should regard it as only a start. As Indonesia closes in on its goal of becoming an industrialised nation, Australia is well placed to help supply your demand for intermediate and capital goods, services and technology. Dr Habibie's visit last year [1995] identified some of the scope for this. Greater cooperation is possible in areas like education, health, tourism, infrastructure, housing and business and financial services.

My Government comes to office with a mandate to undertake some important reforms which I think will make Australia a more dynamic economy and an even more attractive economic partner.

Mr President, just as Australia and Indonesia have come to see the mutual benefits of harnessing our economic complementarity, we have come to see the sense in close security cooperation. Our expanding security links and the recent Agreement on maintaining security reinforce the confidence we have in each other. The Agreement has my Government's strong support. It underlines that the security of each country is important to the other. It sends the message that at a time of strategic change Australia and Indonesia are committed to cooperating in order to promote regional stability.

These shared interests and views are being strengthened by increasing contacts between Australians and Indonesians. Our expanding tourism, business and education links promote much better understanding of each other. More Indonesians and Australians than ever before are learning about each other's country, language and culture. The confidence we have in each other and overall compatibility of our policy choices has made us good partners in regional affairs as well as bilaterally.

Mr President, there is nothing new about Australia's active involvement in the Asia-Pacific region. Since the Second World War, Australian governments of all parties have recognised Asia's importance to Australia's future and have worked to strengthen links with the region. Geography dictates nothing less. Our security is closely affected by what happens in Asia. Our economic stake in the region is massive: more than 60 per cent of Australia's merchandise exports go to East Asia, accounting for nearly 12 per cent of our GDP. In turn, we are an important economic and security partner and a source of technology, skills and education for many countries in Asia.

We do not claim to be Asian. Like every other country in the Asia-Pacific, we bring our own distinct culture, attitudes and history to the region.

I do not believe that Australia faces a choice between our history and our geography, between our links with European and North American societies on the one hand and those with the nations of Asia on the other. Neither do I see it as a matter of balancing our interests in Asia against or with our interests in the rest of the world.

Neither do I see Australia as a bridge between Asia and the West as is sometimes suggested. Rather I believe that our geography and history are elements in an integrated relationship with our region and the wider world. Our links with Asia add something to our links with the rest of the world, and vice versa. For example, our close association and alliance relationship with the United States contribute to the prosperity and stability of the region.

My Government is committed to being an active participant in regional affairs, and in this I am confident that we can work closely with Indonesia. Indonesia played a key role in the settlement in Cambodia, and we cooperated closely with you.

Mr President, it was under your leadership at the 1994 leaders' meeting in Bogor that APEC set the historic goal of free trade in the region by 2010-2020. Australia strongly supported that goal at the time. My Government remains committed to it. I look forward to discussing with you how Australia and Indonesia can work together at this year's leaders' meeting at Subic Bay to make progress towards it.

As neighbours, Australia and Indonesia have a close interest in the success of the other. We should support each other's efforts.

We have to recognise that each country brings different strengths to the relationship. We should acknowledge each other's achievements. We should not presume to have the answers to each other's problems.

We are very different and we cannot expect always to see eye to eye. No country can be asked to deny its history, principles or culture. But when disagreements emerge, they should be seen in the context of the overriding mutual interests we share and the immense benefit of a close relationship between us.

Mr President, the key to any friendship is a shared long-term commitment to each other's well-being. I believe that commitment exists in Indonesia. I want here tonight to renew it on behalf of Australia.

# Australia and Britain Today

## The Contemporary Partnership
## in a new International Environment
## London – 23 June 1997

In 1997, John Howard, Prime Minister of Australia since 1996, was invited to deliver the Sir Robert Menzies Memorial Lecture at the Menzies Centre for Australian Studies, King's College, London. Addressing the topic of the contemporary partnership between Australia and Britain, the Prime Minister acknowledged that whilst each country remained deeply engaged with its own region of the world, the contemporary Anglo-Australian relationship was marked by many shared interests. In addition to the obvious ties of history, culture, language, sport, the Crown, the Commonwealth of Nations and numerous people-to-people links, Howard reminded his audience that Australia and Britain still shared close defence and security ties as well as a high level of investment in each other's economies. Acknowledging his counterpart, Tony Blair, as the newly-elected Labour Prime Minister of Britain, Howard saw their recent elections to office as a fresh opportunity to positively reset Anglo-Australian relations. Instead of allowing political differences between Canberra and Westminster to dominate unduly, the relationship would be mature and flexible enough to accommodate shared interests and values.

After just 15 months in office, I come to the United Kingdom as the head of a still relatively new government in Australia to visit a brand new government here in Britain.

I have had a very valuable discussion with Tony Blair, the new Prime Minister, and I was struck immediately by the warmth of his attitude towards Australia and his desire to enforce strong continuing Anglo-Aus-

307

tralian relationships under our two new governments. In fact, one of the ironic characteristics of Anglo-Australian relations at a political level, in the last twenty years, was, of course, that for most of the time that Britain was governed by a Conservative Government, Australia was governed by a Labor Government. And there has in each country in recent times been a juxtaposition of political leadership and I certainly see it as one of my principal responsibilities, indeed a principal commitment, in developing the relationship to ensure that the political divide, whilst always understood and respected, does not blur overall the greater commitment to building a still stronger relationship between our two societies.

I told Mr Blair that I was convinced of the contemporary relevance of the relationship between our two countries and I was very strongly committed to building a modern relationship with Britain. That relationship is becoming less and less amenable to false caricatures than it has ever been. It is more open and more balanced. It is modern and dynamic.

I am convinced – and I think I can say that Tony Blair shared my view – that the relationship between Australia and the United Kingdom is a considerable asset to both of us as we move into the 21st century. …

Australia's destiny is tightly bound up with that of her region. Likewise, the destiny of the United Kingdom is tightly bound up with the future of Europe. Nevertheless Australia and the United Kingdom have important interests in each other's regions – whether we are geographically part of them or not. History shows events in Europe can affect Australian interests in profound ways, as events in Asia can affect the United Kingdom. We need the markets of both to prosper.

These interests, and the roles we play in our respective regions, constitute compelling reasons to keep the friendship between Australia and the United Kingdom up to date and active and to use it to help shape our futures in a positive way.

We have the tremendous asset that no two countries in our respective regions know each other better, trust each other more, and have closer relationships than Australia and Britain. This underlines a point the Australians here will know I often make: and that is Australia faces no choice between her history and geography.

I believe that the interplay between our bilateral links and the role that each of us performs in our respective regions will be an increasingly important element in our future relationship.

Each nation will be building on a profound economic, political and human investment we have already made and have in the other. Britain is the second largest investor in Australia. It is the largest investor in Australia's manufacturing industry, providing nearly 40 per cent of the total direct foreign investment in manufacturing. After the United States and the Netherlands, Australia rivals France and Germany as the next largest foreign investor in the United Kingdom.

The continuing relevance of our bilateral relationship is also apparent in important defence and security ties, and in our co-operation on many global issues through the United Nations, the Commonwealth and other forums.

It is also evident, of course, in the enduring ties that will continue to bind peoples: the shared values and aspirations, the historical and institutional associations, the ties of family and community, and the links established by cultural, educational and sporting exchanges.

It would be easy with a history as rich as the one shared by the United Kingdom and Australia to allow that history to dominate our perspectives of the relationship. It is therefore important that we keep our understanding of each other contemporary and forward-looking. For that reason, it is most fitting that the Australian and British governments are co-operating in mounting the New Images promotion. We are sharing the challenge of communicating up-to-date perceptions of our economies, our societies, our directions and our peoples.

For the same reason, I am delighted to have had the opportunity provided by the Menzies Centre for Australian Studies to make my own contribution to that endeavour and to underline my confidence in the contribution that both Australia and the United Kingdom can bring, not only to a more secure and productive future for our respective region, but also, with our interplay on each other, a more secure and productive future for our two societies and our two nations.

# What being a Neighbour is Really About

## Sir Edward "Weary" Dunlop ASIALINK Lecture
## Melbourne – 11 November 1997

In the Sir Edward "Weary" Dunlop[41] ASIALINK Lecture established to encourage eminent Australians to present their vision for Asia-Australia relations, the Prime Minister canvassed the approach of his government to Australia's relationship with Asia. Howard paid tribute to Dunlop's far-sighted concern for the well-being of Australia's neighbours in the Asia-Pacific. To honour his legacy, Howard committed his Government to cultivating fruitful relationships with the nations of Asia. Regarding Australia's "engagement with Asia" as "our highest foreign policy priority", he contended that "Australia's economic and political destiny is naturally closely tied up with her immediate region". In his approach to Asia, Howard drew not only on Dunlop's legacy but also on the example of Sir Robert Menzies who pursued a "good neighbour" policy of providing Australian aid and security to developing South-East Asian nations in 1950s and 60s. While Howard stressed the imperative of engaging with Asia, he enunciated what would become his Government's "Asia first, not Asia only" foreign policy. According to this principle, Australia would deepen its economic and defence ties with Asia whilst maintaining strong relations with traditional allies in Europe and North America.

Life is all about personal courage, about character, about the capacity to do the right thing, to care for one another in times of trial and times of

---

[41] Sir Edward "Weary" Dunlop (1907-1993) was a distinguished Australian surgeon, war hero and humanitarian, credited for fostering closer Australian ties with Asia in the post-war years.

difficulty. No figure in Australian history more perfectly and completely personified the injunction to care for others in dire need than "Weary" Dunlop. He did that and he did it in a way that has won him the affection, not only of those he preserved in life but of an entire nation. ...

"Weary" Dunlop became a leading light in the Asia-Australia Society. He played a very active role in the Colombo Plan. Under the Plan, Dunlop shared his energy and his phenomenal surgical skills with the peoples of Thailand, Sri Lanka and India. He later returned to an Asian theatre of war to help the wounded in Vietnam. ...

So on this Remembrance Day, before this audience, what is it that we can learn from Dunlop's legacy?

It is perhaps the true meaning of being a neighbour. Dunlop understood that being a neighbour has less to do with geography than it does with actions, that being a neighbour meant respecting the qualities and cultures of others as well as lending a hand so as to turn regions into neighbourhoods. ...

Australia has a vital interest in her neighbours succeeding in transforming their economies. They must become more open and have sustainable patterns of growth. Sixty per cent of our exports go to East Asia. Through our participation in the International Monetary Fund (IMF) support packages for our neighbours and our practical help at a technical level – through, for example, the Reserve Bank – we are making a real difference to the region's prospects.

The point I want to emphasise, however, is that recent events have surely shown that Australia should not regard itself as an anxious outsider in her region. Our actions build on a long and honourable tradition – which "Weary" Dunlop personified and successive governments of all political persuasions have followed since the War – of conscientious and reliable support and neighbourly behaviour towards our partners in the region.

We have demonstrated beyond any doubt that we are a reliable regional mate. And I am pleased that this has been recognised in the region both in the personal comments that have been made by regional leaders to myself and other government ministers and in the regional press. We have acted from a sense of regional mutual obligation that is the foundation of any community. And of course we would like to think that our neighbours would be there when we need them.

Another important point to emerge from the present economic problems in the region is the need for Australia to think of herself as a citizen of the world. Australia's economic and political destiny is naturally closely tied up with her immediate region.

I am unequivocally committed to deepening our engagement with the countries of Asia. However, in pursuing this objective the Government will not neglect Australia's interests elsewhere. Our policy is Asia first or Asia plus, not Asia only.

Over 60 per cent of the direct investment Australia sends abroad is steered towards Europe and the United States. Over 60 per cent of the direct investment we receive from abroad comes from the United States and Europe. Moreover, these economic links contribute profoundly to the manufacturing base of our economy and our technological leadership in the region. ...

This highlights perhaps Australia's greatest strength: we occupy a unique intersection of history, geography, cultural, political and economic circumstance. There is no other country in the world which has such an asset. It is an immense strength and never a weakness.

Some are inclined to see the economic, cultural and political differences between Australia and the countries in our region as a problem – or as worrying gaps that should be narrowed by changing ourselves. Nothing could be further from the truth.

European and American linkages enhance rather than encumber or diminish the role we play in our region. Equally, an understanding of the region adds value to our relationship with the United States, Britain and Europe. For example, during my recent visit to Washington, President Clinton accepted my suggestion that it might be useful for Australia, with its different perspectives on Indonesia, to share its views with the United States. Australian and United States officials subsequently had some discussions which I think will make some small contribution at least to understanding between two important friends of Australia.

312

We share interests with our neighbours in a stable and prosperous region and we are an active and highly regarded participant in building the region's future. Our unique characteristics and our linkages with other parts of the world – in cultural, political and strategic terms – make this contribution especially effective and make it especially highly regarded in the region.

This is demonstrated at a political level by the commitment to partnership with us by Japan and by the recent responses of countries such as Indonesia and Thailand to our assistance. It is demonstrated through the close defence relationships we have with regional countries such as Malaysia and Singapore. It is demonstrated by the large number of students from the region studying at Australian institutions. It is demonstrated at the most important level by the large numbers of immigrants from our region who have made their homes in Australia and who are playing an influential and welcome part in shaping and building Australia's economy and society.

Our success in creating a successful, diverse, tolerant and united nation is an immense achievement. It is a beacon in our region and the world. Those who seek to diminish that achievement do Australia a great disservice.

Our success reflects the aspirations and values that "Weary" Dunlop held dear and so remarkably fulfilled in his life. Our success is also founded on a political heritage that has given our society a stability and security that has been unmatched anywhere in the world....

The Coalition regards our engagement with Asia as our highest foreign policy priority. We are inextricably linked with Asia for the long term. Recent currency turbulence in the region reminds us that our prosperity as well as our security is linked with the region. We seek closer engagement in Asia because of the profound benefits which can flow from countries in the region as well as the realisation of our mutual interests. ...

On this Remembrance Day, the legacy of "Weary" Dunlop provides us with an opportunity to appreciate what is precious about Australia: our political and economic stability; our international linkages; our

313

skills and technology; our diversity; and, above all, our values as individuals.

The region welcomes us for what we are and what we stand for.

It was for the same reason that the region opened its arms to "Weary" Dunlop. The foundation for his respect and understanding of others was the deep understanding of his own worth and that of his own history, culture and values.

"Weary" Dunlop personified the mateship which lies at the core of Australian values and our sense of nation. He revealed to us what being a neighbour is really all about.

# Cherishing the Australia-Israel Friendship

## Melbourne – 22 November 2000

When the modern state of Israel was inaugurated in 1948, Australia was one of the first countries formally to recognise the new Jewish homeland. In the ensuing post-war years, Prime Minister Robert Menzies cultivated warm relations with both Israel and Australia's own Jewish community. Prime Minister John Howard likewise enjoyed a personal rapport with members of Australia's Jewish community and emerged in public as a firm ally and advocate of Israel. In this address, the Prime Minister praised the immense contribution of the Jewish community to Australian life and culture, with Jewish Australians excelling in many fields of endeavour from military life to academia and the judiciary. Meanwhile, with the volatile geopolitics of the Middle East threatening the security of Israel, Howard promised that his Government would support the territorial integrity of Israel and affirmed the right of Israelis to live in peace and safety within the boundaries of their own country. While standing strong with Israel, Howard also acknowledged the right of the neighbouring Palestinian people to live peaceably within their own state. Aside from admiring its resilience, Howard's affection for Israel was based on the many similarities he saw it as sharing with Australia, especially its commitment to liberal democracy and the rule of law.

I went to Israel long before my entry into Australian politics. In part that visit was inspired by some deep friendships that I had formed with members of the Australian-Jewish community, first at Sydney University and, more generally, within the community afterwards. It was an experience that reminded me of the great tenacity and capacity to survive which has had to be a hallmark of the existence of the State of Israel since its formation in 1948. It brought home to me for the first time in a very vivid way how important that part of the world has been to the creation of many of the spiritual streams of the entire world. The contribution that it made not only to Judaism but also to Christianity and to Islam. …

So it was with a great sense of anticipation and genuine warmth that I went to Israel for the first time as Prime Minister of Australia. I preceded my visit to Israel with a visit to Gallipoli on Anzac Day and subsequently to the battlefields of the Western Front in France. I was reminded on both those occasions of how deeply entwined and embedded in the history of this country is the contribution of the Jewish people. One of the seven Australians who won a Victoria Cross at Lone Pine was Jewish; and the greatest field commander of the First World War, and arguably Australia's greatest Jewish son, was General Sir John Monash. Those references are a metaphor for the partnership that we have enjoyed down through the years, for the contribution that Jewish people have made to our country and the way we have worked together to shape the destiny of this most tolerant of nations.

The situation in the Middle East now is nothing short of heart-breaking. The sense of optimism and hope that was clearly present in April and which I experienced and, might I say, to demonstrate my understanding of how very committed to the peace process, are not only the people of Israel but also the Jewish community here in Australia. I remember announcing for the first time on Melbourne radio that I would, when visiting Israel, go and see the Chairman of the Palestinian Council, having previously been unwilling to invite him to visit Australia because I did not believe the peace process had advanced far enough.

I was questioned about the wisdom or, perhaps, the consistency of that decision and I responded to the interviewer to the effect that circumstances had changed and it was in the interests of the peace process that all of those who were friends and staunch allies of Israel, as well as acknowledging the legitimate aspirations of the people, the Palestinian people, to have their independence, that we should all get together and do what we could to encourage the peace process. I was greatly encouraged to know that later in the day both Mark Liebler and Colin Rubinstein rang the station to express support for the decision that I had taken. That demonstrated the passionate desire of the Jewish people of Australia as well as the desire of so many around the world to see the peace process succeed.

I was encouraged to visit Yasser Arafat. I was encouraged by the Government of Israel. I was accompanied on that visit by members of the Australian Jewish community. I still have a photograph of the Chairman, Isi Liebler, and myself. It was a reminder of how close in a sense the world had come to achieving an absolutely wonderful breakthrough, and to see that now in great peril is tragic and heartbreaking to so many people.

But we must not surrender hope because, when you surrender hope, then you are ultimately giving in to those who do not ever want to see peace. I do not believe any prime minister of Israel could have offered more than did Ehud Barak at Camp David. He went 90 per cent of the way in relation to territory and he was agreeable to joint suzerainty in relation to Jerusalem. It was an offer that should have been accepted and it is tragic in the extreme that it has not been accepted. But we must, all of us who remain staunch and reliable friends and allies of Israel, continue in our different ways to encourage diplomatically, and otherwise, the resumed move towards peace.

In the end, I believe there is a deep desire, certainly in the hearts of the people of Israel and I believe also in many Palestinian hearts for peace. That is what I find as I move amongst the different communities here in Australia. People are tired of the killing, they are tired of the terror, they are tired of the insecurity and they want a brighter future for their children. I believe Barak displayed very great courage and he should be encouraged for the efforts that he has so far displayed.

All countries have a responsibility to urge commitment, renewed commitment, to the peace process. Only today I received a letter from the Prime Minister of Israel detailing the terrible circumstances of the bombing of the bus carrying those children in Israel. Yet despite the understandable anger expressed in that letter, there was a continued commitment to the process of achieving peace.

My message to you, ladies and gentlemen, is two-fold, in two senses. It is a personal message from John Howard, a longstanding friend of the Jewish community of Australia and a longstanding admirer of what Israel has achieved in such tremendous adversity in the last 50 years.

It is also a message from the Prime Minister of Australia on behalf of the Government and the people of Australia, that we admire the contribution of your community to our country and to our country's history. We admire the way in which you have contributed to every facet of Australian life, to the values of family, of hard work, of loyalty, of charity and civic decency that your community has always been famed for. It is also a message of renewed hope, I suppose, that somehow the peace process in the Middle East can get back on track. And I believe that there is residual goodwill in the appropriate areas for that, with appropriate application, to be achieved.

Your contribution to Australian society has been immense. And the contribution of the Jewish people around the world, to wisdom and to culture and to learning, has been absolutely legendary. That great and famous part of the world has given great gifts to the people of the world. And that makes the present time of peril and present time of distress all that much harder to bear. But the hallmark of the Jewish people and the hallmark of the State of Israel has always been faith and commitment and tenacity. You, and they, have displayed it in the past and I know it will continue.

Often in life, when all apparently seems lost, out of that sense of despair, new hope can be retrieved. All of us must hope that that will be what occurs in the Middle East. All of us must hope and pray, in our different ways and according to our different faiths, that that can be brought about. Because the desire for peace is very deep, and it is very strong and the desire of the friends of the Jewish people and the friends of Israel, all around the world, not only to continue to enjoy their great company and their great contribution to our different societies, but also the desire to see the homeland of the Jewish people in Israel live in security and peace, that desire is very strong.

My Government will always remain committed to the territorial integrity of Israel, the right of the people of Israel to live in peace behind secure, defined and defendable boundaries. We also recognise, as we have for many years, the proper and legitimate right and aspiration of the people, the Palestinian people, to aspire to have their own state. And we feel for them in relation to the suffering and the aspirations that they legitimately have. We can all hope that good men and women will triumph, and goodwill and the desire for peace will in the end win out.

It was an honour for me to represent our country in Israel as the Prime Minister of Australia. The vitality of the State of Israel; the obvious and the overt friendship of the people of Israel towards the people of Australia; the burgeoning information technology and other economic links; the honour conferred on me by the Bar-Ilan University, and the particular pleasure that I derived from being accompanied and assisted when the degree was conferred on me by two distinguished members of the Australian Jewish community. All of that left an indelible impression on me.

Israel has been a wonderful source of inspiration to the Jewish people of the world, it has been a wonderful example of racial harmony and tolerance, and of openness and a willingness to receive people from all around the world, not unlike our own country. As many people have remarked, there are many similarities, and of course many differences, between our two societies. We are both robust democracies, we sometimes have noisy parliaments, both of us. We have a very strong commitment to the rule of law, we each have a very strong sense of independence, and a willingness to defy difficult odds.

It is a close friendship and it is a friendship that I hope I have made a small contribution towards nurturing and improving. I will remember with very great affection the three visits I have paid to Israel. None will be remembered with greater pride than the most recent one, because I not only went there as John Howard, a friend and admirer of the State of Israel, but I also went there as John Howard, Prime Minister of Australia, a strong, reliable and faithful ally and friend of Israel.

# Australia's International Relations

## Ready for the Future
## Canberra – 22 August 2001

In this address to the Menzies Research Centre, Prime Minister Howard set out his Government's wide-ranging foreign policy agenda for Australia in the 21st century. Recognising that the world was "framed by the forces of globalisation", the Prime Minister assured Australians that the nation stood poised to succeed on the world stage in an era of rapid change. As a life-long supporter of free trade and open markets, the Prime Minister was optimistic that globalisation would be a positive force for both Australia and the world. Internationalisation of trade and the integration of world markets would not only increase living standards in poorer countries but auger well for Australia's own productivity, trade and future prosperity.

In this globalised environment, Australia needed to calibrate its international relations to serve both its own national interest and the peace and prosperity of the wider world. In a departure from the multilateral approach typically favoured by Australian Labor governments, the Prime Minister laid emphasis on Australia maintaining strong bilateral relationships with its major trading partners, especially Japan, China, the United States and the European Union. At the same time as enhancing these bilateral ties, however, the Prime Minister also appreciated the importance of multilateral forums such as the United Nations and the Commonwealth of Nations to furthering international peace and cooperation. As Australia faced both the challenges and opportunities of globalisation, he reminded the nation that its greatest resource was always its people.

At the beginning of the 21st century, Australia is an active player in a world vastly changed from that which existed even a decade ago. It is a world no longer divided along defined bi-polar lines and one in which the United States holds a pre-eminent position, both economically and militarily. ...

Australia stands confidently positioned to succeed in an era of globalisation – both to handle its challenges, and to seize its opportunities. It is my firm belief that globalisation is a process that provides major opportunities for this country, and for all countries, to grow and improve the standards of living of their peoples. Importantly, it provides opportunities for the poor as well as the rich.

The opponents of globalisation, the self-styled champions of the poor and the marginalised, speak for no-one but themselves. They certainly do not speak for the world's developing nations. They seek to deny those countries the benefits of more open markets for the goods they produce; of international investment flows and the jobs they create; and of technologies and the new industries they stimulate.

It is no coincidence that those developing countries that grew fastest over the last forty years and achieved the greatest reductions in poverty are those that developed sound institutions, forcefully pursued export opportunities and aggressively utilised the market openings made available to them....

Developing countries that are integrated with world markets have seen average incomes rise, and inequality fall, for the majority of their population. Countries open to international trade have achieved double the annual average growth of other developing countries that have not. Opponents of globalisation are arguing for a return to protectionism. On the contrary, developing countries need more, not less, market liberalisation to meet their needs.

Many developing countries are denied the opportunity to trade their way to sustainable growth and higher "core labour standards" because of the barriers in much of the developed world to their exports, particularly in agriculture.

According to a World Bank study to be released later this year, current levels of protection in developed countries cost the developing world more than US$100 billion – that is, twice the amount of total aid they receive.

Although the nation-wide benefits of globalisation are immense, some groups of people can be left behind by economic and technological change. It is an important part of a country's successful management of the process that the needs of these people are met.

Governments must speak out about the reality of globalisation, and carry their people with them in meeting its challenges. Failure to do so is ultimately a failure of national trust and responsibility.

In the broadest sense, Australia's international relations shape the prosperity and security of Australians. First, the basics need to be right. Particular emphasis needs to be given to the self-reinforcing links between the strength of the national economy, the effectiveness of foreign and trade policy, and capabilities of the Defence Force. ...

Second, we need to find the right balance in the conduct of our foreign relations between the principles we believe in, and a pragmatic and clear-eyed defence of the national interest. Our commitment to democracy, to fundamental human rights, to freedom of speech, freedom of the press, and the independence and authority of the rule of law must not be compromised. That said, our relations with countries having different cultural and political traditions must be based on mutual respect. We will give them the same respect and acknowledgment of sovereign authority that we ask be given to us.

There will be times, such as in East Timor, when we must reach out to assist the vulnerable who need and deserve our assistance.

### Key Relations

The maintenance of strong bilateral relationships remains a cornerstone of this Government's foreign policy approach. Asia is of vital importance to us, it lies at the forefront of our policy focus. The region has huge potential and, despite recent difficulties, has taken some major strides down the path of political and economic reform.

The nations of Asia matter because they are important political partners with whom we have worked for many years to build a more stable and secure region. They matter because of where they are. Their proximity inextricably links their future prosperity and security with ours. And they matter because of what they are – our largest export markets and the source of much of our investment and imports.

Japan is Australia's key economic partner, our best customer by far, and our closest diplomatic partner in Asia. We have watched with concern, the malaise of the Japanese economy and been encouraged by the determination of Prime Minister Junichiro Koizumi to overhaul Japan's political and economic structures.

The fact that there are no major problems in the economic and political relationship between Australia and Japan should not be cause for complacency. Prime Minister Koizumi and I agreed that we must be attentive and vigorous in ensuring that this key relationship is kept in good repair. As part of a broader effort to this end, we will continue to outline the benefits of a bilateral trade and investment facilitation agreement with our Japanese friends.

China's growing influence and economic strength is giving it a greater say in the region and the world. We value the positive role China can play. The relationship between an increasingly confident China and a globally preponderant United States is the key to stability in the Asia-Pacific region. Australia is a close ally of the United States; we have a fast-growing economic partnership with China. We have a major stake in China's successful integration into the world economy, and in seeing these two powers working together for the common good.

Australia's own bilateral relationship with China is more productive, realistic and sustainable than at any time since the establishment of diplomatic relations in the 1970s. We are direct with China about differences in values and seek to manage these differences sensibly. We have said clearly to China that we will adhere to our One China policy and have resolved differences of interpretation with firmness and courtesy. Both we and China are keenly aware of the potential benefits of strategic economic cooperation, including in key sectors like energy.

The relationship we have with the United States is the most important we have with any single country. This is not only because of the strategic, economic and diplomatic power of the United States. But, of equal, if not more significance, are the values and aspirations we share. Our fifty-year-old alliance retains its relevance and vitality in the post-Cold War world and makes an important contribution to stability in our region. It gives us access to technology and information that strengthens our ability to pursue our interests. It showed its worth in the events surrounding the East Timor crisis. And, as the recent visits by Colin Powell, the Secretary of State, and Donald Rumsfeld, the Secretary of Defense, reminded us, Australia is of diplomatic and strategic importance to the United States.

Our relationship is more than a security alliance. It is based on ties of friendship built up through common struggle over the century against threats to security and freedom in many parts of the world.

My visit to the United States in a little over a fortnight's time will be a valuable opportunity to recognise formally the significance of the ANZUS alliance and its ongoing relevance. It will also allow us to explore new ways of strengthening an already vigorous relationship, particularly in the trade area.

The European Union is a major economic player in the world and remains vital to our interests. It is Australia's largest economic partner, our largest merchandise trading partner, our largest market for services exports, our largest source of foreign investment and Australia's second largest investment destination. Its influence stretches far beyond its borders, shaping the institutions of the countries of the former Soviet Union, Africa and the Middle East.

Making Australia's voice heard in Brussels is one of the most important diplomatic tasks we face.

Closer to home, Indonesia's transition to a modern, inclusive, decentralised democracy after thirty years of autocratic and centralised rule is one of the most momentous global developments since the fall of communism. Its stability and well-being are vital for Australia, our region and beyond. We will give Indonesia our attention, respect and assistance. Having frankly acknowledged the inevitable political strains over East Timor, we are ready to move to a new phase in the bilateral relationship.

I hosted President Wahid's visit to Australia in June this year, the first by a President of Indonesia to Australia for more than a quarter of a century. And I responded swiftly and positively to President Megawati Sukarnoputri's generous invitation to visit Jakarta – the first by a foreign head of government since her election.

The openness and candour now being demonstrated between us augers well for a future relationship based on what I have termed "positive realism". This should not be a relationship burdened by the kinds of unrealistic expectations that featured so prominently at certain times in the past. Rather it should be based on a realistic appreciation of the differences between our two societies and cultures, but positively focussed on our many shared interests and on a mutual respect for each other.

### Regional Stability

Australia's security environment is affected by increasing instability and unpredictability in our near-Pacific neighbourhood. We have a substantial and special responsibility in the vast expanse of the South Pacific. A number of these countries face formidable challenges. The problems are complex, the breakdown of law and order, severe social stresses within complex communal structures, and the uneven course of economic and social development.

We have provided and will continue to provide strong support for Prime Minister Morauta's economic and political reforms in Papua New Guinea. This country remains a special place for Australia, one for whom we retain a unique interest and enduring responsibility.

We have shown commitment and perseverance in Bougainville to good effect. In the Solomon Islands we moved quickly to deal with the crisis of spiralling civil war. And in Fiji we have worked hard for the peaceful reinstatement of constitutional democracy.

Many of these small island states are economically vulnerable and politically fragile. They will need support from Australia and others, including the United Nations, the Commonwealth, Europe and other donors.

Yet, only the countries of the South Pacific can find the solutions. Australia cannot, nor would we attempt to determine the course of events in the region. We will help where we can, and generously. But our role in the South Pacific must be based on recognition by the countries of the region that independence means taking responsibility for their own destinies and a commitment by their governments to work in the best interests of their people.

### Global Engagement

The resources and attention of the Government must also focus on global issues that affect the lives of Australians and further the values that they believe in. I have called on the United Nations to focus on its core strengths and responsibilities, including peaceful resolution of disputes, disarmament, human rights and relief of suffering and want.

Australia has been a steadfast and important supporter of the United Nations since its establishment. Given our support for UN operations throughout the world, and particularly in East Timor, none could doubt our commitment to remain so. We are keen, however, to work with others to ensure it is an organisation well-structured to meet the challenges of the future and that the views of democratically-elected governments are given sufficient weight...

In October this year, in Brisbane, Australia will host the Commonwealth Heads of Government Meeting, the largest gathering of world leaders ever held in this country. The Commonwealth is not a rich countries club. It is a dynamic international organisation of over 50 countries, most of them developing nations, which brings together one-third of the world's people with a shared heritage and values.

The Commonwealth played a crucial role in decolonisation, dismantling apartheid in South Africa and returning Nigeria to civilian government. It is working for a return to democracy in Fiji and for stability in the Solomon Islands. Many of its members are small states, struggling with basic problems of building democratic governments and fighting against corruption. The Commonwealth has a proud record in addressing the needs of these small states and ensuring their voices are heard in international forums like the United Nations.

The Brisbane Commonwealth Heads of Government Meeting will tackle practical issues of good governance, economic development, poverty reduction and international peace and cooperation. ...

## *Trade Relations*

I said earlier that flexibility and responsiveness to rapidly changing conditions must remain the hallmark of our foreign policy and this is particularly true in regard to Australia's trade relations.

Our exporters are now more successful than ever, assisted by a competitive Australian dollar and the tax reforms put in place last year. In 2000 Australian exports grew by 25 per cent to reach a total value of $143 billion, the best export growth for 21 years. Australian exporters have a right to expect their government will be as committed and as creative in finding solutions, as they themselves are. We will not be hamstrung by ideology in the trade arena, but will pursue our economic interests internationally in a clear sighted and flexible way.

Our aims remain clear and unambiguous – to open markets for Australian goods and services and for fair and transparent trading arrangements. And we will work through whatever medium to achieve those ends.

We continue to give the strongest support to the multilateral trade rules of the World Trade Organisation. This is not, as I have said, because of an ideological fixation on multilateralism. It is because those rules, though imperfect, provide an important protection against the unfair, and sometimes predatory, behaviour of others....

APEC remains the peak organisation of the Asia-Pacific region. It continues to struggle with the challenge of an internal trade liberalisation agenda. APEC, however, remains a critical player in expressing the region's trade and economic priorities. We will continue to argue that APEC should lend its substantial weight to the early launch of a new trade round. It has also embarked on an important trade facilitation and capacity building programme aimed at freeing up the movement of goods, capital and people among its members.

We are also actively pursuing bilateral and regional free trade agreements, wherever we see solid and practical gains that can be delivered more quickly than through the WTO....

## *Conclusion*

Our world is framed by the forces of globalisation. Liberated from the strictures of the Cold War, it is less threatening but less certain. Our own region is one characterised by change and, to some extent, unpredictability. These are not, however, tendencies to fear, so long as you have the credentials and institutions to deal with them.

Australia stands poised, not merely to survive in this environment, but to prosper. Our economy is flexible and resilient. Our national political, legal and financial systems are transparent and robust. Our foreign and trade policy goals are clear and focussed on the national interest. Our political and diplomatic resources are substantial, appropriately deployed, and internationally respected. We have strong alliances and healthy bilateral relationships. We have a military force capable of defending our shores if necessary, and of contributing to the security of our region.

And our people remain, as always, our greatest resource.

We understand the challenges of our environment, and have the capacities and the confidence to succeed.

# Countering Terrorism and Promoting Globalisation

## New York City – 1 February 2002

In a show of solidarity with those who had perished from the recent terrorist attacks on New York City on 11 September 2001, the World Economic Forum held its 2002 meeting in New York rather than its usual location of Davos, Switzerland. Applauding this gesture, Prime Minister John Howard reflected on the spectre of terrorism and the need for a concerted global response. After assuring the United States of Australia's unequivocal partnership in the fight against terrorism, the Prime Minister contended that it would be mistaken to view globalisation as the source of the simmering discontent which bred terrorist activity. On the contrary, the liberalising phenomenon of globalisation had been a force for good in unlocking the potential of underdeveloped countries to realise economic progress and affluence.

By availing themselves of freer trade and open markets, countries such as China and India were able to lift millions of their own people out of poverty. Thus, with the resurgence of terrorism and the festering of anti-globalisation sentiment, the Prime Minister called on the leaders of the free world to prosecute a much more convincing case for what he termed a "humanising globalisation". By so doing, they could advocate the palpable benefits internationalised markets had brought, and would continue to bring, to poorer countries.

Firstly, can I join others in congratulating Davos for its emphatic act of comradeship and empathy with the people of New York and the people of America in shifting this conference to this extraordinary city. I

329

congratulate the Secretary of State [Colin Powell], and his fellow countrymen and women, for the extraordinary resilience with which they have responded to those quite extraordinary events.

I have periodically been asked why Australia, geographically so remote from here, is so heavily involved? We are heavily involved for three very important reasons. The first and most important of those is that, in every single conceivable way, I saw, and most Australians saw, what occurred as being as much an attack on our way of life as it was on the American way of life. We do not delude ourselves, or only a few Australians delude themselves, that we are in some way immune from such a potential attack. It could have been on Sydney or it could have been on Melbourne.

We also have a very long-standing defence, and close friendship and alliance with the United States. A few days after 11 September, our two governments agreed for the first time in its 50 years of existence to invoke the ANZUS Treaty, the security pact that binds the United States and Australia together. The fact that it was invoked for the first time in its history is a measure of the depth and the seriousness of the Australian response.

There are other dimensions to the terrorist attack and the threat of terrorism not only here but around the world. Australians, particularly amongst its young, are much travelled and many of us saw the attack as not only an awful attack on a huge metropolis but as an attack on the capacity of the world to maintain its human mobility. That is, the easy movement of people, particularly amongst the young, which has become a constant characteristic of the experience of nations such as ours in the decades that have gone before us. For those reasons we saw ourselves needing to be part of the response as much as, indeed, the nations of Europe and the other close allies of the United States.

I think it has been an extraordinary coalition and the United States deserves congratulations for the diplomatic and military skill with which the coalition has gone forward. It has achieved very early and very widespread success, but I will join others who are saying that the campaign against terrorism is by no means over. I think we must recognise that the possibility of activity elsewhere in the campaign against terrorism is very real and it would be failing to understand the character of what we are facing if that were not recognised.

I share the views of other speakers about the need to find greater and more effective responses to poverty around the world. We should be careful not to see globalisation itself as a cause of the anger which, in turn, has produced terrorist behaviour. The failure of globalisation is not so much that its value is not there. If there is a failure in relation to globalisation it is a failure of business and political leadership all around the world to advocate more effectively its benefits. The reality, as so many of you will know, is that if the benefits of globalisation could be extended through such things as the removal of many trade barriers to developing countries, then their economic fortunes would be very significantly enhanced by globalisation.

It is necessary, however daunting the task is, to try and find a solution to the hideously intractable problem of the Middle East. That can only be upon the basis of an absolute acceptance without qualification of the right of Israel to exist unmolested within secure and defensible boundaries, and equally to recognise the legitimate aspirations of the Palestinian people for a homeland. It is a tragedy that what looked so bright and aspiringly hopeful in the Middle East only a little over a year ago has now turned into such an awful nightmare. But all of those who have any influence on that troubled part of our globe have an ongoing responsibility to do what they can, however difficult it may seem, to bring about that peace. That will make a contribution.

The coalition has been an extraordinary success out of great difficulty and travail. Those terrible events have encouraged people to talk together about what they have in common more than perhaps they have done for a long time.

On a personal note, I attended the APEC meeting in Shanghai in October 2001, which was attended by President George W. Bush and President Vladimir Putin and the President of China and the Prime Minister of Japan and so many other leaders. We saw people whose views on many issues may be different talking together and making common cause about what they could do to mobilise the world against terrorism. That was a source of encouragement, even inspiration, at a difficult time and a reminder that out of awful tragedy new alliances and new momentums can be generated. ...

I do not think you can effectively pursue the goal of a fairer world and thereby remove some of the bases of the emergence of terrorism without an infinitely more successful prosecution of policies of more open trade. I said in my introductory comments that the developed world, the wealthy nations of the world, could do more to help the developing countries by the removal of trade barriers than they could by several multiples increasing the amount of official development assistance which is now provided to developing countries. And the last 30 or 40 years of the world's economic experience is replete with examples of countries which have pursued more open trade policies and have lifted people out of poverty. It is also important in relation to poverty to bear in mind that we have made progress.

There is always a danger, when we talk about poverty, of repeating scenarios of despair, of talking as if no progress has been made. The reality is that progress has been made and if you adopt proper measures according to absolute numbers you can clearly argue that there has been a great deal of progress made and trade and openness of trade play an enormous part. The most voluble point in relation to globalisation vis-à-vis the cry of the poor of the world is that remaining punitive trade barriers of many of the richer countries of the world do work an injustice to some of the developing countries. Thus, in a sense, insofar as those who argue that globalisation is the problem, the answer is more globalisation through an even more open trading approach.

We do not, as political leaders, business leaders in capitalist society, we do not do a good enough job of explaining the benefits of globalisation. We lose the argument, the rhetorical argument, all too frequently, to political anarchists who try to lay at the feet of globalisation all the sins of the world. It plays a very big part, not only in substance but speaking, as all of us are, as practising politicians. The political challenge is to win – to use that old cliché – the hearts and minds of people about the benefits of globalisation. We are too defensive, we all too readily think that humanising globalisation is to concede some of its critics' arguments. Humanising globalisation is to point out the benefits it has brought to poorer countries over the last decade or more and the benefits it can bring even more to those countries in the years ahead.

# Counting on Each Other
# when It Matters Most

## Washington DC – 12 June 2002

In June 2002, John Howard was afforded the rare honour of addressing the United States Congress. He was only the third Australian leader to do so after Robert Menzies had addressed Congress twice in 1950 and 1955, followed by Bob Hawke in 1988. The Prime Minister of Australia was also the first international leader to address Congress since the terrorist attacks of 11 September 2001.

The Prime Minister followed the tradition of his predecessors by speaking warmly of the enduring Australian-American friendship. He reminded his audience that even before the formal signing of the ANZUS Treaty in 1951, Australians and Americans had enjoyed a close relationship dating back to 1918 when they had fought together in the Battle of Hamel on the Western Front. Punctuated by frequent applause and standing ovations, the warmest response was reserved for his words on Australia's immediate solidarity with the United States in the wake of the terrorist attacks.

He recalled that the US-Australia alliance had been forged not only through shared experiences in war and peace, but by the common values of liberal democracy, the importance of the family, the critical role of the individual in society, a firm commitment to free enterprise capitalism and the spirit of volunteerism.

Mr Speaker, Mr President of the Senate, distinguished members of the House of Representatives and the Senate of the Congress of the United States, may I say how very touched I am by the warmth and generosity of your welcome.

I appreciate very deeply the honour that you have extended to me today and, more importantly, the honour you have extended to my country, Australia. Can I, on behalf of over 19 million freedom-loving Australians, convey to you their deep affection and their warm greetings and their sense of solidarity and friendship.

The bonds between Americans and Australians are as strong as they are genuine, and that is because we share so many values in common. A belief that the individual is more important than the state; a belief that strong families are a nation's greatest resource; a belief that competitive capitalism is the real key to national wealth; and a belief that decency and hard work define a person's worth, not class or race or social background.

My friends, let me say to you today that America has no better friend anywhere in the world than Australia. Australians and Americans enjoy each other's company. We share a love of sport and in some of them we are fierce competitors, and we even, from time to time, share the Academy Awards.

When I last came to this great chamber of democracy on 12 September last year, the smoke still hung in the air over New York and Washington. Brave and courageous policemen and firemen, with no regard to their own safety, searched in the hope of finding survivors. The scale of loss and destruction was yet to be fully calculated.

In seeking justice and not revenge, in choosing calm consideration over blind fury, in turning to friends before turning on enemies, the United States over recent months has led a great reaffirmation of all of those great values and principles on which both of our societies are based.

America fought back magnificently – and in the process has won the admiration of the world. You demonstrated to the world that where fundamental freedoms flourish, evil men can do their worst, cause death and devastation but, in the end, they will never win.

In his inaugural address, George Washington spoke of the destiny of the American people to preserve "the sacred fire of liberty". That promise has been kept for more than two centuries – but never more so than since the appalling events of September 2001.

Through these times, Australians have shared your shock and anger and have been partners in your resolve. We have taken our place beside you in the fight against terrorism, because what happened last year in the United States was as much an attack upon our nation and the values that we hold dear, as it was upon yours. As we meet, Australian and American troops are fighting side by side in Afghanistan, and it is our constant prayer that they all return safely home to their loved ones.

In these past months, President Bush has displayed the tenacity, the strength and the depth of character of a very great leader. He is also applying those great qualities to the tensions in the Indian sub-continent between India and Pakistan and the intractable situation in the Middle East.

It is a special privilege for me to return to this historic place, to address the representatives of a great nation whose people we hold in such high regard and who we feel great warmth and affection towards.

Like you, Australia enters the new century strong and prosperous. Over the past decade, the productivity and growth of our economy has been ahead of most other developed nations. Our pioneer past, so similar to your own, has produced a spirit that can overcome adversity and pursue great dreams. We have pursued a society of opportunity, fairness and hope, leaving – as you did – the divisions and prejudices of the Old World far behind.

Like your own, our culture continues to be immeasurably enriched by immigration from the four corners of the world. We believe, as you do, that nations are strengthened, not weakened, broadened and not diminished, by a variety of views and an atmosphere of open debate.

Most of all, we value loyalty given and loyalty gained. The concept of mateship runs deeply through the Australian character. We cherish, and, where necessary, we will fight to defend the liberties we hold dear.

Australian and American forces fought together for the first time in the Battle of Hamel, in France, in World War I. The date of the attack – 4 July 1918 – was deliberately chosen by the Australian Commander, General John Monash, to honour your countrymen. One of the Australian units held in reserve for that attack was the Third Pioneer

336

Battalion, and it had a young signalman called Lyall Howard. He was my father.

From that moment to this, we have been able to count on each other when it has mattered most. Let me say, and I know I speak on behalf of all of my fellow Australians, that we will never forget the crucial help that America extended to us during the darkest days of World War II. Without that help, our history and our society would have been totally different.

Successive generations of Australians and Americans have fought side by side in every major conflict of the twentieth century – in the jungles of New Guinea, in Korea, in Vietnam, in the Gulf, in skies and oceans around the globe and now, in another new century, among the rock-strewn mountains of Afghanistan.

The ANZUS Treaty of 1951 pledged each country to come to the aid of the other if it were under attack. So it was, that in a United States Air Force plane made available to me on 12 September last year to enable me to return to Australia, and high above the Pacific Ocean, I informed the United States Ambassador to Australia, Tom Schieffer, that it was our intention, for the first time in the 50-year history of the ANZUS Treaty, to invoke that Treaty in response to the attack upon America.

America was under attack. Australia was immediately there to help.

My friends, both of our societies are built on a deep respect for the worth of each individual. "The worth of a state, in the long run", wrote John Stuart Mill in 1859, "is the worth of the individuals composing it. ...a state which dwarfs its men in order that they may be more docile instruments in its hands even for beneficial purposes – will find with small men no great thing can really be accomplished".

America and Australia are societies which extol the precious worth of each individual man and woman.

Like you, I see family life at the heart of a nation's existence. Not only does the family nurture and educate our children but it provides emotional anchorage for all of us as we travel through life. The strength of the family goes beyond the spiritual and the emotional. United, caring families are the best social welfare system mankind has ever devised.

Both of our societies draw great strength from the spirit of volunteerism. The huge, exuberant success of the Sydney Olympic Games in 2000 owed a lot to the warmth and infectious dedication of tens of thousands of volunteers. They gave the Games a sense of exhilaration and joy which contributed enormously to their success. Edmund Burke once called voluntary groups society's "small platoons". They are in fact the living tissue between the government and the people. ...

Our relationship has been long. The ties between us are strong. The bonds, on a people to people basis between Americans and Australians, are deep and rich. This relationship is nourished by many things. It is nourished by shared history. It is nourished by common commitment to democratic ideals and values. It is nourished by our deep and resolute commitment to the role of the individual in society and the place of the family in the national framework of both of our nations.

I express to you on behalf of my fellow countrymen and women a sense of commitment to the constant struggle to preserve democracy and freedom around the world. I say it with great warmth because there is nothing false or phony or lacking in spontaneity in the relationship between our two peoples. It is not contrived. It is genuine. We like each other and we do not mind saying it.

Could I say to you today that as we move forward into this new century, we do so in the knowledge that no matter what will happen – and there will be many paths of difficulty requiring courage and grit and sacrifice – we travel through the century in the constant company of a true and great friend.

May God bless the peoples of America and Australia.

# Globalisation and the
# Eradication of Poverty

## Sydney – 31 March 2005

The Lowy Institute, an independent think tank endowed by Frank Lowy to conduct research into international issues from an Australian perspective, invited Prime Minister Howard to share his perspective on "Australia in the World". In the presence of Lowy and his family, the Prime Minister told the Institute that his Government had "rebalanced Australia's foreign policy to better reflect the unique intersection of history, geography, culture and economic opportunity" the country represented. He reiterated his Government's commitment to both globalisation and the strengthening of bilateral ties with nations in Asia, the Pacific and Europe. In a wide-ranging reflection and assessment of international developments, the Prime Minister spoke of Australia's need to come to terms with the resurgent threat of terrorism, and the need for its successful elimination, the rise of China as an economic powerhouse, the simmering tensions on the Korean peninsula and the transformation of neighbouring Indonesia into the world's third largest democracy. In the midst of these challenges and opportunities, the Prime Minister called on Australia to be "an anchor of stability and prosperity in our region". In so doing, it would serve as a positive contributor to world peace and cooperation.

Winston Churchill once said that: "We make a living by what we get, but we make a life by what we give". The Lowy Institute for International Policy is testimony to the generosity of a man whose life is a compelling Australian story of hard work and global achievement.

Frank Lowy came to our shores in 1952. Behind him lay a childhood darkened by the Holocaust and service in the fight for a new-born Israel. But this young man's eyes were fixed firmly on the future, and Frank's journey from delicatessen-owner in Sydney's west, to head of the world's largest retail property group, has made him an aspiring corporate legend. Now, with a grand investment in ideas, he has added a new chapter on patriotism in a remarkable contribution to Australia in the world....

When I became Prime Minister nine years ago, I believed that this nation was defining its place in the world too narrowly. My Government has rebalanced Australia's foreign policy to better reflect the unique intersection of history, geography, culture and economic opportunity that our country represents. Time has only strengthened my conviction that we do not face a choice between our history and our geography.

History's legacy is a global outlook. We are, overwhelmingly, a country of migrants and their descendants. We are an open economy, dependent on global markets. We are a Western liberal democracy with a profound interest in the structures and ideas that govern the international system.

It is true that Australia's most immediate interests and responsibilities will always be in our region. But we have global interests that require strong relationships with all centres of power.

This is clear from our economic interests. Australia's largest trading partner as a single entity, is the European Union. Our largest investment partner is the United States. Our largest export market and our fastest growing economic relationships are in Asia. The Middle East is one of our most rapidly growing markets for advanced manufactures over recent years.

In a world more interconnected than ever before, the balanced alignment of Australia's global and regional engagement is a measure of our strategic maturity.

My address tonight naturally focuses on relationships and issues that are fundamental to Australia's security and prosperity. ...We should start by reaffirming the power of globalisation to lift the dead hand of poverty around the world. Our development debate must recognise that trade barriers in the developed world cost poor countries more than twice the amount of the official aid they receive.

The greatest contribution nations can make to alleviate poverty is to slash trade barriers and conclude the Doha round of global trade negotiations at the earliest opportunity. We must break the back of these negotiations by December when World Trade Organisation (WTO) ministers meet in Hong Kong. With 70 per cent of the world's poor dependent on agriculture for their livelihood, deep cuts in farm protection and subsidies are essential if Doha is to live up to its promise as a "development round".

Some will say, "well, he would say that wouldn't he". It is true, Australia stands to benefit from freer trade, including in agriculture. But we do argue the case having seen the benefits to our own economy from cutting tariffs and quotas over many years. Australia's economy today is among the most open in the developed world and the OECD estimates that our agricultural sector is second only to New Zealand in the low level of subsidies it receives....

All these global challenges, and many of the world's biggest strategic imponderables, are to be found in our part of the world. History will have no bigger stadium this century than the Pacific Rim. Great power dynamics sit side-by-side with new transnational threats, the strongest of states together with some of the weakest; rapid globalisation alongside unique and ancient cultures; traditional concerns with sovereignty along with nascent regionalism and institution-building.

Asia is poised in coming decades to assume a weight in the world economy it last held more than five centuries ago. It is also home to eight of the world's ten largest standing armies and, after the Middle East, the world's three most volatile flashpoints – the Taiwan Straits, the Korean peninsula and Kashmir.

Clearly, the stakes are large and will test the strategic maturity, restraint, and adaptability of all nations.

Australia approaches our rapidly-changing region with clear assumptions and strategies – and with a sense of optimism. We recognise Asia's diversity – taking account of how differences in power, institutions and aspirations shape regional politics. We seek to engage most substantially with those countries with which our primary strategic and economic interests reside. We believe that what matters most for our regional engagement is the substance of relations between countries, more so than any formal architecture of diplomatic exchange. We recognise that advancing our security and prosperity in the region requires a balance of principle and pragmatism. And we adopt a flexible approach to this task – one that combines bilateral, regional and multilateral instruments and that elevates results over process.

This last point is worth exploring from a wider standpoint. Australia recognises that there are cases where the United Nations can leverage effective cooperation for peace and security, as was demonstrated successfully in East Timor. But we also know that there are times when this is not possible, as we saw in the Balkans. Australia supports multilateral arms control and non-proliferation regimes. We are, as I noted earlier, an active player in global efforts to reduce trade barriers. We continue to work towards an effective global response to climate change – but one that does not unfairly compromise the competitiveness of Australian industry.

But just as Australia does not face a choice between our history and our geography, nor do we face a choice between multilateral institutions and alternative strategies to pursue our nation's interests. Our counter-terrorism strategy in South-East Asia is an excellent example of Australia's mutually reinforcing global, regional and bilateral activism. Australia has built a network of bilateral counter-terrorism arrangements with regional partners and allies. Ten agreements stretching from Fiji across to India provide the means by which security agencies and police forces cooperate closely. It is at this operational level where the greatest dividends in the fight against terrorism can be secured. At the regional level, Australia is engaged through the ASEAN Regional Forum, APEC and the Asia-Pacific Group on Money Laundering. None of this work comes at the expense of action as part of a global counter-terrorism coalition, including through the United Nations.

Simultaneously, Australia has moved to enhance its ability to influence and work with the United States in meeting this terrorist threat. Our alliance with the United States has long been a pillar of Australia's security and the stability of our region. In the age of terrorism, having privileged access to United States military and intelligence assets is vital to disrupt and destroy terrorist networks in South-East Asia.

From the moment of our election in 1996, as a deliberate act of policy, my Government intensified Australia's post-Cold War relationship with the United States. Australia today has never been better placed to put our views to the United States – and have them heard – including on regional issues where we might not see eye to eye. From where I sit, the claim that the war on terror has distracted US policy-makers from Asia is a hollow one. In fact, we have seen the United States strengthen its regional alliances in recent years, while expanding cooperation with countries such as Singapore and India. If anything, the larger trend is towards Washington engaging more purposefully with Asia. This has led to a more balanced American world-view when compared with its understandably Eurocentric focus of last century.

Underlying strengths, including technological dynamism and demographic trends, mean that the United States will continue to be the world's dominant global power and economy. It will remain critical to continued growth and development in our region. In this context, the Australia-US Free Trade Agreement has given our country a new platform for future prosperity. Australia's capacity, simultaneously, to deepen relations with the United States and with countries in Asia is an important yardstick of our strategic maturity as a nation. Compared with a decade ago, there is now a deeper appreciation of how close links with the United States are a plus and not a minus in forging stronger links in Asia.

Next month, I will visit Japan and China, highlighting the importance Australia places on strong relationships with these hinge powers in North-East Asia. The Australia-Japan relationship continues to evolve in new directions off the back of our long and mutually beneficial economic relationship. Australia has no greater friend in Asia than Japan, our largest export market for almost forty years, and a strategic partner for regional peace and prosperity. In July 2003, Prime Minister Koizumi and I signed a Trade and Economic Framework Agreement as the basis for defining the future course of our economic relationship. Both sides have now completed our joint study under the Agreement and Australia seeks an ambitious outcome from this work.

Today, the three great Pacific democracies, the United States, Japan and Australia, are working more closely than ever on shared security challenges – especially terrorism and weapons proliferation. Our Trilateral Security Dialogue has added a new dimension to the value all sides place on alliance relationships. Within the framework of its alliance with the United States, Japan has taken on important out-of-area security responsibilities in recent years, including in East Timor, Afghanistan and Iraq. This quiet revolution in Japan's external policy, one which Australia has long encouraged, is a welcome sign of a more confident Japan assuming its rightful place in the world and in our region.

When we think about the future of Australia in the world, we inevitably think of a world where China will play a much larger role. Australia's relations with China have bulked large during my time as Prime Minister. China's rise is steadily reshaping our world. In the last two years, China has accounted for a quarter of world growth and a similar share of growth in global trade. In the next decade, it will likely overtake Germany to become the world's third largest economy after the United States and Japan. Since my Government has been in office, Australia's trade with China has trebled, to the point where today it is our third largest trading partner. With the completion of our joint feasibility study on a free trade agreement, we now have an opportunity to strengthen this relationship further into a true partnership for prosperity. I hope to affirm this partnership when I meet Chinese leaders in Beijing next month. But I also want to assert that China will remain a large and growing partner for Australia whether or not we negotiate a Free Trade Agreement.

Australia welcomes China's constructive approach to a range of security matters in recent years, from the war on terror, to the Korean peninsula, to maritime security in South-East Asia. In the context of our one-China policy, we continue to urge restraint and a peaceful resolution of issues across the Taiwan Straits. Clearly, a large part of the burden of such restraint is borne by the relationship between China and the United States.

It would in my strong view be a mistake to embrace an overly pessimistic view of this relationship, pointing to unavoidable conflict. Australia does not believe that there is anything inevitable about escalating strategic competition between China and the United States. In recent years, both sides have shown themselves keen to cooperate on common interests and to handle inevitable differences in an atmosphere of mutual respect, a point stressed repeatedly by Condoleezza Rice during her recent visit to China. Australia is encouraged by the constructive and realistic management of this vital relationship. We see ourselves as having a role in continually identifying, and advocating to each, the shared strategic interests these great powers have in regional peace and prosperity.

Closer to home, the world's largest Muslim-majority nation is progressing through a democratic transition as profound as any we have witnessed in our lifetimes. Australia has a huge stake in Indonesia consolidating its place as the world's third largest democracy and one of Asia's great democracies. In my view, Indonesia has not received enough credit for the political reforms that have taken root in the face of far-reaching economic and security challenges. The 2004 elections reaffirmed the strength of moderate Islam in the face of terrorism and extremism. Australia welcomes the steps taken by President Susilo Bambang Yudhoyono to give effect to his vision of a "safe, just and prosperous" Indonesia.

We are particularly encouraged by the steps towards good governance as a means of underpinning sustained economic recovery and macroeconomic stability. Australia today is working closely with Indonesia on its road to a strong, united and democratic future. As we are at Indonesia's side at a time of natural disaster, so we stand ready to forge a closer partnership for our shared future. I know that I speak for Australia in saying that we look forward to welcoming President Yudhoyono to our country within the next few days.

Australia's other relationships in South-East Asia display important underlying strengths. Beyond counter-terrorism, Australia is working closely with our neighbours on shared security challenges. Free trade agreements with Singapore and Thailand have added new momentum to our shared agenda of opening markets and spreading prosperity. Australia and Malaysia have now completed scoping studies on a possible FTA in advance of Prime Minister Abdullah Badawi's visit to Australia next week, the first official visit by a Malaysian Prime Minister in more than 20 years. ...

In our near neighbourhood, Australia has turned its power and purpose to the governance challenges faced by many states in the Pacific. Our leading role in the Regional Assistance Mission to the Solomons has helped to restore law and order. In Papua New Guinea, our Enhanced Cooperation Programme is strengthening law enforcement and tackling corruption, assisting with economic and public sector reform, and improving border management and transport security. Australia will soon have some 210 police and 64 officials in frontline positions within the PNG police force and public service.

Again, a note of realism is called for. We should not underestimate the depth and the complexity of the problems faced by PNG and other Pacific states. Progress will likely be uneven and will only be made if all parties accept ownership of solutions to institutional weakness...

We have learned that, if we make the right choices, Australians can shape our environment and our destiny, not simply be takers of trends set elsewhere. We have learned that global engagement is demanding work requiring large resources, great stamina and reserves of patience.

This can only be sustained through constant dialogue with the interests and instincts of the Australian people. It is something that my office requires me to think about every day. How to explain the need to work with friends and allies to help nourish democracy in places that seem so very far away. How to make the case for open markets to workers worried about their jobs in a global economy. How to tell a taxpayer that we must help build better institutions abroad even as our needs seem so pressing at home.

Australia will be engaged most intensively on challenges in our own region – cooperating with others to rip up terrorist networks in Asia;

seizing opportunities for economic integration; and bringing a new intensity to state building in our neighbourhood. But we have learned also that the old boundaries that shaped our thinking – between domestic and foreign policy; regionalism and globalism; realism and idealism – are fuzzier now. This may prove disorienting for some. But my sense is that Australia has found new clarity of purpose in these uncertain times.

By getting things in order at home, we can be a more active partner abroad. By meeting the challenges of globalisation, we can be an anchor of stability and prosperity in our region. By honouring our history, defining our interests and upholding our values, we can make this a better world – not just for us, but for all. ...

# IX

# Anniversaries and Australian Achievements

# Building a United, Happy and Successful Nation

## Brisbane – 25 January 1999

With the support of the Menzies-led Opposition, Australia's post-war Chifley Labor Government passed the *Nationality and Citizenship Act* 1948. Coming into effect on 26 January 1949, the new law created, for the first time, a distinctive category of Australian citizenship which meant that Australians would be simultaneously Australian citizens and British subjects. The legislation was enacted in response to the 1948 Prime Ministers' Conference which determined that the United Kingdom and all self-governing dominions should each introduce a separate national citizenship.

For the Prime Minister and the Minister for Immigration, Philip Ruddock, the fiftieth-anniversary of this milestone was cause both to celebrate and reflect on what it meant to be an Australian citizen. With Australia's present citizenship laws reflecting the egalitarian character of the nation, Howard prided himself on the fact that every citizen could regard themselves as equally Australian, whether they were born abroad or in Australia with a native ancestry dating back thousands of years. The capacity for Australia over the past five decades successfully to absorb immigrants from over 140 countries across Europe, Asia and elsewhere stood as eloquent testimony to the durability and flexibility of Australian citizenship.

This is a special two-headed event, to use sporting parlance; it is an opportunity to commemorate the 50th Anniversary of the separate establishment in 1949 of Australian citizenship. The moment at which, legally, we ceased all to be in the absence of separate national citizenship, British subjects, and became as well Australian citizens. But it would be wrong, and a total misreading of the history of our country, to imagine for a moment that the Australian national identity started with the formal proclamation of the legal identity of Australian citizen. Those who trace the history of our nation will, I think, agree that the true identity of an Australian citizen and a man or woman of the Australian nation was forged long before 1949.

This celebration is an opportunity to do a number of very simple things. It is an opportunity for all of us, as Australians, to reflect upon the extraordinary good fortune that has come our way to be the citizens of this country. There is no country on Earth as fully endowed with the good things of life as our nation. It is also an opportunity to acknowledge a simple reality, and that is, there is no hierarchy of descent when it comes to being an Australian citizen. Whether our ancestors were here thousands of years ago, as in the case of the original Australians, the Indigenous people, whether our ancestors came in the 19th century, or whether we or our ancestors are amongst the millions of Australians who have flocked to this country since the end of World War II, we are equally together, one no better than the other, all Australians.

Those who have come recently and embraced this nation as theirs, have as much right as I or anybody else in this audience to claim this country as their own, to respect and abide by its laws, and to seek the shelter and the protection which comes with being a citizen of Australia.

The third thing that this occasion allows us to do, in our own different way, is to conjure up what is the greatest of all the Australian achievements. I think the Australian achievement as a collective expression is a marvellous way of describing what we have done. But we all, in a sense, assess that achievement in our own personal way, and no one individual assessment is better than the next person's. I do not believe in a society where there has to be a defined, handed down, for all purposes definition of what is the Australian spirit or what does Australia represent. We all have our own experiences; we all have our passions and our own definition of that.

351

To me, one of the many great things about the Australian achievement is that, better than most nations on Earth, we have been able to blend the best of our past to build such a contented, tolerant and united present. We have borrowed much and we have enjoyed much from our British and other European heritage. Respect for law, the parliamentary institutions, the freedom of the press, the great inheritance of English literature which is the basis of our common national language.

But we have been wise enough as a people to reject the pretentions and the class structures which were endemic in many of the nations of Europe. We have continued a great bond with the people of North America and we share with the peoples of North America the great traditions of liberal democracy. To complete it here, we are in the Asia-Pacific region and, in recent years, we have been enriched by the migration to our country of tens of thousands of people from the different nations of Asia. They have given us living person-to-person links with that part of the world.

When you add that to the rich tradition of our Indigenous heritage, we have built something on this continent of ours that no other nation has been able to achieve. We have developed traditions of mateship, of tolerance, of tenacity, of courage, of the volunteer spirit that I think makes every individual Australian immensely proud.

I am passionately proud of my Australian heritage. I respect the heritage of my parents, and I honour the respect that other Australians have for the heritage of their parents coming from different parts of the world. There is no nation that has so successfully brought together people from 140 or more different origins, or source-countries, as well as Australia has.

So, on this, the eve of Australia Day 1999, the last Australia Day that I will see that will not have a two in front of it, can I say to all of you, that in our different ways, let us celebrate what it is like to be an Australian. Let us reflect upon the immense privilege of being an Australian citizen. Let us reflect upon the bounty of the Australian nation and let us acknowledge the contribution that our forefathers have made to the building of such a united, happy and successful nation.

It is an immense privilege for me as Prime Minister to be part of this observance of the 50th Anniversary of the establishment of separate Australian citizenship. It is a great occasion. I wish all of you well and, along with all of you, I rejoice in the great achievement, the great miracle of individual Australian citizenship over the last 50 years.

# Celebrating the Constitution of Australia

## London – 5 July 2000

In July 2000 John Howard, the Prime Minister of Australia, led a bipartisan delegation to London to mark the centenary of the *Commonwealth of Australia Constitution Act,* passed by the Parliament of the United Kingdom on 9 July 1900. Accompanied by four of his predecessors, John Gorton, Gough Whitlam, Malcolm Fraser and Bob Hawke, the Prime Minister met again with his British counterpart, Tony Blair, and two of his predecessors, Sir Edward Heath and Baroness Thatcher.

In proposing the toast to the Lord Mayor and Corporation of the City of London at a banquet at the Guildhall, London, Prime Minister Howard spoke not simply of the Australian Constitution's legal birth but of the nation's broader British inheritance, the traditions of parliamentary democracy, the rule of law, the freedom of the press and the English language. While he acknowledged that Australia owed much to Britain, he also pointed out that the British people owed a great deal to the people of Australia. Over the course of the last century, Australia had arguably been Britain's greatest military ally. Howard reminded his audience of the enormous contribution Australian services had made to the allied war effort in both major world conflicts.

While the Prime Minister's delegation to London attracted some public criticism for the expense involved, Howard believed that it was fitting for a self-respecting nation such as Australia to honour its historical milestones, not least the legal conception its own nationhood one century ago at Westminster.

My Lord Mayor, your Royal Highness, Lord Chancellor, Lord Chief Justice, the Chief Justice of Australia, your Graces the Archbishops of Canterbury and Brisbane, to the ministers of the British Government, and the Leader of the Opposition, to the Premiers of the States of Australia, and the Chief Minister of the Northern Territory, and especially do I acknowledge the presence of two former Prime Ministers of Great Britain, Baroness Margaret Thatcher and Sir Edward Heath, and I acknowledge the presence of my predecessors – John Gorton, Gough Whitlam, Malcolm Fraser and Bob Hawke.

Mr Lord Mayor, you do our country and those who have come to London this week, in a very bipartisan fashion to represent Australia, to commemorate that great event 100 years ago, great honour in this banquet that you have given tonight. Because today is the day 100 years ago that the Act of the British Parliament, establishing the Constitution of the Commonwealth of Australia, passed through the House of Lords. It followed the efforts of five, then colonial, soon to become Australian, statesmen of that era; Barton,[42] Deakin,[43] Fysh,[44] Dickson[45] and Kingston.[46] Two of them became Prime Ministers of Australia.

They did not come in anger. They did it in terms of the essential quest to obtain the approval of the British Parliament for a constitution which had already been approved by the people of the colonies at successive referenda. They did not come in anger and they did not leave disappointed. It is a matter of interesting historical record that the principal point of dispute between them and the then Colonial Secretary, Joseph Chamberlain, was about the circumstances in which an appeal might lie

---

[42] Sir Edmund Barton (1849-1920) served as the first Prime Minister of Australia for the (Liberal) Protectionist Party from 1901 to 1903.

[43] Alfred Deakin (1856-1919) served as Prime Minister of Australia for the (Liberal) Protectionist Party for three separate terms, 1903 to 1904, 1905 to 1908 and then 1909 to 1910.

[44] Sir Philip Oakley Fysh (1835-1919) served as Premier of Tasmania and as a member of Australia's first federal ministry in the government of Sir Edmund Barton.

[45] Sir James Robert Dickson (1832-1901) served as Premier of Queensland and was the lead Queensland advocate for Australian Federation.

[46] Charles Cameron Kingston (1850-1908) served as Premier of South Australia and as a minister in the Barton Government.

on certain matters from a decision of the High Court of Australia to the Privy Council.

That, in a sense, summed up the character and the relationship between the people of the emerging Commonwealth of Australia and successive governments of the United Kingdom. At every stage of our constitutional development, it had been the wish of successive British governments to give us what the people forming Australia wanted.

As I speak to you tonight, I try and think of those things that crystalise, not only the Australian achievement, because it has been an immense achievement of the last 100 years, but also to think of the character of the relationship between our two great societies.

We have so much in common, and it is impossible in a gathering such as this, in a place such as this, at a time such as this, not to think of the great inheritance that the people of Australia have with from the people of Britain. The rule of law, the sense of civic duty, the robust political discourse, even exchange, the great gift of parliamentary democracy, the wonderful inheritance of the English language and all the culture that surrounds it. We owe a great deal to the people of Britain and we owe a great deal to the British inheritance.

But it has been a two-way partnership. The people of Britain, as the Lord Mayor was kind enough to acknowledge, owe a great deal to the people of Australia. We Australians never forget the contribution that Australian servicemen made in defence of liberty alongside the service men of the United Kingdom. In 1914, a nation of just 2.5 million males contributed a volunteer army of almost 400,000. It was an extraordinary demonstration of the commitment of the people of our nation at that time, and that was to be repeated in World War II. If I can think of perhaps the greatest moment of shared achievement of the people of Great Britain and the people of Australia, it was the way in which they stood alone, but for a few other societies of common values at the time, in defiance of Nazi Germany in the darkest days of World War II. It will always be one of the greatest achievements ....

But as the Lord Mayor has acknowledged, it is not only a relationship that is steeped in history and some tradition and a reverence for a shared culture and a shared inheritance, it is also a vibrant, contemporary relationship. Like any good relationship, you need a combination of shared values and history and also a touch of mutual self-interest, and both of our societies recognise that. The commercial links between our two societies are great indeed. Australia is now surpassed by France only in terms of wine exports to your country. Although it is properly understood that Australia's great export customers are to be found in the Asian region, it is nonetheless a fact of life that 70 per cent of the outward foreign investment from Australia goes to a combination of the United Kingdom and the United States....

It is a fact of life, and a fact of history, that the thing that in the end that will bind two countries together more than anything else is the values that we share in common. We can have our differences as we do on trade. You can have, as you do, a great emphasis on your links with the nations of Europe. We can have, as we properly do, a great emphasis on our links with the nations of Asia.

In many ways, Australia occupies something of a special cultural and economic intersection in the world. We are, in so many respects, a projection of Western civilisation in our part of the world – we share an inheritance together. We have great and enduring links with the people of Britain and the rest of Europe. We have very close associations with the people of North America, but we are in the Asia-Pacific region. Some 800,000 Australians speak an Asian language, and we have a very rich history over the last one hundred years of absorbing people from 140 nations in the world. One of the great boasts of the Australian achievement over the last one hundred years has been our capacity to take people from every corner of the Earth, and to blend them into a united harmonious community – a community that respects the different cultural characteristics and inheritances of the people who comprise the modern Australia, but, nonetheless, a society that binds them together with a set of common values.

But it is the values that bind us more than anything else. What I would like tonight to be seen as, is not only a celebration, but a very gracious honouring by the people of this magnificent city, in this magnificent setting, of the contribution that Australia has made to the world over the last 100 years and the scale of the Australian achievement during that time. It is an achievement which must be put against our share of errors, particularly the way in which we have on so many occasions mishandled the treatment of the Indigenous people of our country. We are like any other nation, not without our errors and our blemishes, but it has been a hundred years of great achievement.

It has also been a one hundred year journey between Australia and the people of the United Kingdom. A journey which has taken many characteristics, shared and often vigorous encounters on the sporting field, vigorous political and trade disputes, but the common thread that has kept us together during all of those years has been the values that we share in common. There are not too many societies that can look the world in the eye and say we were continuously democratic throughout the whole of the 20th century. You can count those societies on the fingers of your two hands and we, the people of Australia, and you, the people of the United Kingdom, comprise two of those societies.

So can I say to our British friends tonight that we thank you for the honour that you have paid to our country, and we in Australia honour the contribution that the British inheritance has given to our society. We think of the values that we have in common. We reflect upon the way in which we have together defended those values in moments of great challenge and great crisis.

We rededicate ourselves to a pursuit of those common values of political liberty, of individual freedom, of the rule of law, of freedom of the press, a respect for the strength of the parliamentary system, and the importance in our lives of civic duty and civic commitment. They are great values, they are ageless values. They are values that are as relevant to this part of the world as they are to any other part of the world. They are values that I believe the people of Britain, and the people of Australia, will always have in common. They will always act as binding cement between the people of our two societies.

# Women's Action Alliance
## 25th Anniversary
### Melbourne – 12 October 2000

The Women's Action Alliance (WAA) was founded in 1975 as a nation-wide advocacy group for the interests of Australian women. Reflecting the liberal principles of Menzies, the WAA had the two-fold aim to raise the status of women in the Australian community and to strengthen Australian families as the basis of society. With the Howard Government evidently bringing these two aims to bear on its social policy approach to women and families, the Prime Minister had a natural affinity with the WAA and spoke warmly of its ideals and advocacy work.

In this address to the Alliance, the Prime Minister spoke of the need to celebrate the gains made by women in professional and public life whilst also cherishing the family unit as a stabilising influence in the life of the nation and its people. To help realise both of these ideals, Howard spoke of how his recent reforms to the taxation system would afford greater freedom for parents to organise and structure their working and family lives. Speaking about family life, he again alluded to the fact that he saw himself as a liberal in economic policy and a "modern conservative" in social policy. In what might have appeared to be a contradiction in terms, Howard defined a modern conservative as somebody who cherished traditional values and institutions, such as the family, but did so in a way that made them relevant and applicable to modern times.

Celebrating 25 years of an organisation is always a special moment. But when one thinks of all of the things that have happened in political and national and social life in this country and around the world, the last 25 years have been an extraordinary period. It almost exactly – not totally but almost exactly – mirrors the period of time that I have been a member of the House of Representatives. I was elected to the House of Representatives as the Member for Bennelong in May 1974, half way through the three-year term of the Whitlam Government. I will come to politics gently in a moment, but it does represent a very remarkable period of change in Australian society.

Many of those changes have been very positive, a lot, many would argue, have not been so positive. It has been a period of time that has seen furious debate on social issues. It has been a period of time when major economic change has brought about very significant social change.... Many of the legitimate goals of equality of treatment and opportunity have now been achieved. That does not mean that men and women either within or outside of the paid workforce are treated equally or are afforded equality of opportunity. But it does mean that we now live in a society that recognises that the aspirations and the horizons of women have changed for all time.

It is also a society, I know, and particularly your organisation, that would argue that although those horizons have properly changed, that does not alter the fundamental and enduring value of many of the institutions of our society. I know to an organisation such as your own, as to the Government and as to my own personal political philosophy, the family unit remains the central and most stabilising influence in the life of the nation and in the lives of most Australians.

The challenge of government in the 21st century is to recognise that and support the fact that the family remains the most important group unit in our society. It continues not only to provide most people within our community with the immediate source of their emotional and, often their spiritual being and sustenance, but it is also something that in economic terms provides the best social welfare system that mankind has ever devised.

What we all must recognise is that although the family remains central to our lives, and central to what we think of ourselves, how we learn to relate to each other, and how we learn to relate to our fellow human beings, it is now operating within a very different environment than what it was 25 or, indeed, 50 years ago. It is no less relevant, it is no less important, it is no less held dearly by the community, and one of the things I find fascinating is that whenever a survey is done of the aspirations of young people within our community, you normally find, at the very top, the aspirations of personal happiness, security, family life and stability, all those things that you tend to associate with traditional attitudes towards family life within our community.

What I think we draw from that is that people still want the stabilising influence of family in their lives. They still see it as the most immediate source of support though families today are going to operate under different rules. Family members are going to relate to each other differently. The opportunities for family members are going to be different and particularly the opportunities for women are going to be different.

Many of the things that were spoken of as the goals of your organisation, and many of the things that we have achieved, if I may say so, together, in areas such as taxation are all built around a very important philosophical notion. That philosophical notion is the notion or concept of choice. The driving force of so much of the philosophy of the party that I am privileged to lead, the Liberal Party of Australia, is a belief that the most important thing we can provide to the Australian community is to give to the men and women of Australia the maximum range of choices that we possibly can. I have been a long-term advocate of greater equity and justice within the taxation system for different family formations.

I do not think governments have a right to tell families how to organise their paid and unpaid working lives. I do not seek, as Prime Minister, to say to parents of young children, you should have this or that child-care arrangement; that is not my right. But it is my responsibility as far as possible to allow parents in Australia to exercise the choice they want in relation to their child-care arrangements. If they want child-care to be in the form of homecare by one or other parent on a full or substantially full-time basis, they should not suffer a severe economic penalty if they elect to go down that path.

I believe that the changes we have made have reduced that penalty. I do not think I can say it has disappeared altogether but certainly it has been substantially reduced. It remains our goal to maintain choice. We do not mandate conduct. Rather, we facilitate choice.

That same commitment to choice underlies the attitude of the Government in another very important area that touches the lives of all families and that is the area of education. The Government believes very strongly that Australian parents have the right to choose the education they think best suits the interests of their children. I do not believe in commercial monopolies, nor do I believe in education monopolies. We have in many ways the best mixed system of government and independent schools to be found anywhere in the world.

We have provided a climate for growth of choice against the back drop of a well-funded, strongly supported government education system. I speak myself as totally the product of the government education system of New South Wales, a quality of education to which I remain indebted to the schools that gave me that education. But I believe, very strongly, that we should always provide parents with the maximum level of choice. The new funding arrangements, introduced by the government and currently before the Senate, have been the subject of some debate within Parliament and within the media in recent weeks. The aim of those policies is to increase the choices available to Australian parents. The aim of those changes is not to confer privilege on small sections of the Australian community but to expand the choices available. We have done so by introducing new funding arrangements and new measurements of the capacity of parents to pay, and we believe that, as a result of those new arrangements, there will be far greater choice available to Australian parents....

Can I say to you that although I have not said a lot about the economic condition of the country, I am sure that you would all agree that the capacity of a government and the capacity of a country to deliver stable economic conditions, strong economic growth, rising job opportunities, lower interest rates and low inflation, all of those things, create better conditions for Australian families. One of the things that gives me a great deal of pride is that today we have a set of figures on unemployment which shows not only an unemployment level of 6.3% over the last month but also the lowest level of youth unemployment that we have had since 1978. Those figures represent, if I can put it, the flesh and blood of economic policy and economic achievement.

We hear a lot these days about whether we have become a society which is obsessed with economic efficiency and economic achievement. I can understand why people occasionally express concern about a tendency by some to be preoccupied with economic outcomes because running an efficient economy is never an end in itself. I do not seek a strong growing stable efficient Australian economy in order to please the economic purists of the world or of the International Monetary Fund. I do it because I see it as a way of delivering a better life for individual Australians and for their families. Because of more people in work, more satisfying work, more career opportunities, more family opportunities, they are the outcomes, they are the flesh and blood of strong economic policies and effective economic achievement.

I have often been asked to describe, as best I can, the broad philosophical goals and objectives of the Government that I lead. I have sought to describe the modern Liberal Party of Australia as being very much a Party that believes in principles of economic liberalisation when it comes to economic policy, and a Party that believes in modern conservatism when it comes to social policy. What I mean by modern conservatism in social policy is that we are a government that believes that there are some enduring values and some enduring institutions in our community – just as relevant and as precious and as valuable to us in these early months of the 21st century as they have ever been. But, equally, we live in a society where the conditions in which those institutions operate and contribute to human happiness and human fulfilment are different from what they were a generation ago. The challenge of modern society is always to maintain the enduring value and importance of institutions such as the family, but ensure that we do it in a way that retains its relevance and its support and its value for the modern community.

Organisations such as your own do recognise that. You are not arguing that the conditions in which families operate are the same now as they were when your organisation was formed. Having achieved some of your goals, you are now very sensibly moving on to others and I congratulate you for that. It does mirror in a very significant way the approach that the Government has taken to many important elements of social policy in Australia....

Can I thank the Women's Action Alliance for the contribution that it has made to economic and social debate in Australia. Can I encourage you to continue your work; can I encourage you to find new forms of advocacy; can I encourage you to continue to put them to my Government and any future government of Australia. We may not agree with everything but we certainly will always listen to you.

We will always respect your commitment to family life, your commitment to effective choice for men and women and your belief, a belief that the Government shares, that there are some enduring institutions in our society which are as relevant and as important today as they have ever been. The support of those institutions is very important to the future of the whole of the Australian community.

# Valedictory Speech

## House of Representatives
## Canberra – 9 December 2004

In this end-of-year valedictory speech to the House of Representatives shortly after his fourth election victory, the Prime Minister set aside the usual "cut and thrust" of politics to reflect on some of the deeper spiritual and social issues of importance to Australians. With Christmas approaching, he spoke of the religious significance of the celebration of the birth of Jesus of Nazareth. For Howard personally, this had special meaning given his own Christian beliefs and upbringing. Conceding that he was a less than perfect Christian, Howard would reflect in *Lazarus Rising* that "the fundamentals of Christian belief and practice" he had imbibed from his formative years at Earlwood Methodist Church remained with him "to this day". At a national level also, the Prime Minister appreciated the importance of this religious faith to millions of Australians. Although acknowledging that Australians were not typically given to public displays of religiosity, he held that the quiet yet earnest Christianity of many had been a tremendous "force for good" in the nation. The Prime Minister maintained that a religiously diverse society such as Australia could still honour its Christian inheritance in a way that respected the religious, or non-religious, beliefs of all. In addition to its spiritual dimension, the Prime Minister reminded his colleagues that the Christmas season was a time to cherish the bonds of family and children. In his desire to bring civility to the often rancorous atmosphere of parliamentary proceedings, he introduced the tradition of shaking hands with the Leader of the Opposition.

As the House comes to an end for this year, in the tradition, I would like to extend first to you, Mr Speaker, brief though your occupancy in the chair has been, the very best of good wishes for Christmas and the New Year. To thank you for your many courtesies already afforded to me and the House, and to wish you and your family every happiness over the Christmas break. To the Clerks, to Ian Harris and to Bernard Wright in particular, both of whom exemplify the very best traditions of independence and integrity in the discharge of their duties, we owe a very special thanks. …

I especially say to the new members: "Welcome. I hope you have been made welcome". Speaking for myself on behalf of the Coalition, I express my pride in the quality of the new members that have come into the Government ranks. They come from very diverse backgrounds. They bring different talents and different skills and their own different personalities. Some of them came easily, and some of them had two fights. I can think of one who did: he had a preselection fight and then he had an election fight. For others, it all suddenly happened in a rush. I can think of somebody who falls into that category. I can think of other members who had to work very, very hard for eight, nine or 12 months to win seats from the other side of politics. One succeeded a very distinguished member of this House who had been a wonderful colleague for a number of years. They have all brought something new and something different. That is what this Parliament must do: it must reflect the breadth of the Australian community. …

I particularly welcome the new members who have joined us. They represent a different perspective but, nonetheless, I know they come here determined to make an impact and determined to change things for the better. All people, with a few exceptions, come into this place determined to try and improve life for their fellow citizens. I do not think we do each other any good by suggesting that there is total malice residing in the breasts of our opponents and total merit residing on our side of politics. People are really motivated to go into public life for the very best of reasons, and most people I have met in this place have got that motivation.

This is, of course, an occasion of the year that celebrates the birth of the most significant figure in human history, Jesus of Nazareth. It is an occasion to acknowledge the spiritual component of our lives. That is not compulsory. We live in a society where faith is a matter of personal choice, and millions of Australians lead their lives according to the Christian religion. A smaller, but nonetheless totally respected, number lead their lives according to other faiths. Many choose not to lead their lives according to any faith at all. That is entirely a matter of personal choice. One of the driving philosophical forces of Christianity is individual choice and free will, and faith in the Christian sense is based very much on an individual choice and an individual embrace of a set of spiritual values.

For my part I have endeavoured, completely inadequately, to live as best I can according to the basic tenets of the Christian religion. It is not something that most Australians choose to wear on their sleeve quite as much as some from other countries do. It does not alter the fact that there is a deep deposit of spirituality in this country which is a very, very strong force for good. For all the brickbats that have been hurled at the Christian churches and for all their failings, and for all the failings, personal sins and indiscretions of some of their members, it remains the fact that the Christian religion is the greatest force for good, progress and dignity of the individual in this nation. There is no force which is greater for the enhancement of individuals and the liberation of the human spirit.

I think it is important at a time like this for those who attest to that view to express it, as I do, but I do that in no sense of stricture against those who hold a different point of view. I respect very strongly the secular traditions of this country. I will never be one that will seek to define the worth of somebody's contribution to public life according to whether or not they hold a particular religious point of view. We are a society that respects all religions, but we should respect our own history and our own traditions. We should not run away from the influence of Judeo-Christianity on this country. It has been an enormous force for good and it has shaped not only the individual lives of people but also

367

the character of our nation. We will be a poorer nation if we shrink from an understanding of that influence and from the impact that it has had.

In that spirit, can I wish all members of the Parliament the very best for Christmas. Have a good time with your families. I intend to. I intend to have a holiday, and I hope the Leader of the Opposition [Mark Latham] does. I mean that sincerely; I do not mean that in any facetious sense. He has a young family. I remember what it was like when my children were that age. It is important that we do spend a lot of time with our children, particularly at that age. As they get older they spend a little less time with you, I can report, but nonetheless quite a bit. The bonds that develop with your children at the age that the Leader of the Opposition's are at are the bonds that make it the case that when they have grown up to adulthood, they still want you around—selectively and occasionally, as we all understand. To have a good relationship with your adult children is the most satisfying thing that you can have in life because it is a completely consensual, voluntary thing, and it is based upon mutual respect and the compatibility of personalities.

I wish the Leader of the Opposition well. I wish all of my parliamentary colleagues well and, as was a tradition that I developed with one of his predecessors, I extend a handshake to the Leader of the Opposition, wish him well for the Christmas period and look forward to seeing him back in the New Year.

# INDEX

# Acknowledgements

I wish to acknowledge the following people for their invaluable assistance in the composition of this volume.

First, I wish to recognise my supervisor and Executive Director of the Menzies Research Centre (MRC), Nick Cater, for providing me with the inspiration to embark on the timely project of researching and publishing a series of noteworthy speeches by Australia's second longest-serving Prime Minister. With this publication, these selected speeches of John Howard can be once again read and appreciated. Nick's encouragement and guidance throughout this project has been invaluable and much appreciated.

I would like to thank my wonderful colleagues at the MRC, Kay Gilchrist, Rick Umback and Michelle Ko for their encouragement and abiding interest in this publication.

I especially appreciate the genuine interest and support of the former Prime Minister himself, the Honourable John Howard, OM, AC. At all times, I have valued his generous availability, personal warmth and civility as I have interviewed him about the art and practice of prime ministerial speech-making. I would also like to thank his personal staff, Ruth Gibson, Sally Murphy and Joshua Anderson for their courtesy and assistance.

I am very grateful to John O'Sullivan, CBE, for his Foreword. Written by a fellow John Howard admirer and one of the great conservative columnists and public intellectuals of the English-speaking world, this foreword provides a fitting adornment to the volume.

With the proofreading, editorial fine-tuning and presentation of the volume, I am indebted to the editorial expertise and generous time of John Nethercote, Adjunct Professor, Canberra Campus, Australian Catholic University. His meticulous proof-reading of the manuscript and welcome advice about design and layout have been invaluable.

In bringing this volume to print, I am grateful to Dr Anthony Cappello and the team at Connor Court for overseeing the process of publication with their professionalism and precision.

I conclude by offering my profound appreciation to my family and friends who have supported me through this endeavour with their love, good humour, interest and encouragement.

**David Furse-Roberts**
**Canberra**
**February 2018**